THE WAY TO GOD
ACCORDING TO THE RULE OF ST. BENEDICT

*by*

ABBOT EMMANUEL HEUFELDER, OSB

# THE WAY

## ACCORDING TO THE

# TO GOD

## RULE OF SAINT BENEDICT

*by* EMMANUEL HEUFELDER OSB

*Translated by* LUKE EBERLE OSB

*with a translation of*
**The Rule of Saint Benedict**
*by* OSWALD HUNTER BLAIR OSB

Cistercian Publications
Kalamazoo, Michigan
1983

*The Way to God According to the Rule of St Benedict*
is number Forty-nine in the Cistercian Studies Series.

A translation of *Der Weg zu Gott,* published by
Echter–Verlag, Würzburg, West Germany.

Available in Britain and Europe
from A. R. Mowbray & Co., Ltd.
St Thomas House   Becket Street
Oxford OX1 1SJ

**Library of Congress Cataloguing in Publication Data**

Heufelder, Emmanuel Maria, 1898–1982.
    The way to God according to the Rule of Saint
Benedict.

    (Cistercian studies series ; no. 49)
    Translation of: Der Weg zu Gott.
    Bibliography: p. 301
    1. Benedict, Saint, Abbot of Monte Cassino. Regula.
2. Spiritual life.  I. Title.  II. Series.
BX3004.Z5H4613 1983   255'.106   82-17823
ISBN 0-87907-849-9

*Typography by Gale Akins, Kalamazoo*
*Printed in the United States of America*

# TABLE OF CONTENTS

# Foreword

T HAT A PERSON 'TRULY SEEK GOD' (RB 58) was
for St Benedict the fundamental characteristic of a
genuine monastic vocation. His own life had as its
substance and purpose what he demanded of priests who
might belong to his monastery, since they, in virtue of special
privilege, were expected to be exemplars of holiness: 'to
advance ever more and more in godliness' (RB 62). Through
his Rule St Benedict has led on the way to God not only his
monks but also countless persons in the world who seek God.

In our times, in many ways so similar to the times of
St Benedict, there seems to be a new openness to the dynamic
unity and simplicity of the way to God which the benedictine
Rule presents. Pope Benedict XV declared, on entering upon
his pontificate, that he had chosen the name of the Patriarch
of Western Monasticism because he wanted to lead to God the
era then just beginning as once St Benedict had led his
contemporaries to God. This book attempting to portray
'the way to God according to the Rule of St Benedict' should
need no justification.

In his Rule Benedict did not seek to present a theory of
the spiritual life, but simply to offer a practical program for
persons wanting to live the christian life fully. Nevertheless
all his specific directives are backed by clear insight into the
essence and the mysteries of the spiritual life. This insight was
deepened by years of intensive study of Holy Scripture,
ecclesiastical writers, and monastic pioneers. It was confirmed

and crowned by the experience of coming to know all the stages of the way to God in his own search and struggle. What St Benedict in chapter 64 of his Rule requires of the abbot, that he 'be learned in the Law of God, that he may know whence to bring forth new things and old', applied to himself in a pre-eminent degree. The Holy Rule is not only a deep mine of practical wisdom for life as such, but also gives us an understanding of the essential elements of perfection and sets up a well-ordered structure of the spiritual life.

To point out these elements and this structure is the purpose of the present work. Its starting point is always the text of the Holy Rule, which in turn rests on the Word of God in Holy Scripture. The commentary on the text of the Rule is intended to be nothing more than the setting for the jewel. It seeks to disclose the hidden meaning and content of the Rule's wording, which is generally concise, and to make abundantly clear what this master of the spiritual life wished to say. It may also, we hope, be an incentive to the reader to walk the way of the Rule, to make its purpose and goal his own.

The thoughts presented in this book—like the Rule itself—should therefore not be read hastily but should be inwardly digested, assimilated and consequently put into practice. It is one of the basic principles of St Benedict's asceticism—and this will frequently be discussed—that in the spiritual life all mere theory is sterile and that profound understanding comes only with practice.

# PART ONE

# GOD'S CALL

# The Prologue
# to the Monastic Rule
# of St Benedict

*Hearken, O my son, to the precepts of your Master, and incline the ear of your heart; willingly receive and faithfully fulfil the admonition of your loving Father, that you may return by the labor of obedience to him from whom you had departed through the sloth of disobedience.*

AT THE BEGINNING of the way to God stands the word 'Hearken—*Obsculta!*' All spiritual life, indeed all created life, begins with 'hearkening' to the call of God. According to Holy Scripture, all creation is rooted in the fact that God calls and the created being hears this call and obeys it: 'God said: Let there be. And there was' (Gn 1:3ff). 'He commanded and they were created' (Ps 148:5).† In a most profound sense creation means essentially: a summons from God to hear and to do what God has said. It is essential to the creature that from the outset God give it what theology calls *potentia obedientialis:* the capacity to accept God's call and obey it. All development of natural and supernatural life is based upon this capacity.

---

† Psalms have been cited according to the Hebrew enumeration.

If the creature 'corresponds' to God's call, if it 'replies' to
the word of God, if listening turns into obeying, into an act
of obedience, then the creature attains the perfection which
in the mind of God it ought to have. Thus what exists in God
as an eternal idea becomes 'fulfilled in deed', becomes
actuality in time, in the mode of created being. Irrational
creatures cannot do otherwise than accept and fulfil God's
call. 'He calls the light, and it obeys him trembling . . . .
When he calls the stars, they answer, "Here we are!", shining
with joy for their Maker' (Bar 3:33,35).

The free will of rational creatures gives them the possibility
of resisting God's call, of saying, 'I will not serve' (Jer 2:20), instead of responding to it by an act of obedience', the 'labor of
obedience', as St Benedict calls it. This resistance is 'the sloth
of disobedience' wherein lies the very essence of sin. By it the
creature 'departs from God'. God's creative call is displaced
by one's own call, the divine will by self-will. The creature
wants to be its own master, to listen and to obey itself alone.

This attitude, which alienates from God, St Benedict sees
incorporated in that caricature of genuine monachism, the
Sarabaites, who 'without a shepherd, shut up, not in the
Lord's sheepfolds, but in their own, make a law to themselves
in the pleasure of their own desires: whatever they think fit
or choose to do, that they call holy; and what they like not,
that they consider unlawful' (RB 1).

If man wants to return to God from this way of 'slothful
disobedience whereby he had departed from God', he must
above all 'renounce this self-will'. He must 'be converted—
change his mind' (Mt 3:2). He must again listen to God
instead of to himself. He must acknowledge Christ as 'the
Lord and true King' and serve him. This means spiritual
combat, because sinful self-will does not yield its position of
sovereignty without a struggle. Victory in this battle is won
with 'the strong and bright weapons of obedience'. To the
extent that man listens to God and responds to his call, he
will be filled with divine strength and enabled to overcome

in himself everything opposed to God.

> To you, therefore, my words are now addressed,
> whoever you are that, renouncing your own will,
> take up the strong and bright weapons of obedi-
> ence, in order to fight for the Lord Christ,
> our true King.

This interior conversion to God at its very beginning and all the more so in its perfection is impossible for man by his own power. The creature has in itself no power to act. True, by reason of the freedom of will given him by God, he can resist God's call. He is capable of 'the sloth of disobedience' and hence of evildoing. We can obey God and do well only 'with the good things he has given us'. Recognition of this, which is fundamental for the way to God, leads to prayer as the most indispensable of the resources of the spiritual life.

> In the first place, whatever good work you begin
> to do, beg of him with most earnest prayer
> to perfect.

This praying flows primarily from that basic attitude of listening and obeying on which the entire spiritual life is built. By begging in prayer for strength from God, 'that he who has begun the good work will carry it through to completion' (Phil 1:6), we 'incline the ear of our heart' to God again after we have turned away from him through self-will, and we open ourselves to the inflow of his creative power.

The more profoundly we recognize our powerlessness as creatures and our dependence on the grace of God—and Benedict will take us through all the abyss of human nothingness—the more intense will be this turning of our heart (RB 52) to God in prayer, and the more will our heart be enlarged in yearning and alertness (end of Prologue), the more capable of receiving God will we become (*Dei capaces*, as Augustine says), the closer God will be to us with his supporting grace, as promised by a text quoted further on: 'Before you call upon me, I will say to you, "Behold, I am here",' the more energetically and resolutely can we pursue

the way we must follow if we wish to attain blessedness.
*May he who has now vouchsafed to count us in the
number of his children not at any time be grieved
by our evil deeds. For we must always so serve
him with the good things he has given us, that not
only may he never, as an angry father, disinherit
his children, but may never, as a dreadful Lord,
incensed by our sins, deliver us to everlasting
punishment, as most wicked servants who would
not follow him to glory.*

We *must* obey God. This obligation derives from the nature of creation; it gets a special character and urgency from
God's offer of grace by which he has called his creatures to
supernatural life in a personal sharing of his love. God did
not want to be only the 'Lord' of his creatures; he wanted to
become their 'Father'. 'He has vouchsafed to count us among
the number of his children.' And a child must listen to and
obey the one from whom it has received its being and its life.

'All fatherhood takes its name from the Father of our
Lord Jesus Christ' (Eph 3:14). All sonship in the realm of
nature is an 'image and likeness' of the sonship which exists
in God himself, a participation in the eternal sonship of the
second Person of the Godhead. It is in this that the ultimate
and most profound meaning of that 'listening' of which
St Benedict speaks is revealed to us. In God himself there is
one who calls and one who hears. In God himself there is one
who, as Father, utters an eternal divine word, 'Hearken, O my
Son!' and one who, as Son, receives this word and responds,
'Abba, Father!' (Rom 8:15; RB 2). 'In the beginning was
the Word; the Word was in God's presence, and the Word was
God. He was present to God in the beginning' (Jn 1:1-2).
From this speaking and hearing, from this presence of the
Word to the Father, issues the Holy Spirit as its fruit, the
'Spirit of sonship', the Spirit of love, the bond of unity
between Father and Son.

The creative word which God spoke 'in the beginning' of

time is like the resonance of this internal divine utterance and response, the echo as it were of the eternal Word of the Father: 'Through him all things came into being, and apart from him nothing came to be. Whatever came to be in him, found life' (Jn 1:3-4). By partaking in the creative word of God, creatures came into being, receiving natural life and, in accordance with the loving will of God, also supernatural life, 'a sharing in the divine nature' (2 Pt 1:4), in the life of the Son of God. 'And the life was the light of men' (Jn 1:4). The 'Word of God' that lives and works in them is their interior illumination, their divine splendor, the source of everlasting blessedness. That is the 'prologue' to the whole of God's creation, the 'prologue' to the glad tidings of the grace of God who 'has vouchsafed to count us in the number of his children'.

'The light shines on in darkness and the darkness did not comprehend it' (Jn 1:5). The creature's self-will, which turned away from God and thereby became darkened, closed itself to the Word of God, which is light and life. A fearsome thing happened: no response came anymore to the word of the Father. To his call, 'Hearken, my son!' the creature no longer replied, 'Abba, Father!' Man wanted 'to be like God' (Gen 3:5), himself lord and father, himself a call, himself the voice, 'serving his own will'. 'You broke your yoke, you tore off your bonds. "I will not serve," you said' (Jer 2:20).

We sense the terrible mystery of sin. It invades the innermost life of God. It does not want the 'word' to be 'present to God' anymore. It disrupts the dynamic flow of speaking and listening, of calling and obeying, which constitutes the innermost life of God. Sin is actually an attack on God himself, on the heart of the eternal Father. 'You said in your heart: "I will scale the heavens; above the stars of God I will set up my throne . . . . I will ascend above the tops of the clouds; I will be like the Most High!" ' (Is 14:13-14). By this the Spirit of love, of surrender, of blessedness, in whom the Father and the Son have their being, must of necessity be extinguished. By it man, called to participation in the divine life of the Trinity, must of necessity not only 'lose the inheritance of children, but be delivered to everlasting punishment as most wicked servants who would not follow him to glory'.

Only the living Word of God himself could bring man back after his sinful turning away from God. That is why 'the Word became flesh and made his dwelling among us' (Jn 1:14). God's eternal Son became man in order to restore to mankind 'the power to become children of God', to implant them again in the current of life which flows from the Father to the Son and, in the Holy Spirit of self-giving, flows back to the heart of the Father.

Hence the visible coming of the Son of God is the revelation and manifestation of the fundamental disposition of 'the Word that is present to the Father'. Jesus Christ 'did not come to do his own will, but the will of him who sent him' (Jn 6:38). He 'speaks just as the Father has instructed him' (Jn 12:50). He 'cannot do anything of himself'. 'I judge *as I hear*', he says (Jn 5:30). Deep within himself he always listens to what the Father says, and as he hears so does he, 'obedient unto death' (Phil 2:8). This 'obedience unto death' became man's redemption, the beginning of his 'return to him from whom he had departed through the sloth of disobedience'.

Now it is very clear why at the outset of our way to God we find the words, 'Hearken, O my son!'

This call has the same meaning as the one by which our Lord called his disciples: 'Follow me!' It signifies willingness like that of the Son of God 'to listen to the Father and always to do what pleases him' (Jn 8:29). It says that through the grace of Christ 'the ear of the heart' has been opened again to God. And thereby access has been restored to 'the kingdom of God', where the Father utters his eternal Word and this eternal Word is present to God. In the measure that the heart inclines to the call of God by listening and obeying, it participates in the life of the Son of God. What has been said is fulfilled: ' "They shall all be taught by God." Everyone who has heard the Father and learned from him comes to me' (Jn 6:45).

What is promised regarding the Holy Spirit is again fulfilled: 'whom the Father will send in the Son's name and who will instruct us in everything, and remind us of all that the Lord has told us' (Jn 14:26).

The word that Benedict uses for 'hearing' (*obscultare*) really means 'to listen attentively'. Like the ear of the body, the ear of the heart can be more or less finely attuned to the call of God, to the voice of the Holy Spirit. The more attuned the ear of the heart is to this interior enlightenment and instruction by the Spirit of God, the more receptive a person is to 'the inspiration of divine grace' (RB 20). The more he 'lets himself be led by the Spirit of God', the more he becomes 'a son of God' (Rom 8:14).

In this docility toward God, in this willingness to 'hear the word of God and keep it' (Lk 11:28), lies the beginning and the end of the way to God. It is from this that all perfection and holiness grows. It is this docility that Benedict wants to teach us in the Prologue to his Rule and in the Rule itself.

Since all our progress on the way to God depends on this docility and willingness, St Benedict seeks, by means of various mental images and references to the words of Holy Scripture, to awaken and give endurance to such willingness in us. Ever more insistently he points out that our eternal happiness depends on our listening to God and obeying him, and the life-span granted us for this momentous decision is very short. There is urgency in his words. An ardor found in few other passages of the Holy Rule can be felt. He is wholly the 'master and teacher' who wants to sweep his disciples up into his own striving for sanctity. He is wholly the 'loving father' who considers himself responsible for his 'dearest brethren' whom he, as he later demands of the abbot, 'exhorts always to advance in virtue' (RB 2).

*Let us then at length arise, since the Scripture*
*stirs us up, saying: 'It is time now for us to*
*sleep'. And our eyes being open to the deify-*     Rom 13:11
*ing light, let us hear with wondering ears what*
*the Divine Voice admonishes us, daily crying*
*out: 'Today if you shall hear his voice,*
*harden not your hearts'. And again, 'He that*     Ps 95:7,8
*has ears to hear, let him hear what the Spirit*
*says to the churches'. And what says he?*     Rev 2:7
*'Come, my children, hearken to me, I will*
*teach you the fear of the Lord'. 'Run while*     Ps 34:11
*you have the light of life, lest the darkness of*
*death seize hold of you.'*     cf. Jn 12:35

The state of sin, of separation from God, resembles the
condition of someone who is asleep. 'The ear of the heart' no
longer perceives God's call. The eye of the soul sees none of
his light. In slothful torpor (*desidia*) man is at the mercy of
the power of evil, the propensities of passion.

But now God in his mercy has awakened us to new life.
Now his call forces its way powerfully to our ear. Now his
light wants to shine on us again. We must become wide
awake, open our eyes and ears to the light, to the call of
God, and hasten to do what God asks of us.

Repeatedly in the Prologue and in the body of his Rule,
Benedict refers to this 'doing'. Repeatedly he reminds us that
we must put into practice what we hear. It almost seems as
though by this emphasis on action he is protesting against
certain theorists of the spiritual life who say nice things
about the way to God without actually setting a foot on it.
He, on the contrary, never tires of insisting: 'Unless we run
[to God] by our good deeds, we shall by no means reach it
[his kingdom]'. In this he is saying nothing else than what
Christ himself says: 'None of those who cry out, "Lord,
Lord," will enter the kingdom of God but only he who does
the will of my Father in heaven' (Mt 7:21). For there is an

inner essential relationship between 'listening' to God's call and its 'fulfilment in practice'.

Just as in the act of creation the word of God comes to effect only by the fulfilment of what God wills, so too the divine life can become actuality in us only as listening turns into obedience. Listening is the initial opening of our soul to the deifying light and the action of divine grace. Then in the 'doing', God's light and God's power enter into us effectively. Wherefore the Lord says of his teaching: 'Any man who chooses to do his [God's] will, will know about this doctrine—namely, whether it comes from God' (Jn 7:17). This is the kind of 'doing' that Benedict teaches. Such 'doing' reaches into the very depths of the divine essence itself. In God, knowing and willing and doing are ever one and the same. As the theologians put it, God is *actus purus*: purely act, unalloyed actuality. And we are called to be his 'image and likeness'. Hence there follows:

> *And the Lord, seeking his own workman in*
> *the multitude of the people to whom he thus*
> *cries out, says again:†* '*Who is the man that*    Ps 34:12
> *will have life, and desires to see good days?'*
> *And if you, hearing him, answer, 'I am he,'*
> *God says to you: 'If you will have true and*
> *everlasting life, keep your tongue from evil*
> *and your lips that they speak no guile. Turn*
> *from evil and do good: seek peace and pursue*
> *it'. And when you have done these things, my*    Ps 34:13,14
> *eyes will be upon you, and my ears will be*
> *open to your prayers; and before you call*
> *upon me, I will say unto you, "Behold,*
> *I am here".'*    cf. Is 58:9

---

† This question and answer are taken, in accordance with a homily attributed to St Augustine (*Enarratio in psalmum 33*), from Ps 34 (Vulgate 33), which is also the source of the verse quoted in the preceding section: 'Come, my children, hearken to me, I will teach you the fear of the Lord'.

When we listen to God's call, God looks upon and listens to us. If we speak the word indicating willingness, then he too speaks: 'Behold, I am here'. If we do what he wants, then he too does what we want, or rather, he fulfils what he has called us to and what he has promised. Then it is as in the depths of the triune God. The cycle of the divine life, which had been broken by sin, by 'the sloth of disobedience', is restored. The Son does everything 'as he hears'. Therefore he may also say, 'Father, I know that you always hear me' (Jn 11:42).

> *What can be sweeter to us, dearest brethren, than this voice of the Lord inviting us? Behold in his loving-kindness the Lord shows unto us the way of life. Having our loins, therefore, girded with faith and the performance of good works, let us walk in his paths by the guidance of the Gospel, that we may deserve to see him who has called us to his kingdom.*

Ever more clearly and brightly the destination of our path-way looms up ahead of us: eternal life, the beatific vision in the kingdom of God, most intimate union, holy familiarity with him in his dwelling.

> *And if we wish to dwell in the tabernacle of his kingdom, we shall by no means reach it unless we run thither by our good deeds. But let us ask the Lord with the Prophet . . . .*

Let us listen in the depths of our being! Let us seek an answer to the words of Scripture! Benedict wants to teach us this 'listening' in a very practical way by repeatedly putting prayer formulas from Holy Scripture on our lips—here from Ps 15 (V 14)—which express willingness to listen, a yearning for God and his Word:

> *. . . saying to him: 'Lord, who shall dwell in your tabernacle, or who shall rest on your holy hill?' After this question, brethren, let us hear the Lord answering, and showing to us the way to his*

*tabernacle, and saying: 'He that walks without stain and works justice: he that speaks truth in his heart, that has not done guile with his tongue: he that has done no evil to his neighbor, and has not taken up a reproach against his neighbor'.*

The particular directives which issue from the psalm passages quoted by St Benedict, as also the various expressions: 'obedience, labor of obedience, workman, to do good, good works, good deeds, good observance, performance of good works, way of God's commandments, holy observance of the commandments, military service, the Lord's service, fulfilment of duty'† in the last analysis always mean the same thing: that which is the basis of the spiritual life in its entirety and which Benedict wants to teach us in the Prologue to his Rule, namely, total willingness to listen to God and to obey him so that we may become completely free and open to the working of God's grace in us.

The following psalm verse, which Benedict renders freely and enlarges upon,‡ offers him the opportunity to point out the opposite of his doctrine about 'hearing'. There is another voice too which wants to force its way to the ear of the heart, the voice of the tempter who would like to get us off the way to God. From the very outset we have to be deaf to this voice. We may not even let it get near the ear of the heart. As soon as we, with 'the eye of the heart', become aware of the approach of the evil spirit even off in the distance, we have to repulse him with loathing and thus keep the ear of the heart free and open to the voice of God.

---

† *Obedientia, obedientiae labor, operarius, agere bonum, facere bonum, boni actus, bona observantia, observantia bonorum actuum, via mandatorum Dei, sancta praeceptorum obedientia, militaturus, dominicum servitium, officium complere.*

---

‡ It reads, 'By whom the reprobate is despised—*Ad nihilum deductus est in conspectu ejus malignus*'.

Hence Benedict says further about the one who wants to dwell in the royal tent of God:

> *He has brought the malignant evil one to naught,*
> *casting him out of his heart with all his suggestions,*
> *and has taken his bad thoughts, while they were*
> *yet young, and dashed them down upon the*
> *[Rock] Christ.*

In the 'Instruments of Good Works' (RB 4) and later in the fifth degree of humility, Benedict will explain more precisely what this 'dashing upon Christ' means, namely, that we 'lay open to our spiritual father our evil thoughts the instant they come into the heart'. Evidently he sees in this, as in all direction by a 'spiritual father', something very significant for the way to God. So already in the Prologue to his Rule he includes a brief reference to it.

The emphasis which St Benedict had to place upon 'doing good', 'good works', could become a danger: one's own activity may be overestimated, one may forget what this master of the spiritual life already said at the beginning of the Prologue—that we can serve God only 'with the good things he has given us'. The heresies of Pelagianism and Semipelagianism, which had found wide acceptance in monasticism, had shown that it is persons far advanced in asceticism who are specifically exposed to this danger.

So before concluding his insistent exhortation to do good, St Benedict stresses that in the last analysis all spiritual life and all perfection is not the work of man but 'the working of God in us'. Consequently admission to the royal tent of God is attained only by those of whom it can be said:

> *These are they who, fearing the Lord, are not*
> *puffed up with their own good works, but*
> *knowing that the good which is in them comes*
> *not from themselves but from the Lord,*
> *magnify the Lord who works in them, saying*
> *with the Prophet, 'Not unto us, O Lord, not*
> *unto us, but unto your name give the glory'.*    Ps 115:1

*So the Apostle Paul imputed nothing of his
preaching to himself, but said, 'By the grace
of God I am what I am'. And again he says,*     1 Co 15:10
*'He that glories, let him glory in the Lord'.*†     2 Co 10:17

In the 'Instruments of Good Works' (RB 4) St Benedict
expressed these thoughts clearly and forcefully in the words:
'To attribute any good that one sees in oneself to God, and
not to oneself. But to recognize and always impute to oneself the evil that one does.' Again and again in the Holy Rule
this conviction of God's all-embracing activity and of the
absolute necessity of divine grace comes to light. In the key
chapter of the Holy Rule (RB 7) Benedict based the development of his doctrine 'Of Humility' on this conviction. The
more one's ego is 'brought to naught' and the more one lowers
himself in humble self-renunciation, the more powerfully
will the Lord manifest the working of his grace 'by the Holy
Spirit in his laborer, now cleansed from vice and sin'.

So now we have received a clear and unequivocal answer
to our query about the way to God: we have to listen to God
and obey him. We have to open ourselves completely, by
humble willingness, to the action of God's grace. 'By this
labor of obedience man returns to him from whom he had
departed through the sloth of disobedience.'

We see that this doctrine of Benedict is nothing else than
what Our Lord himself says in the gospel about following
him and about the way to the Father. That is why at the end
of his exhortations Benedict puts the words with which our
Lord, in the Sermon on the Mount, concludes his invitation
to perfect discipleship:

---

† Throughout the Prologue, especially in the interpretation of Pss 34
and 15 (V 33 and 14), we gain an insight into Benedict's manner of
exercising his role as teacher in regard to his brothers and sons, indeed
into his own prayer and contemplation. In the words and prayers of
Holy Scripture the depths of the spiritual life are disclosed to him and
from them flow his own prayer and teaching. (See IV, Part 2.)

*Hence also the Lord says in the Gospel: 'He
that hears these words of mine, and does
them is like a wise man who built his house
upon a rock: the floods came, the winds
blew, and beat upon that house, and it did
not fall, because it was founded upon a
rock.' And the Lord in fulfilment of these his*   Mt 7:25
*words is waiting daily for us to respond by
our deeds to his holy admonitions. Therefore
the days of our life are lengthened for the
amendment of our evil ways, as says the
Apostle: 'Know you not that the patience of
God is leading you to repentance?' For the*   Rom 2:4
*merciful Lord says: 'I will not the death of a
sinner, but that he should be converted and
live'.*
                                                Ezk 33:11

Once again St Benedict summarizes his entire teaching
about the way to God and the motives for setting foot on
this way:

*Since then, brothers, we have asked of the Lord who
is to inhabit his temple, we have heard his commands to those who are to dwell there; and if we
fulfil those duties, we shall be heirs of the kingdom
of heaven. Our hearts, therefore, and our bodies
must be made ready to fight under the holy
obedience of his commands; and let us ask God to
supply by the help of his grace what by nature is
not possible for us. And if we would arrive at
eternal life, escaping the pains of hell, then—while
we are still in the flesh, and are able to fulfil all
these things by the light which is given us—we
must hasten to do now what will profit us for
all eternity.*

Who would want to resist the urgency in these words of the
wise 'teacher' and the 'loving father'? Who will not rejoice
that St Benedict volunteers to continue as our teacher in the

spiritual life and our guide on the way to God? Gratefully we hear his declaration:

*We have, therefore, to establish a school of the Lord's service.*

In using the word 'school', this master of the spiritual life doubtless had in mind, along with the ancient schools of the philosophers in which teachers and pupils strove to acquire true wisdom, also the old roman *scholae fabrum,* craft guilds, in which workers in the same handicraft were organized in labor unions. In the 'school of the Lord's service' that he is going to establish, the 'Lord's service' is to be not only taught theoretically but put into practice.

Even more than of these types derived from the earthly sphere of life he may have been thinking of the school into which the God–Man Teacher and Master once admitted his disciples to teach them the 'way to the Father'. It is especially in the chapter on the abbot that he has the image of this school in mind. Therefore what he there says about the abbot applies to Benedict's own teaching: 'He ought not to teach, or ordain, or command anything contrary to the law of the Lord; but let his bidding and his doctrine be infused into the minds of his disciples like the leaven of divine justice.'

It is in accordance with this ideal that in his school of the Lord's service he, as the true 'representative of Christ', wants to 'mingle with the rigor of a master the loving affection of a father' (RB 2 and 64). He assures us:

*In establishing this school we hope to order nothing that is harsh or rigorous. But if anything be somewhat strictly laid down, according to the dictates of sound reason, for the amendment of vices or the preservation of charity, do not therefore fly in dismay from the way of salvation, whose beginning cannot but be strait and difficult. But as we go forward in our life and in faith, we shall with* Mt 7:14

*hearts enlarged and the unspeakable sweetness
of love run in the way of God's commandments; so that never departing from his
guidance, but persevering in his teaching in
the monastery until death, we may by patience
share in the sufferings of Christ, that we may
deserve to be partakers of his kingdom. Amen.*

Already on the first page of his Prologue St Benedict had set the image of 'Christ, our true King' before our eyes. He does so again at the conclusion. Repeatedly in his considerations and exhortations he made reference to Christ. In what follows he will do it frequently. His Rule claims to be nothing else than an attempt to portray as perfectly as possible the ideal of the christian life and to realize it.

That is why Benedict's school is still a source of renewal in the Spirit of Christ even today, not only for his monks but for the entire Church, and that is why his school is accessible to all who 'want to fight for the Lord Christ, our true King'.

PART TWO

# MAN'S RESPONSE

*We have become aware of God's call. Benedict has shown us the basic disposition we must have to accept God's call: willingness to hear and to obey. In the 'school of the Lord's service' we are now entering we shall learn how this basic disposition develops and works out in practice. In three organically connected chapters (4–6) we are shown a threefold way to 'listen' docilely to God, a threefold inner readiness for the action of his grace.*

# Willingness to Do What is Good

*Chapter 4: The Instruments of Good Works*

A GOOD INSTRUCTOR simply takes his apprentice into the workshop and by working with him teaches him the details of exercising his craft or his art and the use of the various tools. So St Benedict too, in the first chapter of his Rule devoted mainly to asceticism, leads us into 'the workshop of the monastery', as he says, puts into our hands 'the instruments of good works', and has us begin working at the 'spiritual craft' immediately.

The figures of speech Benedict here employs resume the theme upon which he laid such stress in the Prologue—that one comes to God only by good works, that the call of God must become effective in action.

We have already spoken of the intimate relationship between 'listening' to God and the practical realization of God's call. Like all life, spiritual life too can develop only through activity, by 'good deeds'. In the doing of what is good, knowledge grows, the will becomes firm, the inner self is formed. 'Any man who chooses to do his will, shall know about this doctrine—namely, whether it comes from God or is simply spoken on my own' (Jn 7:17). Benedict's

biographer, Pope St Gregory the Great, in an Easter homily
says of the Emmaus disciples: 'At hearing God's instructions
they were not yet enlightened but were so by an action; for
it is written: it is not the hearers of the law who are just in
God's sight, but it is the doers of the law who will be justified. Therefore let him who wants to understand what he has
heard hasten to put into effect what he has already been
given to hear'.†

In this sense is St Benedict to be understood when, in a
number of passages in his Rule, he seems to equate perfection with the performance of good works and when, in the
first ascetical chapter of his Rule, he simply, without further
ado, puts 'the instruments of good works' into the hands of
his disciple and tells him to 'employ them constantly'.

By this stress on human activity he does not place himself
in conflict with his own teaching about 'the Lord working in
us'. It is clear that all good action on the part of man flows
simply and solely from the activity of God. ('To attribute
any good that one sees in oneself to God, and not to
oneself'—the forty-second instrument of good works.) It is
precisely by following the inspiration of divine grace (RB 20)
and giving practical effect to God's call by good deeds that
man takes into himself the power of God's grace and makes
it possible for this power of God to continue to work in him.

How then does the will of God make itself known? What
work does he want done? Where do we hear his word so that
we can put it into practice?

We hear the word of God first of all in Holy Scripture. His
will is made known to us in the commandments which God
revealed already in the Old Testament and which the Son of
God complemented and perfected in the New. 'If you wish to
enter into life, keep the commandments' (Mt 19:17). The
primary and fundamental 'instruments of good works'
therefore are:

---

† (*Hom. 23 in Evang.*).

1. *In the first place, to love the Lord God with all one's heart, all one's soul, and all one's strength.*
2. *Then one's neighbor as oneself.*
3. *Then not to kill.*
4. *Not to commit adultery.*
5. *Not to steal.*
6. *Not to covet.*
7. *Not to bear false witness.*
8. *To honor all men.*
9. *Not to do to another what one would not have done to oneself.*
10. *To deny oneself, in order to follow Christ.*
11. *To chastise the body.*
12. *Not to seek after delicate living.*
13. *To love fasting.*
14. *To relieve the poor.*
15. *To clothe the naked.*
16. *To visit the sick.*
17. *To bury the dead.*
18. *To help in affliction.*
19. *To console the sorrowing.*
20. *To keep aloof from worldly actions.*
21. *To prefer nothing to the love of Christ.*

The perfection set as a goal for the monk does not differ essentially from the perfection for which the Christian in the world must strive. For both, perfection consists in 'the Lord's service', in 'the service of obedience to the commands of God' (RB Prologue), in the love of God and of neighbor put into practice (first instrument). That is why the commands and instructions of the Lord which apply to everyone also set the norm for the monk's spiritual striving.

The monk must 'be ever mindful of all that God has commanded' (RB 7, the first degree of humility), he must 'daily fulfil by his deeds the commandments of God' (the sixty-second instrument). In the monk's life the service of obedience demanded of all Christians should find expression in an especially articulate way. In virtue of his state the monk has the obligation, solemnly vowed, to fulfil the law of God perfectly and 'to be holy' (RB 61). Consequently, the monk must not only observe the commandments of God in all fidelity down to the last 'jot and title', without 'breaking even the least significant of these commands' (Mt 5:19). He must also strive to fulfil the commandments of God wholly in the new spirit which our Saviour proclaimed in his Sermon on the Mount, rather than in the Old Testament imperfect concept of law.

In the life of the monk, who no longer has anything in common with the activities and spirit of the world (RB 20), the 'Spirit of Christ' (Rom 8:9) must be able to act without hindrance or competition. Permeated with 'the love of Christ above all', the monk stands ready for every sacrifice entailed by self-denial in order to follow Christ (RB 10). Indeed, he endeavors 'to dash down on the [Rock] Christ all evil thoughts the instant they come into his heart' (RB 50) in order to be perfect, as his divine Master was.

Thus the monk, 'in the love of Christ' (RB 70), fulfils the commandments of God, especially 'the new commandment' of the Lord—the commandment to love both neighbor and enemy—whose faithful observance St Benedict never ceases to inculcate:

22. *Not to give way to anger.*
23. *Not to harbor a desire of revenge.*
24. *Not to foster guile in one's heart.*
25. *Not to make a feigned peace.*
26. *Not to forsake charity.*
27. *Not to swear, lest perchance one forswear oneself.*
28. *To utter truth from heart and mouth.*
29. *Not to render evil for evil.*
30. *To do no wrong to anyone, indeed, to bear patiently wrong done to oneself.*
31. *To love one's enemies.*

*32. Not to render cursing for cursing, but rather blessing.*

*33. To bear persecution for justice's sake.*

It is not only from the 'divinely inspired books of the Old and New Testaments, which are a most unerring rule for human life' (RB 73) that Benedict takes his 'instruments of good works'. Many of his exhortations are taken from the teachings 'of the holy catholic fathers' (*ibid.*). For God, in his Church, never ceases to speak in sacred tradition, through the saints, through masters of theology and the spiritual life. 'What book of the holy catholic fathers does not loudly proclaim how we may by a straight course reach our Creator? Moreover, the *Conferences of the Fathers,* their *Institutes*† and their *Lives,* and the Rule of our holy father Basil‡—what are these but the instruments whereby well-living and obedient monks attain to virtue?' (*ibid.*).

This appreciation and utilization of 'sacred catholic tradition' by St Benedict, resulting from his listening to it in faith, gives his teaching its depth and sureness, inserting it into the living stream of divine life which is the bond of union in the 'communion of saints'. From the ascetical and monastic life of christian antiquity he took over what was of lasting value, synthesized it in accordance with his own call from God, refashioned it where it seemed necessary to do so, and now hands it on to those who want to follow him on the way to God. This too is an 'instrument of good works'—not to look for one's own way in the spiritual life but to stay within the sacred tradition of the Church and the directives of proven masters.

---

† Two works of John Cassian (d. about 435) which treat of the spiritual life in its entirety as well as describe the interior and exterior life of Egyptian monks. They exerted an extraordinary influence on monasticism.

‡ St Basil the Great (d. 379), patriarch of eastern monasticism, in many areas of his two Rules provided a model for St Benedict, who therefore calls him 'our father'.

Anyone who has a longing for the word of God will therefore 'willingly listen to holy reading' (RB 56) and endeavor
to hear God's voice in it. That is why in his monastic schedule
Benedict assigns a very large place to spiritual reading and
presupposes that there will be a library in his monasteries
(RB 48).

*34. Not to be proud.*

*35. Not given to wine.*

*36. Not a glutton.*

*37. Not drowsy.*

*38. Not slothful.*

*39. Not a murmurer.*

*40. Not a detractor.*

Is there need for such warnings among the 'work tools of
the spiritual craft'? A competent teacher of the spiritual life
must see and show human nature as it is, in all its frailty and
sinful tendencies caused by sin, which man can overcome
only with the help of divine grace. Hence among the decisive
'instruments of good works' are the following:

*41. To put one's hope in God.*

*42. To attribute any good that one sees in oneself
to God, and not to oneself.*

*43. But to recognize and always impute to oneself
the evil that one does.*

To conquer our nature's weakness resulting from original
sin there is need of strong motivation for aspiring to God.
St Benedict urges us to meditate on the Last Things, as he
had recommended already in the Prologue:

*44. To fear the Day of Judgment.*

*45. To be in dread of hell.*

*46. To desire with a special longing everlasting life.*

*47. To keep death daily before one's eyes.*

In addition St Benedict lists for us some particulars that
are no less powerful in warding off spiritual dangers and in
exercising us in all sorts of 'good deeds'.

*48. To keep guard at all times over the actions of*

one's life.

49. To know for certain that God sees one everywhere.

50. To dash down on the [Rock] Christ one's evil
thoughts the instant that they come into
the hearts:

51. And to lay them open to one's spiritual father.

52. To keep one's mouth from evil & wicked words.

53. Not to love much speaking.

54. Not to speak vain words or such as move to
laughter.

55. Not to love much or excessive laughter.

56. To listen willingly to holy reading.

57. To apply oneself frequently to prayer.

58. Daily to confess one's past sins with tears and
sighs to God, and to amend them for the time
to come.

59. Not to fulfil the desires of the flesh: to hate
one's own will.

60. To obey in all things the commands of the
abbot, even though he himself (which God
forbid) should act otherwise; being mindful of
that precept of the Lord: 'What they say, do
ye; but what they do, do ye not'.

61. Not to wish to be called holy before one is so;
but first to be holy, that one may be truly so
called.

62. Daily to fulfil by one's deeds the commandments of God.

In subsequent chapters of the Holy Rule, especially in
Chapter 7, we shall find all these particularized instruments
organically united and integrated into the structure of the
spiritual life. It is primarily as real *instruments* that we are to
regard them here; as enabling and helpful equipment, their
use in 'the faithful performance of good works' (Prologue)
will become for us as routine and self-evident as is the use of

his tools to an artisan. For instance, if a temptation against purity assails us, this resolve should immediately come alive in us:

*63. To love chastity.*

If thoughts of hatred, jealousy, envy, or arrogance arise in us, if we are in danger of in any way violating fraternal charity and the duties we owe to the community, then 'as it were naturally and by custom' (RB 7) we should take hold of the 'instrument' required by the situation and without delay perform the act of virtue it embodies:

*64. To hate no man.*

*65. Not to give way to jealousy and envy.*

*66. Not to love strife.*

*67. To fly from vainglory.*

*68. To reverence the seniors.*

*69. To love the juniors.*

*70. To pray for one's enemies in the love of Christ.*

*71. To make peace with an adversary before sunset.*

If we were minded actually to employ these instruments to the letter at all times, if for example when enmity threatened we would immediately pray for each other 'in the love of Christ', if in case of a quarrel both parties would do everything 'to make peace before the setting of the sun', how we would grow interiorly day by day and necessarily come nearer to God. By such faithful use the individual instruments become ever more familiar to us and at the same time disclose ever more clearly their meaning and importance for our spiritual life in its entirety.

Human misery and frailty will of course weary us again and again. Human strength simply does not suffice to pursue the way of virtue to the end. So the last of all the 'instruments of good works' and at the same time the most indispensable and the most beautiful, is this:

*72. And never to despair of God's mercy.*

This instrument refers our 'good works' to the source from which alone they derive their strength and their worth—from

'God who prepared for us in advance good deeds, that we may walk in them' (Eph 2:10).

The chapter on the instruments of good works recalls in its make-up the collections of sayings which were widespread in pagan antiquity and by means of which popular philosophy offered people wisdom of life and principles of proper conduct. Even the term 'instrument' in this sense was current. Seneca speaks of 'instruments for a happy life'. With St Benedict this form found its ultimate development:

*Behold, these are the tools of the spiritual craft.*

Benedict offers more than a mere collection of sayings. He really puts 'tools' into our hands to accomplish 'the good works whereby God is reached'. The more faithfully we employ them, the more expert do we become in the 'spiritual craft'. And the more capable do we become, by the grace of God, of making our life a work of art: conforming ourselves to the image and likeness of God.

How happy we shall be on the day of reckoning before God if what we have become through faithful employment of the 'tools of the spiritual craft' is manifestly in conformity with the eternal idea of us in the mind of our Lord and Creator, the divine Artist, if what we have become is what was intended by God's call to us.

*If these tools are constantly employed day and night, and duly given back on the day of judgment, they will gain for us from the Lord that reward which he himself has promised, 'which eye has not seen, nor ear heard; nor has it entered into the heart of man to conceive what God has prepared for them that love him'. And the workshop where we are to labor*    1 Cor 2:19 *at all these things is the cloister of the monastery, and stability in the community.*

The last sentence leads over to Chapter 5, 'Of Obedience', which gives to the basic law of the spiritual life, that of 'hearing and obeying', a new dimension and new fruitfulness.

# ʿObedience

# Without Delay'

## CHAPTER 5: OF OBEDIENCE

TO LISTEN TO GOD and immediately 'respond to God's call by our deeds' (RB Prologue) or, to stay with the metaphor of Chapter 4, to 'employ the instruments of good works constantly day and night', is the simple formula to which St Benedict has reduced christian life in practice.

The will of God, as expressed in the divine command-ments and other directives for virtuous living drawn from Scripture and tradition, does indeed afford a general norm for our life, and more particularly indicates the limits whose overstepping is 'disobedience' and hence sin. Nevertheless there is still much room for human liberty. Anyone who has grasped the mystery of 'listening' feels constrained to place his whole life, in its every phase and manifestation, under obedience to God's will and, in imitation of our Lord, to do 'as he hears'.

As a matter of fact, Christ has shown us a way in close imitation of himself to render an obedience embracing our entire life by the observance of the evangelical counsels: poverty, chastity and obedience. St Benedict sees in these three counsels merely three different forms of 'belonging to God'. By detaching himself from material goods through voluntary poverty, by sacrificing his body through chastity, and by surrendering his will through obedience, man makes himself wholly free for God.

At the same time, it seems to St Benedict that the surrender of the will through obedience, in which the surrender of material goods and of the body is rooted, is so much 'the first degree of humility' and the epitome of all the evangelical counsels that, of these three counsels, he has his monks expressly vow only obedience (RB 58). In Chapter 33 he determines the content of monastic poverty thus: 'They are not allowed to keep anything which the abbot has not given, or at least permitted them to have . . . . Let none presume to give or receive anything without leave of the abbot, nor to keep anything as their own . . . since they are permitted to have neither body nor will in their power'. Obedience then is also the basis of poverty, and all three counsels mean that man sacrifices his ego† entirely so that in its stead God may be all in all.

> *The first degree of humility‡ is obedience without delay. This becomes those who hold nothing dearer to them than Christ, and who on account of the holy servitude which they have taken upon them, either for fear of hell or for the glory of life everlasting, as soon as anything is ordered by the superior, suffer no more delay in doing it than if it had been commanded by God himself. It is of these that the Lord says: 'As soon as the ear heard he has obeyed me'. And again, to teachers he* says: 'Whoever hears you hears me'.*    Ps 18:44    Lk 10:16

Listening and obeying now receive a new and thoroughly practical definition and substance. From now on it is no

---

† Throughout this book, 'ego' means not the self, as used by modern psychology, but the 'self-centered self', the false self.
‡ Here for the first time St Benedict brings in the concept of humility, whose full import is not unfolded until Chapter 7 of the Holy Rule. 'First degree' here means that in the way to God it is the basic degree and in practice the most important. On the 'ladder of humility' in Chapter 7, obedience makes its appearance as the third rung.

longer only in certain divine commandments and in directives sanctioned by tradition that we hear the voice of God. Now we are faced by a man who has authority over us, and we believe· of this 'superior' that he 'holds the place of Christ' (RB 2), that God has given him a mandate and a mission on our behalf, that through him God makes his will known to us. If we listen to him and obey him, therefore, we are listening to God and obeying God: 'The obedience which is given to superiors is given to God' (RB 5).

WHAT IS THE BASIS OF THIS FAITH?

It is a law both of the natural and of the supernatural order into which God has placed us that the way from God to us and from us to God constantly passes through human mediators. It is in this way that the natural life of creation and the supernatural life of grace are given to us.

But there is *one* man whom God has made 'mediator' in a unique way, and through whom he has spoken to man—'the one mediator between God and men, the man Christ Jesus' (I Tm 2:5). By way of the apostles and their successors, to whom our Lord addressed the words, 'He who hears you, hears me' (Lk 10:16), this representative function issues from Christ and goes through the whole structure of his mystical body, the Church. Since the *corpus monasterii*—the monastic body, as St Benedict calls the monastery (RB 61)— is a replica of the entire body of Christ, the monk too recognizes in the abbot, as the visible head of the monastery he has entered, 'the representative of the person of Christ, and therefore calls him Lord and Abbot—not that he has taken it upon himself, but out of reverence and love for Christ' (RB 63).

> Such as these [who believe this] therefore imme-
> diately [upon receiving a command] leaving their
> own occupations and forsaking their own will,
> with their hands disengaged, and leaving unfinished
> what they were about, with the speedy step of

*obedience follow by their deeds the voice of him*
*who commands; and so as it were at the same*
*instant the bidding of the master and the perfect*
*fulfilment of the disciple are joined together in the*
*swiftness of the fear of God by those who are*
*moved with the desire of attaining eternal life.*

Only by faith in the supernatural life flowing from divine love can such 'obedience without delay' be understood. Where this faith is lacking, obedience like this can never be grasped. To someone who has faith, this divine representation is as real as anything else belonging to the world of faith. Likewise the actual rendering of this obedience 'in the swiftness of the fear of God' is self-evident, as Benedict describes it, to him. When God calls, there can be but one response: obedience without delay.

In the area of freedom, where no express divine commandments or directives show the way, the voice of God can now be discerned, through the instrumentality of a human superior as God's representative. No longer is there any sphere of life in which one cannot follow the call of God directly or indirectly. Now one can always act according to 'what he hears'. Now the exhortation of Chapter 4, 'To obey in all things the commands of the abbot' (RB 4.60) has found its real significance and its inner connection with that other exhortation, 'Daily to fulfil by one's deeds the commandments of God' (RB 4.62).†

---

† In their literal sense these statements apply in the first instance to someone engaged 'in the Lord's service in the cloister of the monastery'. But they can also serve as norms for the Christian in the world. Everyone is under obligation to obey, in a variety of situations in the family, in society, in professional life. All these obligations to obey are seen by the Christian in the light of God (it is exactly this that distinguishes him from the non-christian) and in the light of what our Lord said to Pilate as the representative of the civil power: 'You would have no power over me whatever unless it were given to you from above' (Jn 19:11). Thus he can always somehow discern the will of God in these obligations to obey and can, in the spirit of Benedict,

### WHY DOES ANYONE UNDERTAKE SUCH OBEDIENCE?

Monks, says St Benedict, render this obedience 'on account of the holy servitude which they have taken upon them, either for fear of hell or for the glory of life everlasting'. They know that the 'sloth of disobedience' leads away from God and to eternal damnation, but that 'by this path of obedience they shall come unto God' (RB 71).

> *These, therefore, choose the narrow way, of which the Lord says: 'Narrow is the way which leads unto life'; so that living not by*    Mt 7:14 *their own will, nor obeying their own desires and pleasures, but walking according to the judgment and command of another, and dwelling in community, they desire to have an abbot over them.*

Romano Guardini makes a profound statement† about the motive of our Lord's Incarnation: 'But love does such things!' That applies as well to monastic 'obedience without delay'. Love needs no further explanation or justification. One who is 'moved with the desire of attaining eternal life', who 'holds nothing dearer to him than Christ', and who is conscious of having been called by Christ to go this way, 'does things like that'.

> *Such as these without doubt fulfil that saying of the Lord: 'I came not to do my own will, but the will of him who sent me'.*    Jn 6:38

---

act according to 'what he hears'. Here too it is apparent that monastic asceticism does not essentially differ from that which constitutes the way to God for every Christian. It is precisely the concept of authority and obedience which emerges from the Rule of St Benedict that is decisive and basic for the christianization of life, of the family, ultimately of every relationship of authority and obedience. The fact that in the Middle Ages emperors and kings saw the Rule's directives for the abbot as a model for rulers is solid confirmation of the universal christian import of these sections of the Rule.

† *The Lord* (English translation, Chicago: Regnery, 1954) p. 15.

In this obedience there is an especially close resemblance to Christ (Phil 2:5ff), something that binds the monk very intimately to the Son of God who 'was obedient unto death'. In this obedience the spirit of sonship, of being a child, manifests itself in an extraordinary way. To be a son means, of course, to have a father, to listen to this father and 'always to do what pleases him' (Jn 8:29). That is why 'the abbot is called by Christ's name, as the Apostle says: "You have received the spirit of the adoption of children, in which we cry Abba, Father".' (RB 2).

A sacred mystery of faith and love comes to light here. 'He who hears you, hears me,' our Lord says to his disciples in the passage which St Benedict quotes as the justification for monastic obedience. 'He who welcomes me welcomes him who sent me' (Mt 10:40) occurs in a similar context.

Monastic obedience unites abbot and monks in a wonderful oneness of faith and love which is a reflection and emanation of the unity of Father and Son in the Trinitarian life of God. The abbot becomes the 'father of the monastery' (RB 33), the 'spiritual father' of his monks (RB 49), privileged to be their guide to the divine life given them in Christ (Gal 4:19, 1 Cor 4:14-15) if they let him lead and direct them as did Paul his converts. In this way the monastic family, grounded in obedience, grows into a profound union of grace with the eternal Father and his Incarnate Son.

Something of the blessed security in the will of the Father which fills the earthly life of our Lord, something of the strength which flowed to him from oneness with the will of the Father, then overflows into the life of the monk as well. But it will do so only if obedience is taken as seriously as Christ practised it, even obeying his Father's visible representatives to whom 'he was subject' (Lk 2:51, Jn 19:11), and if obedience proceeds from that inner joy and self-surrender which characterized Christ's obedience to the Father because he loved him: 'The world must know that I love the Father and do as the Father has commanded me' (Jn 14:31).

Therefore Benedict concludes his chapter on obedience with the words:

> But this very obedience will then only be acceptable to God and sweet to men, if what is commanded be done not fearfully, tardily, nor coldly, nor with murmuring, nor with an answer showing unwillingness; for the obedience which is given to superiors is given to God, for he himself has said: 'He that hears you, hears me'. And it ought to be given by disciples with a good will, because 'God loves a cheerful giver'. For if the disciple obeys with ill-will, and murmurs not only with his lips but even in his heart, although he fulfils the command, yet this will not be accepted by God, who regards the heart of the murmurer. And for such an action he shall gain no reward; nay, rather, he shall incur the punishment due to murmurers, unless he amend and make satisfaction.

*Lk 10:16*

*2 Co 9:7*

There is something delightful about this cheerful obedience, this security in the Father's will, about being able to submit one's whole life, even its least activities, to a higher 'judgment and command', always to act 'without delay' according to 'what one hears'. How free for God does the one become who is always obedient in this way, 'in the swiftness of the fear of God'!

It is also something surpassingly great to have the privilege of being a 'father' to others in this way, of being the 'voice of God', and to be allowed to take into one's hands the will of free persons as a sacred sacrificial gift in order to present this will to our Lord as an offering of love.

But it is frightfully serious, and ominous as well, to be thus set over others as a superior, and the burden which this obedience imposes upon the superior is much greater than the burden it imposes upon the one who obeys.

St Thomas Aquinas says: 'One man's will can be the rule of another's will only in so far as our neighbor's will adheres to God's will' (*Summa Theologica 11-11 q. 37, a. 1, ad 1 et 2*). In exercising his delegated duties, however, the superior hardly ever receives any indication directly from God as to what he is to proclaim as the will of God in a particular case. So it is by other means that he must strive for the greatest possible uniformity with the will of God.

He must be so 'learned in the law of God' (RB 64) that he 'ought not to teach, or ordain, or command anything contrary to the law of the Lord; but let his bidding and his teaching be infused into the minds of his disciples like the leaven of divine justice' (RB 2). He must endeavor to lead so pure and holy a life, he must seek to abide in so dynamic a union with God, that 'joined to the Lord', as St Paul says, 'he may become one spirit with him' (1 Cor 6:17), and his thinking and willing and commanding may simply flow out of this union with God. Of all the community he must have the finest sensitivity for what is the will of God at any given moment. He must continually be alert and attentive and open to the possibility that God may be speaking to him.

Should a monk come from another monastery 'and if reasonably and with humility he reprove and point out what is amiss, let the abbot prudently mark his words, in case God has perhaps sent him for this very end' (RB 61). The abbot is to 'do all things with counsel', and he must, 'as often as any important matters have to be transacted in the monastery . . . call all to council, because it is often to the younger that the Lord reveals what is best' (RB 3). Therefore, just as the brethren look to the superior to hear God's call from him, so must the superior be receptive in regard to the brethren in order, perhaps, to hear from them what God wants.

The monastery is not a collectivist community in which the individual loses his identity, but an organism in which each member has his own special God-given character, his own special function, his own special grace 'for the common good' (1 Cor 12:7), 'to build up the body of Christ' (Eph 4:12). Christian community does not annul the dignity and the personal God-willed character of the individual, but on the contrary brings them to full development, just as in God himself the most sublime unfolding of personality is consonant with supreme oneness.

The most difficult task of the superior as head of the 'monastic body' is to recognize the personal call of God addressed to each individual member of the community, to give guidance to the individual in conformity with this special mission, and to incorporate it into the community in such a way that the individual and the community thereby grow in the manner willed by God. Consequently he must 'accommodate and suit himself to the character and intelligence of each', he must 'adapt himself to many dispositions' (RB 2).

This obedience of the superior can become far more burdensome than the obedience of the monk, which has its limits in adaptation to the 'character of the superior'. Both superior and subject are thus subject to obedience on a higher level. In his own way and in accordance with his position, each listens by way of the other to God himself: the superior in order to make the call of God known; the subject in order to comply with the call of God. So it is that both say with Christ the Lord, 'It is not to do my own will that I have come, but to do the will of him who sent me' (Jn 6:38).

The import of this concept of authority extends far beyond the monastery. Here lies the christian solution for all conflict between authority and freedom, between ruling and serving. Here the Lord's teaching about duty and dignity and power in his realm is put into practice: 'Anyone among you who aspires to greatness must serve the rest; whoever wants to rank first among you must serve the needs of all. The Son of Man has not come to be served but to serve' (Mk 10:43-45).

How the one and the other converge in the will of God when difficulties arise, how in the last analysis both commanding and obeying are listening to God, is wonderfully demonstrated by Chapter 68 of the Holy Rule:

#### IF A BROTHER BE COMMANDED TO DO THE IMPOSSIBLE.

*If on any brother there be laid commands that are hard and impossible, let him receive the orders of him who bids him with all mildness and obedience. But if he sees the weight of the burden altogether exceeds his strength, let him seasonably and with patience lay before his superior the reasons for his incapacity to obey, without showing pride, resistance, or contradiction. If, however, after this the superior persists in his command, let the younger know that it is expedient for him; and let him obey for the love of God, trusting in his assistance.*

The subject has the right to ask the superior, with due respect, to reconsider whether he is not demanding something 'impossible', something that cannot or should not be done because it does not correspond to the will of God. But the subject may not simply refuse to obey. He must keep the will to obedience basically intact and must therefore receive the orders 'with all mildness and obedience'.

For his part, the superior is duty-bound to give the subject a hearing, to examine in God's sight 'the reasons for his incapacity to obey', to 'listen' anew for what is God's will. Then if after this re-examination the original decision is sustained, the subject can be firmly convinced that the implementation of the command corresponds to the will of God and is therefore 'expedient for him'. Then he has no choice but to 'obey for the love of God', for that supreme motive which is the root of this obedience, 'trusting in the assistance of God' who also gives the strength to accomplish what his will requires.

Anyone who in this way obeys God's representative at all times 'with no more delay than if the command had come from God himself' (RB 5), will necessarily become ever more ready and able to listen for God's call in all circumstances and to follow it without hesitation; such a person will necessarily, as St Benedict says in Chapter 71 of his Rule, 'by this path of obedience come unto God'.

# The Practice of Silence

*CHAPTER 6:* DE TACITURNITATE

'OBEDIENCE without delay', 'which Chapter 5 of the Holy Rule demands, could be called a concentration of all interior and exterior faculties in perfect submission to the call of God. It is not an end in itself, and may never be. 'The obedience which is given to superiors is given to *God.*' It is the exercise and expression of unconditional and all-embracing readiness to render obedience to God. The monk obeys 'as if the command came from God'. This is '*militia*–military service', the obedience of the soldier: schooling, training, preparation for final commitment to God's direct service 'in order to fight for the Lord Christ, our true King' (RB Prologue).

Since for the proper exercise of obedience not the external command of the superior but the internal call of God is decisive, next to obedience St Benedict places *taciturnitas*– the practice of silence.

*Let us do as says the prophet: 'I said, I will
take heed to my ways, that I sin not with my
tongue, I have placed a watch over my mouth;
I became dumb and was silent, and held my
peace even from good things'. Here the          Ps 39:1,2
prophet shows that if we ought at times to
refrain even from good words for the sake of
silence, how much more ought we to abstain
from evil words, on account of the punishment due to sin. Therefore, on account of the
importance of silence, let leave to speak be
seldom granted even to perfect disciples,
although their conversation be good and holy
and tending to edification; because it is
written: 'In speaking much you shall not
avoid sin'; and elsewhere: 'Death and life are    Pr 10:19
in the power of the tongue'. For it becomes       Pr 18:21
the master to speak and to teach, but it
beseems the disciple to be silent and to listen.*

Benedict must have considered what he says here very
essential and fundamental, for he devotes a special chapter
to 'the practice of silence', as he does to obedience. Silence
does indeed have an inner and direct connection with the
basic disposition which is indispensable to the way to God.
Benedict indicates this connection in the statement: 'It
beseems the disciple to be silent and to listen'.

Everything depends on our listening to God, on our
becoming ever more alert to his call. But it is in
stillness that God speaks. Anyone who wants to hear
him must be able to keep silence. God speaks from
within. Anyone who wants to hear him must turn
inward and detach himself from what is 'without', from
things and people: 'I will hear what God proclaims'
(Ps 85:8).

Silence, of course, does not mean merely 'not speaking'.
The practice of silence implies love of quiet, in which the

call of God becomes perceptible. It is the disposition of a person who is waiting for God's call, who opens himself to hear the voice of God. It is the disposition of the 'disciple who is silent and listens' in order to 'learn from the Father' (Jn 6:45). 'Whoever would hear God speak, for him must all voices become mute' (Meister Eckhart).

All those to whom God's call has ever come have been led by God into solitude, into the desert: Moses and Elijah and all the prophets, including the greatest of them, John, the precursor of the Lord, Paul, and Benedict, Francis, and Ignatius. There is no saint through whom God has spoken to man, not one, who has not done 'what the prophet says: "I became dumb and was silent and held my peace".'†

Perhaps there is nothing which for modern man has lost its meaning as much as quiet, silence, has. In treating of prayer (RB 20) St Benedict says that we should expect to be heard 'not for our much speaking' but 'in all lowliness and purity of devotion'. Is our entire spiritual life not more or less dominated by this 'much speaking'? Herein lies one of the principal reasons for the sterility and futility of much well-intentioned effort to make progress on the way to God. We assume that correct prayer consists of our speaking, our telling God what we have at heart. And yet, what can we tell him that he does not already know? Should we not much rather listen for his word? 'An interior listening for God to speak' is prayer much more than 'many words'; it is a praying whereby we simply turn our inmost being toward God, open ourselves interiorly to him and give ourselves to

---

† Ps 39.2. See Guardini, *Wille und Wahrheit* (Mainz, 1958) 42: 'Silence is the expression of an inner condition . . . . Quiet means not merely the absence of speech; it is something in itself. It is an inner presence, a depth and fulness. Quiet is the tranquil flowing of the hidden life. What it is in the sight of God we learn from these words in the Book of Wisdom: "When peaceful stillness compassed everything and the night in its swift course was half spent, your all-powerful word bounded from heaven's royal throne" (18:14–15)'.

him 'in purity of devotion'. 'What is it I must do, Lord?'
(Acts 22:10). 'Speak, Lord, your servant is listening' (1 Sm
3:9). 'I have come to do your will, O God' (Heb 10:7). 'I am
the servant of the Lord. May it be done to me as you say'
(Lk 1:38).

Such prayer issues from silence, from sacred stillness in the
presence of God, and in stillness such as this God speaks to
the heart and begins to work in it. The most important element of the practice of silence is that we learn how to be in
the presence of God in this way, keeping quiet and listening.
Then we shall also understand what St Benedict in general
says about 'much speaking' and 'silence'.

He speaks of 'conversation that is good and holy and
tending to edification, for which, on account of the importance of silence, permission is to be seldom granted even to
perfect disciples'. Here he is referring to the 'spiritual conversations' which from the earliest days of monasticism had
great importance. Benedict considered the exchange of ideas
about God and spiritual matters in such conversations worth-
while. He recommends the assiduous reading of the *Conferences of the Fathers* which Cassian compiled as the fruit of
his travels among the monasteries of the East.

Every year Benedict met with his sister, Scholastica, to
'spend the whole day in the praise of God and in holy
conversation'. At their last meeting it turned out that,
because of his sister's love and the power of her prayer, 'they
spent the whole night in vigil and comforted each other
with holy converse in spiritual things'.† But he did this
'seldom'—once a year. This once was so meaningful, so
gratifying, because it was filled with and permeated by a
year's silence. It was like a seed's bursting forth after long
months of quietly maturing, to grow, to blossom, and to
bear fruit.

---

† Gregory the Great, *Dialogues* II.33, translated by Dom Justin
McCann, *Saint Benedict by Saint Gregory the Great* (Worcester:
Stanbrook Abbey Press, 1951) 64.

Our words about spiritual matters are often wanting in depth and effect because they have not matured and grown in the stillness of silence. They lack the power of which Gregory speaks at the conclusion of his biography of St Benedict: 'Let us by silence renew the power of speech'. No one nowadays wants to wait and 'to be silent and listen as beseems the disciple'. Everyone wants to be a master as soon as possible and 'to speak and teach'. In spiritual conversation, too, there is less concern about hearing and speaking the word of God than about making one's own word heard and offering one's own opinion. How then is God's word to become audible and alive in us? This is why St Benedict demands that all use of speech, especially dialogue on things spiritual, be done in the spirit of humble obedience.

> *And therefore, if anything has to be asked of the superior, let it be done with all humility and subjection of reverence.*

Here, as at the beginning of Chapter 5, the saint again refers to 'humility', which for him is the entire inner disposition we have to acquire. In connection with the completion of his structure of the spiritual life (the ninth to eleventh degrees of humility) he will again speak of what he has anticipated here, because from the very beginning of the spiritual life the practice of silence is of great importance for further progress in the 'school of the Lord's service'.

Perhaps Benedict would have said the same things not only about 'much speaking' but also about 'much reading' (and 'much writing') if it had been as easy and common then as it is today to disseminate thoughts and words in print. How significant and provocative, in contrast to the hastiness and profusion of our spiritual reading, does this simple directive sound: 'In the days of Lent, let each one receive a book from the library, and read it all through in order' (RB 48), that is, one should read the book very thoroughly in the stillness of this holy season, and assimilate it.

The master of the spiritual life concludes his instructions on the practice of silence with a peremptory prohibition of all useless and senseless talk:

> *But as for buffoonery or idle words, such as move to laughter, we utterly condemn them in every place, nor do we allow the disciple to open his mouth in such discourse.*

To anyone who has learned really to observe silence and knows the power of the word that issues from sacred stillness, every senseless use words is like a desecration. The word born of silence is something great and holy. It is a revelation of the spirit. It is, in a very profound sense, an echo of the almighty divine Word which the eternal Father utters (Jn 1).

We are beginning to discern how meaningful and important the chapter 'Of the practice of silence' is. If the word of God is to come through to us, we have to seek the sacred silence in which God speaks to the heart. In silence we must 'hearken to the precepts of the Master, incline the ear of our heart, willingly receive the admonition of our loving Father' in order to 'fulfil it faithfully and return by the labor of obedience to him from whom we had departed through the sloth of disobedience' (RB Prologue). In this way the great ground swell of the Holy Rule becomes ever richer and fuller. 'In quiet and in trust lies your strength' (Is 30:15).

# PART THREE

# THE ASCENT
# TO GOD

# The Degrees
# of Humility

## HUMILITY

WHAT ST BENEDICT has so far said already contains the seed of perfection, and yet in a sense is no more than a preparation for what constitutes the essence of perfection properly so called. It is indeed a part of the way to God, but merely the approach to the foot of the mountain on which stands the tabernacle of God. The real ascent now lies just ahead of us.

Through the practice of good works the 'sloth' of the old man has been vanquished; man has been conditioned to do good. By means of obedience, self-will has been forced from its fundamentally domineering role. Man is now interiorly open to God's call, ready to follow it 'without delay'. There is sacred silence, and in it God's call is perceptible.

Now God can speak and act. Herein really lies the essence of perfection. It is not man who makes himself perfect; it is God who makes man perfect. Spiritual life and christian perfection are, in the last analysis, not man's doing but, as St Benedict has already said in the Prologue, 'the working of God in us', the development of 'the good things he has given us'. Therefore 'these are they who, fearing the Lord, are not puffed up with their own good works, but know that the good which is in them comes not from themselves but from the Lord'. For 'apart from me you can do nothing,' says the Lord (Jn 15:5).

The purpose and goal of all spiritual striving, then, is this: to give oneself wholly to God, to let God act in oneself, to make oneself free for and receptive to 'the inspiration of divine grace', as Benedict says (RB 20). 'All who are led by the Spirit of God are sons of God' (Rom 8:14).

So, to come right down to it, God is all—man is nothing. Everything good in us is God's work. Borne along by the power of his love, all we can do is to cooperate humbly with his grace (cf. Eph 2:10). Therefore if the monk 'sees any good in himself, he must attribute it to God, and not to himself'. Man can also, to be sure, refuse to cooperate with God's grace. That is then his own work: let him 'recognize and always impute to himself the evil that he does' (RB 4).

This being so, man—in accordance with the nature of the creature and the nature of grace—faces the decision whether or not he wants to acknowledge this dependence on God, the Creator and the Giver of grace. Because of his free will, man can also rebel against accepting grace at all. He can—and this is the essence of all sin—follow the example of Lucifer who did not submit in humble acquiescence to grace but in blasphemous pride 'wanted to be like God'.

This pride, this self-exaltation, does not, of course, lead to true exaltation, but, on the contrary, to degradation. By it man, in fact, separates himself from the very source of his life, from the creative power which called him into being. As a result he will be like a child torn from its mother before it is able to live by itself.

*The Holy Scripture cries out to us, brethren,*

*saying: 'Everyone who exalts himself shall be*
*humbled, and he who humbles himself shall*
*be exalted'.† In saying this, it teaches us that*
*all exaltation is a kind of pride, against which*
*the prophet shows himself to be on his guard*
*when he says: 'Lord, my heart is not exalted*
*nor my eyes lifted up; nor have I walked in*
*great things, nor in wonders above me'. For*     Ps 131:1
*why? 'If I did not think humbly, but exalted*
*my soul: like a child that is weaned from his*
*mother, so will you requite my soul.'*           Ps 131:2

These words of the Psalmist express simply and profoundly that fundamental and definitive disposition of humble docility whereby the soul opens itself to the 'spirit of
sonship' in order to be 'led by it' (cf. Rom 8:14). The most
profound expression of this humble docility ever spoken by a
human being are the words of the Mother of God: 'I am the
servant of the Lord. May it be done to me as you say'
(Lk 1:38). By these words Mary opened her entire being in
humble obedience to the gracious love of God. She wanted
only to be a servant, a handmaid, wholly submissive and
ready for everything God willed to do in her and through
her. And so the Word could be made flesh and dwell in her.

This fundamental and definitive disposition which man

---

† This statement of Our Lord is recorded three times: at the end of
the parable of the Pharisee and the tax collector (Lk 18:14), in connection with the banquet at which those invited sought the first place
(Lk 14:11), and in a major discourse 'to the crowds and his disciples'
(Mt 23) in which Jesus contrasts the spirit of the Pharisees with the true
godly spirit. The Pharisees 'believed in their own self-righteousness
while holding everyone else in contempt' (Lk 18:9). In conceited self-
justification they boasted of their works, which in reality were
nothing in the eyes of God. This pharisaical spirit is the most
pronounced and evident antithesis of christian humility. Humility
makes man aware that God is all, and man is nothing. The pharisaical
spirit is the ultimate pitfall of all serious striving for virtue. Hence our
Lord's hostility to it.

must offer to God is called *humilitas* by Benedict, 'humility', which expresses submissiveness in contrast to the arrogant 'I will not serve' of the first man. The latin word *humilitas,* whose root meaning is lowliness, abasement, implies other aspects of this fundamental disposition and it is to these that Christ made reference when he spoke of self-abasement, as he does in the passage with which Benedict begins his chapter on humility, or when he discourses on 'self-denial, renunciation of self', on 'losing one's life', on relinquishing all possessions as a prerequisite for being his disciple and for possessing the kingdom of God (Mt 16:24,25; Lk 9:23,24; 14:33; Mk 8:34,35; Jn 12:24,25). What he always meant is essentially what Benedict wanted to express by *humilitas:* that man in his sinful pride must bow low before God, that he must sacrifice his haughty ego, 'so God may be all in all' (1 Cor 15:28). That is the core of christian humility, of benedictine humility.

Actually man should not have a feeling of 'abasement' when he strives for the basic disposition of humility before God. He should have this disposition *velut naturaliter,* quite naturally, as self-evident, St Benedict says at the end of his chapter on humility, for it is rooted in the natural relationship of man to God and is therefore wholly consonant with truth.

Through sin this original order of nature was perverted. The human will lost the orientation to God proper to its nature and became 'self-will' alienated from God. Restoration of right order and 'return to God' is possible only if man renounces his own now sinful will (RB Prologue), only if the God-defying ego is driven from the eminence it has arrogated to itself, only if it is brought low. Ever since the first sin the basic disposition of humility during life on earth can no longer be separated from what the word *humilitas* expresses: abasement, humiliation, renunciation of self.

That is why Christ the Lord himself chose the way of humility for mankind's redemption, the way of voluntary, expiatory abasement so graphically described by St Paul in that passage of Philippians (2:5ff) which St Benedict quotes in the third degree of humility:

> *Your attitude must be that of Christ: though he was in the form of God . . . he emptied himself and took the form of a slave . . . humbled himself, obediently accepting even death, death on a cross! Because of this, God highly exalted him . . .*

It is not merely a verbal sameness which connects this pauline text with our Lord's words about self-abasement and exaltation, quoted at the beginning of the chapter on humility, and with Benedict's own comments. Paul and Benedict mean the same thing: 'Your attitude must be that of Christ!' The humility of the Holy Rule is nothing other than the imitation of the humble, obedient, crucified Saviour. By this way of 'abasement' we shall with him attain 'heavenly exaltation'.

> *Wherefore, brothers, if we wish to arrive at the highest point of humility, and speedily to reach that heavenly exaltation to which we can only ascend by the humility of this present life, we must by our ever-ascending actions erect such a ladder as that which Jacob beheld in his dream, by which the angels appeared to him descending and ascending.*

Because it is so difficult for man weakened in intellect and will by original sin to grasp the fact that true exaltation can be attained only through humiliation, and because at the same time everything depends on our acceptance of this truth deep within ourselves, St Benedict makes use of an uncomplicated metaphor whose meaning even the simplest, most unsophisticated person can understand—the image of Jacob's ladder with ascending and descending angels. This simultaneous ascent and descent are for him a vivid picture of what the Word of the Lord wants to express: 'Everyone who exalts himself shall be humbled, and anyone who humbles himself shall be exalted' (Lk 14:11, 18:14).

> *This descent and ascent signifies nothing else than*
> *that we descend by self-exaltation and ascend by*
> *humility. And the ladder thus erected is our life*
> *in the world, which, if the heart be humbled, is*
> *lifted up by the Lord to heaven. The sides of the*
> *same ladder we understand to be our body and*
> *soul.*

The fundamental and definitive disposition of humility must permeate our outward and inward life. It must fill the soul and overflow from it to the body and thus take hold of man in his entirety.

> *In these sides [of the ladder] our divine vocation*
> *has placed various degrees of humility or disci-*
> *pline, which we must ascend.*

Ever new depths into which he must descend are disclosed to someone who walks the path of humility; ever new heights to which the grace of God is beckoning are shown him. Ever more relentlessly and radically man learns 'to renounce his own will', until God's will has wholly displaced it. Ever more clearly he recognizes the nothingness of his own existence; ever more overwhelmingly God's greatness looms before him, the incomprehensibility of his gracious love, the dazzling holiness of his being. More and more man 'loses his life'; more and more powerfully God's life flows into him.

There is no limit to this descent into the depths of created nothingness, or to the elevation into the fullness of divine being. So it is that at the conclusion of his Rule (RB 72) Benedict can assert that he proposes to teach only 'a beginning of holiness', the initial basic steps or degrees of the way leading upward to God. The benedictine tradition holds that these twelve steps or degrees of humility include everything in the way of devotion and acquiescence that man can offer in response to the grace of God.

What St Benedict says to us by this figure of the ladder of humility, he derived in substance from the living Word of

God in Holy Scripture, from the practical experience of monasticism before him, and from his own inner struggles and battles. It is this which gives his doctrine on humility its power of conviction. Here too is given the key to understanding this doctrine. Its meaning is not disclosed to someone who is looking for a theory of the spiritual life—that was far from St Benedict's mind—but only to someone who wishes 'to reach that heavenly exaltation by the humility of the present life' and is therefore resolved to conduct himself in accordance with these directives. If we want to understand the way to God which Benedict points out in his degrees of humility, we have to walk it courageously even though in some details the full meaning of his directives may be hidden from us for the time being. What this master of the spiritual life is telling us will then really become for us 'the way to God'.

# Walking in the Fear of God

## THE FIRST DEGREE OF HUMILITY

*The first degree of humility, then, is that a man, always keeping the fear of God before his eyes, avoid all forgetfulness.*

GOD IS THE SUPREME goal we seek to attain. What is more natural than that we should always have this goal before our eyes and never forget it? But why should fear first and foremost dominate our thinking about God?

The concept a person has of God is decisive for his spiritual life. It does not even occur to most people to call to mind that they are dealing with God, with a Being who surpasses all our concepts, with God who, as St Benedict says, is 'the Lord God of all things' (RB 20). He is Lord in the absolute sense of the word: upon him we are dependent down to the utmost depth of our being; he has unrestricted dominion over us; to him we are obligated for all that we are and have; he can give us commands and precepts which it is our unconditional duty to heed and fulfill.

At the beginning of our way we must become fully aware that it is this God with whom we are dealing. Hence the first degree of humility states:

> *The first degree of humility, then, is that a man, always keeping the fear of God before his eyes, avoid all forgetfulness; and that he be ever mindful of all that God has commanded, bethinking himself that those who despise God will be consumed in hell for their sins, and that life everlasting is prepared for them that fear him.*

Upon the infinite Being we call God and upon the fulfilment of his commands depends our eternal destiny. This God can make us eternally happy or he can damn us for all eternity. One or the other he will do.

It is terrifying to be subject to such a Being, to know that God has irrevocably destined me to unending existence, to eternal life or, if I am unworthy of that, to eternal damnation. The words of our Lord come to mind: 'Fear him who can destroy both body and soul in Gehenna!' (Mt 10:28).

Within ourselves we should ponder each of these words; we should let them work on us in quiet meditation. Then we shall experience how fraught with meaning every single word is. Then something of God's majesty will flash upon us. Then we shall become conscious of his incomprehensible reality. Over us will come a salutary fear that we might, by some neglect of his commandments, by some sin, offend this tremendous, almighty God, who will in the future admit us to bliss or sentence us to damnation. Once anyone is seized by this fear,

> *keeping himself at all times from sin and vice, whether of the thoughts, the tongue, the hands, the feet, or his own will, let him thus hasten to cut off the desires of the flesh. Let him consider that he is always beheld from heaven by God, and that his actions are everywhere seen by the eye of the Divine Majesty, and are every hour reported to him by his angels.*

How terrifying is this glance of God which penetrates all things, even our most secret thoughts!

> *This the prophet tells us, when he shows how God is ever present in our thoughts, saying: 'God searches the heart and the soul'. And*    Ps 7:9
> *again: 'The Lord knows the thoughts of men.' And he also says: 'You have understood*    Ps 94:11
> *my thoughts from afar off'; and 'Man's*    Ps 139:2
> *thought shall praise you'.*    Ps 76:10

We have to think these words through very slowly and let them work on us. God's glance penetrates to the utmost depth of our soul. We can hide our thoughts from man, and how glad we are that we can do so, glad that our fellowmen know nothing of our frequently selfish, proud, uncharitable thoughts, but 'the Lord knows the thoughts of men. You have understood my thoughts afar off. Man's thought shall praise you.' 'The eyes of the Lord, ten thousand times brighter than the sun, observe every step a man takes and peer into hidden corners. He who knows all things before they exist, still knows them all after they are made. The sinner says to himself, "Who can see me? Darkness surrounds me, walls hide me; no one sees me; why should I be afraid to sin?" He does not understand that the eyes of the Lord see all things' (Sir 23).

> *In order, therefore, that he may be on his*
> *guard against evil thoughts, let the humble*
> *brother say ever in his heart: 'Then shall I be*
> *unspotted before him, if I have kept myself*
> *from my iniquity'.*                                   Ps 18:23

This thought, that we are constantly in the sight of God, must have made an impression on St Benedict and he must have experienced its beneficial effect profoundly. Clearly he considered it of great importance that we make this thought our own, way down deep within ourselves, for there is hardly any other single point in his Holy Rule that he develops so extensively.

Every movement of our will likewise lies open before God. He knows all the self-seeking, self-willed, perverse tendencies in man. In nothing do we deceive ourselves so easily as in regard to the purity of our intentions. We do not deceive God. How we shall one day tremble at the judgment when in the light of God we recognize our will as perverse and dishonorable and self-seeking! St Benedict continues:

> *We are, indeed, forbidden to do our own will*
> *by Scripture—which says to us: 'Turn away*
> *from your own will'. And so too we beg God*        Sir 18:30
> *in prayer that his will may be done in us.*
> *Rightly therefore are we taught not to do our*
> *own will, if we take heed to the warning of*
> *Scripture: 'There are ways which to men seem*
> *right, but the ends thereof lead to the depths*
> *of hell'; or, again, when we tremble at what is*     Pr 16:25
> *said of the careless: 'They are corrupt and*
> *have become abominable in their pleasures.'*        Ps 14:1

What a frightening statement this is: 'There are ways which to men seem right, but the ends thereof lead to the depths of hell'. A person can, through his own fault, delude himself into a false security, considering something to be the way to God which in reality leads away from God. The Sanhedrin thought itself obliged to inflict the death penalty for blasphemy on Jesus for his claim to divine sonship (Mt 26: 65). Our Lord warns his disciples: 'A time will come when anyone who puts you to death will claim to be serving God!'' (Jn 16:2). With inexorable severity Jesus exposed the self-deception to which the Scribes and Pharisees had fallen victim in thought and act (Mt 23).

All these considerations force us to recognize our own unreliability and insecurity, injured as we are by sin and hence always menaced, and humbly to acknowledge the all-merciful love of God which alone can save us.

*And in regard to the desires of the flesh, we must believe that God is always present to us, as the prophet says to the Lord: 'O Lord, all my desire is before you'.* Ps 38:9

Oh, if we humans only knew what power the flesh still has over us, what ugly cravings still come to life in us! 'All my desire is before you.'

*Let us be on our guard, then, against evil desires, since death has its seat close to the entrance of delight; wherefore the Scripture commands us, saying: 'Go not after your evil desires.'* Sir 18:30

How great is he from whom nothing is hidden! God knows all. The whole course of my life lies open before him. One day he will pronounce judgment upon this life: upon my thoughts, the movements of my will, my desires, my actions. Once such thoughts have sprung to life with full force, the firm decision must be made never to offend this all-knowing God, cost what it may.

*Since, therefore, 'The eyes of the Lord behold the good and the evil', and 'The Lord is ever looking down from heaven upon the children of men, to see who has understanding or is seeking God'; and since the works of our hands are reported to him day and night by* Pr 15:3

Ps 14:2

*the angels appointed to watch over us; we
must be always on the watch, brothers, lest,
as the prophet says in the psalm, God should
see us at any time declining to evil and become unprofitable; and lest, though he spare
us now because he is merciful and expects our
conversion, he should say to us hereafter:
'These things you did and I held my peace'.*          Ps 50:21

The great incomprehensible God is good, infinitely good.
He does not want to punish. He does not want to condemn.
He prefers to spare. But it is this very goodness which is for us
a new reason to fear. God does not punish immediately. He
'expects our conversion'. He remains silent. He does not
react to our sins, even big sins, even the sins of those who are
consecrated to him. And, alas, we misinterpret this silence.
We abuse this goodness. We delude ourselves in false security.
Woe to us if we heedlessly live and die in such self-deception,
if this God in his justice must say to us then: 'These things
you did and I held my peace!' O God, how man must
necessarily fear you!

We sense, in this first degree of humility, that this is no
casual exercise of the fear of God, one exercise among others
in the spiritual life, but the foundation for our entire relationship to God, the initiation of a fundamental spiritual
disposition which determines our whole life. Before our soul
the perception of God so blazes up in all its dynamic glory that
its tremendous power can never afterwards escape us. God's
glance struck us and from now on will ever rest upon us.
'Always keeping the fear of God before our eyes, therefore,
we avoid all forgetfulness.' We are thoroughly convinced
'that our actions are everywhere seen by the eye of the
divine Majesty.' We learn for ourselves what Gregory the
Great says of St Benedict: 'He lived alone with himself under
the eyes of the heavenly Watchman' (*Dialogues II.3*).

With overwhelming clarity we become aware and we remain
aware of who it is we are dealing with in the spiritual life:

with the infinite, all-powerful, all-knowing God. We experience something like the prophet Isaiah did when he stood before the thrice-holy God: 'Woe is me, I am doomed! For I am a man of unclean lips' (Is 6:5). Woe is me if I do not stand sinless before this God! 'Only then shall I be unspotted before him, if I shall have kept me from my iniquity.'

In his biography of St Benedict, St Gregory dwells on the statement we quoted above: 'He lived alone with himself under the eyes of the heavenly Watchman'. And in answer to the question of his disciple Peter he gives a more precise explanation of the phrase 'he lived alone with himself' (*habitavit secum*): 'Often because of distractions in our thoughts we are too much carried out of ourselves; although we remain ourselves, yet we are not with ourselves, for we lose sight of ourselves and let our thoughts ramble.' Gregory refers to the prodigal son in the gospel, who left his father's house, went the ways of sin, and thereby lost himself. So it is that Scripture says of him, 'he returned to himself' (Lk 15:17).

The disciplined control of thoughts, desires, movements of the will, which St Benedict in the first degree of humility seeks to instil, brings man back to himself from all distraction and straying, lets him find his true self made in the image of God, and enables him to present himself before God in divinely willed self-possession as a person. St Augustine expresses the same thought when he says in reference to the time of his own estrangement from God: 'You were within and I was outside'.

We are beginning to understand the depth and solidity our spiritual life acquires when we base it on the fear of God. There is no longer any room for sin and indifference and superficiality. That is why St Benedict wants this fear of God to fill and permeate the entire life of the monk: 'Come, my children, hearken to me, I will teach you the fear of the Lord' (RB Prologue).

'In the swiftness of the fear of God' the monk must at all times obey 'without delay' (RB 5). 'Serve the Lord in fear' applies in a special way to the work of God (RB 19). A holy gravity should pervade the monastery, 'the house of God'. An everlasting ban is therefore placed upon 'buffoonery or idle words, such as move to laughter' (RB 6). For the same reason even 'all the vessels and goods of the monastery' must be regarded as belonging to God 'as though they were the consecrated vessels of the altar' (RB 31).

The higher a man is placed, the more important the office entrusted to him and consequently the greater his responsibility before God, the more must he be filled with the fear of God. 'Let there be chosen as cellarer of the monastery a God-fearing man' (RB 31). 'For the sick brethren let one who is God-fearing, diligent and careful be appointed to serve them' (RB 36). 'Let the care of the guest-house also be entrusted to a brother whose soul is possessed with the fear of God' (RB 53). 'With all mildness and the fear of God let the porter give reply' when someone comes to the door (RB 66).

It is 'in the fear of God' that the monastic community is to undertake the most important act it can perform, the election of a new abbot (RB 64). The abbot himself must 'do everything with the fear of God and in observance of the Rule: knowing that he will have without doubt to render to God, the most just Judge, an account of all his judgments' (RB 3). With the most incisive words St Benedict again and again reminds the abbot of the fear of God and of judgment. This is actually the only safeguard he provides against the dangers of the abbot's almost unlimited authority, and Benedict considers this safeguard sufficient to obviate these dangers.

In making the fear of God the foundation of the spiritual life, Benedict is simply following the example of Our Lord. Christ the Lord sent the stern preacher of penance, John the Baptist, ahead of him as a precursor, to open hearts through salutary fear of God, and he began his own preaching of the kingdom with a call to penance and conversion.

Benedict is likewise following the guidance of the Holy
Spirit, who already in the Old Testament, in the Book of
Sirach, sang the canticle of the fear of God and on the first
Pentecost poured out this holy fear upon the Church as a
precious gift. 'Great fear came upon all' recorded the Acts of
the Apostles (Acts 2:37, 43; 5:5, 11). Out of this fear, out of
this seizure by the glory and the nearness of God, love burst
forth, that great apostolic love which set the whole world
ablaze, that great martyr-love which was capable of any
sacrifice, that great brotherly love in which all were 'of one
heart and one mind' (Acts 4:32).

Love needs fear as its forerunner. This is so because the
mystery that God loves us and that we may love him in return
is really much more frightening and sobering than is the fact
that God is 'Lord of all' whom we must fear. Holy fear, 'which
pierces the heart' (Acts 2:37), opens hearts so that the love of
God may be 'poured out in them through the Holy Spirit who
has been given to us' (Rom 5:5). 'Fullness of wisdom is fear
of the Lord; she intoxicates men with her fruits' (Sir 1:14).

Walking in the
Will of God

## THE SECOND DEGREE OF HUMILITY

*The second degree of humility is, that a man*
*love not his own will, nor delight in fulfilling*
*his own desires; but carry out in his deeds*
*that saying of the Lord: 'I came not to do my*

*own will, but the will of him who sent
me'. And again Scripture says: 'Self-will gains*  Jn 6:38
*punishment, but necessity wins the crown.'*

WE COMPARED the spiritual effect of the first degree of humility with what the prophet Isaiah experienced when he was brought into the presence of the thrice-holy God. Recognition of his creaturely nothingness and of his sinfulness overwhelmed him, giving rise in him to a burning desire for purification and sinlessness. God himself satisfied this craving by having an angel touch the mouth of the seer with fire from his altar so that his mouth and heart might be made pure by the cleansing fire of divine holiness. The prophet continued the account: 'Then I heard the voice of the Lord saying, "Whom shall I send? Who will go for us?" "Here I am," I said; "send me!" ' (Is 6:8,9).

In 'the sight of the Divine Majesty' it is not only the desire to purge the soul of all opposition to God's all-holy will that comes to life. Recognition comes, too, that the will of God is the sum total of all holiness, all goodness, all perfection. There is a readiness to surrender self, to abandon self completely to this holy will, a longing to become wholly one with this will—'sharing in the divine will,' as Clement of Alexandria says (*Stromata,* VII 78,4).

From the first degree of humility, then, proceeds the second, consisting in this, 'that a man love not his own will' fixed in the perversion of original sin, 'nor delight in fulfilling his own desires' arising out of the ego alienated from God. But radically and without reserve he replaces self-will with God's will and makes this the norm of his whole life in accordance with 'that saying of the Lord: "I came not to do my own will, but the will of him who sent me" ' (Jn 5:30).

Here too, as in the first degree of humility, there is no question of submission to the will of God in this or that instance as an act of a specific virtue among others, but of a fundamental spiritual disposition governing all our thoughts and actions. It is the organic development and deepening of the spiritual disposition implanted by the first degree of humility. From the fear of sinning against the will of God grows the desire and readiness at all times to fulfil God's holy will as perfectly as possible. 'Walking in the fear of the Lord' becomes 'walking in the will of the Lord.'

We are back to what has been from the outset the keynote of the Holy Rule: the disposition of 'listening and obeying' whereby we 'return to God'. It finds its purest and most perfect expression in the life of the incarnate Son of God. St Benedict now refers explicitly to this model. In the words which St Benedict here puts into the mouth of his disciple, our Lord himself summarized the fundamental motivation for what he willed and did: 'I came not to do my own will, but the will of him who sent me'.

When our Lord speaks of the mission he received from the Father, he refers to the most intimate mystery of his being and his life, to the ultimate purpose of his divine-human existence, indeed to the most profound mystery of the Godhead itself. The mission to which his words directly refer is the Father's mandate for the redemption of the world. But this mission is rooted in a previous and more profound mission, that mysterious procedure (or procession) in the innermost depth of the Godhead, which the doctrine of the Blessed Trinity enunciates. From all eternity the Father utters the Word who 'was present to God in the beginning, and the Word was God' (Jn 1:1).

This Word is the only-begotten Son of the eternal Father, born of him as the reflection of his glory, as the image of his substance. The Father lets the totality of the divine being he bears in himself pour forth into the Son in infinite love. In the same love whereby the Father gives himself to the Son, however, the Son in turn gives himself to the Father, 'hears' the Word the Father utters, receives into himself everything contained in this Word and lets it flow back again to its source. In this mutual love of the Father and the

Son, in the exultant joy of the Holy Spirit, the cycle of the divine life is consummated, Father and Son are one in unending bliss. We see what in the final analysis the will of God is: nothing other than the love of God, that love which unites Father and Son, that love which in the Holy Spirit is a divine Person.

We understand why the incarnate Son of God cannot judge and act otherwise than 'as he hears', why he must be ever attentive to the call of the Father, why he came not to do his own will but the will of him who sent him. Exultation echoes in the Saviour's words when he speaks of the will of his Father. The Father's will is his 'food' (Jn 4:34), his nourishment, his vital energy. For him the will of the Father is nothing else than the Father's love. In fulfilling this loving will of the Father he exercises his own love of the Father: 'The world must know that I love the Father and do as the Father has commanded me' (Jn 14:31).

So it becomes clear why for us a necessary step in the ascent to God is not to love our own will but to embrace and acquiesce with total love to God's will. Indeed, the sacred mission of which our Lord speaks is transmitted to us: 'As the Father has sent me, so I send you. As the Father has loved me, so I have loved you. Live on in my love. You will live in my love if you keep my commandments, even as I have kept my Father's commandments, and live in his love' (Jn 20:21; 15:9,10).

We have come forth from this same love of the Father that was the reason for the creation of Christ's humanity. As children of grace we have been begotten to the supernatural life of divine sonship out of the same love that begot the incarnate Son of the Father. ' . . . that your love for me may live in them, and I may live in them' (Jn 17:26). So we are also 'predestined to share the image of his Son, that the Son might be the first-born of many brothers' (Rom 8:29).

For us too, then, the will of the Father must become 'food', the substance of our life, the law of our life. Only if our life develops in conformity with the creative and grace-giving will of God can it fulfill its purpose, can that which God's love intended when it 'sent' us into the world be realized. Any attempt to live according to 'our own will' and 'our own desires', apart from the will of God, in opposition to it, means separation from the source of our life, and therefore death.

The real purpose of the temptation of Christ was that Satan wanted to divert him from his mission, from the path that the Father had appointed, that he wanted to induce him to go his own way in bringing happiness to mankind. The aim of all temptation is to make us want to 'depart from God', from his will, from the plan that God's wisdom and love has for us. It is the essence of all sin that we become 'disobedient' and rebel against God's holy will, that we want to go our own way and no longer want to fulfill God's command. Such disobedience, however, robs our life of its basic significance, its God-given meaning, and therefore necessarily leads to eternal absurdity and frustration, to 'hell'. Hence 'Scripture says: "Self-will has punishment, but necessity [—submission to the will of God—] wins the crown".'

By fulfillment of the divine will our life 'wins the crown', we accomplish our God-given mission, we give effect to God's call to us. Or rather, the almighty will of God itself gains entrance into us in the measure that we submit to this will, and it accomplishes in us what it wants to accomplish. Someone who has grasped the mystery of the divine will knows that he is directed and sustained by the holy will of God, just as Christ knew he was guided by will of the Father. He knows that back of his life is God's 'will and pleasure' (Eph 1:5) which cannot but be infallibly realized if he himself makes the effort to enter into this will of God.

With pride and joy Paul called himself 'an apostle by the will of God' (Eph 1:1, 2 Cor 1:1). This consciousness of being 'by God's will an apostle of Jesus Christ' was for him the

source of invincible courage and victorious power in all life
situations. We too are what we are 'by the will of God'. If, as
our Lord said explicitly, 'not a single sparrow falls to the
ground without your Father's consent', if 'every hair of your
head has been counted' (Mt 10:29,30), surely there can be
nothing in our life that has not been assumed into the 'will
and pleasure' of God overshadowing our life, that cannot
serve the purpose of divine providence.

Everything that happens to us and around us, our vocation, the people with whom we come into contact, the particular circumstances in which we find ourselves—everything
becomes for us in one way or another the expression of the
divine will. Suffering and sorrow, too, all deviation and error,
all human misery and weakness, indeed even faults and sins,
must in the final analysis serve the ends of the loving will of
God. 'For those who love God'—and enter into the divine
will—'all things work together for good' (Rom 8:28).

From this total submission to the divine will, as taught by
the second degree of humility, comes that absolute trust in
God with which St Benedict's life was filled. What unshak-
able, faith-filled confidence there is in what he says to the
monks who complained about the lack of water in their
mountain monasteries: 'Almighty God has power to supply
you with water even on the summit of the mountain' (*Dialogues* 2.5). And God did produce water in answer to the
saint's trusting prayer.

Out of this same faith-filled confidence issues the directive in Chapter 28 of the Holy Rule regarding those 'who,
being often corrected, do not amend'. If the abbot has done
everything to bring an erring brother back to the right way
and nevertheless 'sees that his labors are of no avail, let him
add what is still more powerful: his own prayers and those
of all the brothers for him, that God, who is all-powerful,
may effect the cure of the sick brother'. Always and everywhere the guiding principle must be 'to put one's hope in
God . . . . Never to despair of God's mercy'. Thus filled with
faith and confidence does the man become who has wholly

abandoned himself to the will of God. 'Necessity wins the crown.'

Everything depends on this—that we consciously, without reserve and in every respect, embrace the will of God, that we never 'love our own will, nor delight in fulfilling our own desires; but carry out in our deeds that saying of the Lord: "I came not to do my own will, but the will of him who sent me".'

The crucial question for the attainment of our goal in life is: 'Lord, what will you have me do?' (Acts 9:6). Our most important prayer is this: 'Teach me to do your will, for you are my God. May your good spirit guide me on level ground' (Ps 143:10). 'Behold I come . . . . To do your will, O my God, is my delight, and your law is within my heart!' (Ps 40:8,9). 'Here I am; send me!' (Is 6:8).

All those whom God has used as instruments to accomplish his works of grace, through whom he has done great things in his kingdom, have been persons who submitted themselves to the will of God, who were unreservedly ready for anything God asked and imposed, who stood before God like the prophet Jeremiah to whom he said: 'To whomever I send you, you shall go; whatever I command you, you shall speak. Have no fear before them, because I am with you' (Jer 1:7,8). 'Necessity wins the crown.'

Furthermore, whenever and wherever a person has become futile, whenever and wherever a created personal being has no longer made sense, it has been because the creature substituted its own will for the divine will, like Adam in paradise, like Lucifer, the adversary of God. 'Self-will gains punishment.'

It was when Mary spoke her *fiat* in unconditional docility and self-surrender, and opened herself completely to the holy will of God that the Holy Spirit came upon her, that the power of the Most High overshadowed her, and that the Holy One was to be born of her (cf. Lk 1:35). Any soul that, like Mary, says its *fiat,* and in the measure that it does so, is made 'full of grace', enters into the inner stream of Trinitarian life, 'participates in the divine will', by being taken up into the mutual self-giving of the Father and of the Son in the Holy Spirit.

'Anyone who loves me will be true to my word, and my Father will love him; we will come to him and make our dwelling place with him. He who does not love me does not keep my words. Yet the word you hear is not mine; it comes from the Father who sent me' (Jn 14:23,24).

Anyone who says, *Fiat voluntas tua*–Thy will be done, likewise says *Fiat caritas tua*–Thy love be done. Anyone who makes the will of God his own, thereby makes the substantial love of God his own, admits God of whom the apostle says, 'God is love' (1 Jn 4:8).

In this love the will of God becomes blessedly unburdensome. It anneals what is hard in it and recasts it into a claim upon 'the glorious freedom of the children of God' (Rom 8:21), into a gently imploring wish which is gladly met. The utter responsiveness of love such as this is expressed in the simple statement by which St Thérèse of the Child Jesus revealed her interior state: 'Since the age of three I have never refused my Lord any wish'. That is the shortest way to holiness: never to refuse God any wish, always to be open and alert for God's call, always to be ready to do his will.

In the spirit of St Benedict's second degree of humility, may we at all times make every effort to 'carry out in our deeds that saying of the Lord: "I came not to do my own will, but the will of him who sent me".' to become persons whose every movement of the will merges into that supreme self-surrender whereby the incarnate Son of God abandoned himself to the Father in the ardor of the Holy Spirit for the salvation of the world.

# Obedience

# unto Death

## THE THIRD DEGREE OF HUMILITY

*The third degree of humility is, that a man
for the love of God submit himself to his
superior in all obedience; imitating the Lord,
of whom the apostle says: 'He was made
obedient even unto death'.*                    *Ph 2:8*

IN OUR ANALYSIS of Chapter 5 of the Holy Rule we have
already noted how monastic obedience gives real substance
to surrender of self to God, how it offers the possibility of
freeing life in its entirety from the tyranny of self-will and
of subjecting it to the divine will through the visible representative of God. We have considered the more profound
aspect of this obedience and the motive of love that leads to
it. It has become clear to us that this obedience whereby
man gives up the core of his being, his own will, can never be
an end in itself but always and merely the manifestation of
submission to God himself.

St Benedict gives eloquent expression to this by the name
he assigns to the superior of the monastic community, the
abbot: 'Let him be called Lord and Father, not that he has
taken it upon himself, but out of reverence and love for
Christ' (RB 63).

'Lord and Father'. This twofold name is in fact the most
concise formulation of St Benedict's concept of God, and it

was paramount in his life and in his teaching. God is Lord in the absolute sense of the word, 'the Lord of all' whom man must fear and serve with total self-surrender. But he is also our Father 'who has vouchsafed to count us in the number of his children' (RB Prologue), who has given us 'the spirit of the adoption of children, in which we cry Abba, Father' (RB 2, Rm 8:15).

For the person who is subject, this twofold name is a constant reminder that 'the obedience which is given to superiors is given to God' (RB 5). The superior, for his part, must be made aware by this title that he is merely the representative of One Higher, that he is obeyed 'out of reverence and love for Christ. Let him be mindful of this, and show himself to be worthy of such an honor' (RB 63).

In the third degree of humility St Benedict now incorporates this obedience into his way to God. What he thereby wants particularly to stress, continuing from Chapter 5, is doubtless the nature of the humility, submission, abasement inherent in this obedience, the spiritual dying which is inseparable from it and which is a reproduction of Christ's obedience unto death.

Monastic obedience is 'self-subjection', 'self-surrender' not only to another's will but, as Chapter 5 has already pointed out, often to 'another's judgment' as well. It embodies in itself a sacrifice which in both substance and duration is all-inclusive; in perfect, all-embracing obedience the monk is to submit himself to the superior. 'Let him be subjected to the punishment prescribed by the Rule, who dares to leave the enclosure of the monastery, or to go anywhere, or to do anything, however trifling, without permission of the abbot' (RB 67). 'They are not allowed to keep anything which the abbot has not given, or at least permitted them to have' (RB 33).

Even good works are worthless in the sight of God if they have been done without the blessing of obedience: 'Let each one make known to his abbot what he offers up [during

Lent], and let it be done with his blessing and permission: because what is done without leave of the spiritual father shall be imputed to presumption and vainglory, and merit no reward. Everything, therefore, is to be done with the approval of the abbot' (RB 49).

We get the feeling that there is something 'radical' here, something that lays hold of our will at its very roots, that really means a spiritual dying. It is 'obedience unto death'.

In the fourth degree of humility where Benedict describes the 'hard and contrary things in this obedience' he quotes the psalm verse, 'For you we suffer death all the day long; we are esteemed as sheep for the slaughter' (Rm 8:36). Here his concept of obedience comes into contact with the age-old monastic idea that the monk is the heir of the martyrs. Whereas the martyr imitates 'Christ's obedience unto death' by a bloody sacrificial death, the monk does so by death in spirit through obedience.

This readiness to die in spirit belongs to obedience to the all-inclusive extent that St Benedict sees and demands. Where obedience is understood and practised and required in the sense of Chapter 5, its character is felt to be less painful, even though 'the earthly man' may ever and again rebel against this 'self-subjection'.

But obedience can become a genuine spiritual martyrdom if the one commanding or the one duty-bound to obey seeks no longer the will of God but himself; if it happens that the superior is no longer 'prudent and considerate in his commands', as Chapter 64 prescribes; if his commanding no longer issues from 'listening to God', from inner union with God and divinely enlightened wisdom. Even so the subject must obey. There is no release from obedience.†

Such obedience is then literally an 'imitation of the Lord,

---

† Unless the superior commands something that is evidently contrary to the will of God. In this case he would cease to be God's representative.

who was made obedient unto death', who still recognized 'the power from above' even in the judge abusing his authority, and in the unjust sentence of Pilate discerned and fulfilled the Father's will. He did this 'for the love of God' and of us. Only from love can such obedience come forth.

When this 'obedience even unto death' is demanded of the monk, he must penetrate deeply into the mystery of our Lord's love-inspired sacrifice. From the cross, strength will come to him so that he too can 'for the love of God submit himself to his superior in all obedience, imitating the Lord'. Blessed by the sacrifice of the cross, his obedience will also share in the fruit of Christ's obedience unto death, in its atoning and redemptive power.

The superior should of course 'always be mindful that his bidding and his doctrine must be infused into the minds of his disciples like the leaven of divine justice and that at the dreadful judgment of God an account will have to be given both of his own teaching and of the obedience of his disciples' (RB 2). A superior who is conscious of this responsibility will never exercise his authority frivolously and without taking thought of God's will.

The superior's task is not made easier if the subject does not show 'all mildness and obedience' called for by the Rule (RB 68), if self-love and pride have robbed the monk of the supernatural point of view, if indifference or even sin have taken from him the supernatural love from which alone genuine obedience can proceed. Then the exercise of authority and the solicitude for those duty-bound to obey becomes a spiritual dying, a martyrdom—all the more so when the abbot recalls that in Chapter 2 St Benedict even makes him responsible for his disciple's obedience. The saint does, however, add: 'Only then [at the judgment of God], shall he be acquitted, if he shall have bestowed all pastoral diligence on his unquiet and disobedient flock . . . . And then at length the punishment of death shall be inflicted on the disobedient sheep.'

We get the feeling that in this third degree of humility too the question is not primarily one of the exercise of obedience in individual instances, but again of creating a disposition of soul wherein the disposition acquired in the first two degrees of humility gains depth and perfection. It is a question of 'perfect obedience, obedience without delay' to God himself, of radical sacrifice of one's own will by the superior as well as by the subject, of complete openness to the call and the will of God.

There is a question of something else: the formulation of the monastic community, the building up of the 'corpus monasterii, the body of the monastery' (RB 61). By imitating Christ's obedience unto death, not only are the head and the members of this body united with each other, but the members are united among themselves too, so that 'all are one in Christ' (RB 2). For it is also the law that 'the brothers must obey one another' (RB 71).

> Not only is the excellence of obedience to be shown by all to the abbot, but the brothers must also obey one another, knowing that by this path of obedience they shall come to God. The commands, then, of the abbot or the superiors appointed by him (to which we allow no private orders to be preferred) having the first place, let all the younger brothers obey their elders with all charity and vigilance.

The following chapter again lays stress on this:

> Let them vie with one another in obedience. Let no one follow what he thinks good for himself, but rather what seems good for another.

That St Benedict sees in this mutual obedience not merely a counsel but an essential element of the monastic community, and hence a strict duty, is evident from the whole of the chapter on obedience to one another, especially from the sharply stated penalties in the second part. If anyone does not want to submit to this law of mutual obedience, 'if anyone be found refractory, let him be corrected'.

And if this structure of mutual obedience, so essential for the stability of the monastic community, is in any way impaired, it must be restored immediately by an act of humility, by sacrificial obedience on the part of the disciple who has the obligation to obey:

> *If a brother is rebuked by the abbot or any of his superiors, for the slightest cause, or if he perceives that the mind of any superior is even slightly angered or moved against him, however little, let him at once, without delay, cast himself on the ground at his feet, and there remain doing penance until that feeling be appeased, and he gives him the blessing. If anyone should disdain to do this, let him either be subjected to corporal chastisement, or, if he remain obdurate, let him be expelled from the monastery.*

From what St Benedict says and the way he piles up expressions, we can sense how important it is to him that this chapter on mutual obedience be taken seriously. The chapter can be understood only in the perspective of the root source from which obedience as such proceeds: from love. Love does such things. Love wants to be 'obedient even unto death'. For the sake of the brothers and the community it unreservedly surrenders self-will. It does not ask who was at fault in the impairment of the structure of obedience. It wants only to repair the breach in the community and 'appease that feeling'.

If the fault, for which the humble act of obedience is reparation, is not one's own, then the expiation taken upon oneself despite innocence ought to reawaken love of obedience in the superior or senior confrère. Such is the love described by the apostle: 'Love is not self-seeking, it is not prone to anger; neither does it brood over injuries. Love does not rejoice in what is wrong but rejoices with the truth. There is no limit to love's forbearance, to its trust, its hope, its power to endure' (1 Cor 13:5ff.).

We sense that where there are no limits to the exercise of obedience, the result must be a community which truly reflects the community of the divine Persons in the Blessed Trinity. Each listens to the other, each gives himself unreservedly to the other. 'All are one in Christ' (RB 2), as Father and Son are one in the Holy Spirit (Jn 17:21).

In such a community too, the power of God's loving will must of necessity manifest itself and, as was the case at Monte Cassino, at Cluny, at Cîteaux, produce marvels of divine life, marvels of sanctity, marvels of unlimited blessing. 'An obedient man shall speak of victory' (Pr 21:28, Vulgate).

# Patience

## THE FOURTH DEGREE OF HUMILITY

THE THIRD DEGREE of humility shows us the way leading to the imitation of Christ, 'of whom the apostle says, "He was made obedient even unto death".' To this, Paul adds the phrase, ' . . . death on a cross!' The climax of the sacrifice which obedience demanded of Christ was the cross. Our own self-surrender through obedience likewise finds its confirmation and completion in the cross, in suffering and enduring, in the patience taught by the fourth degree of humility.

As in all the other degrees, here too the question is not primarily of practicing patience in specific instances but of a spiritual disposition which appropriates and concentrates that of the previous degrees of humility, a question of basic attitudes toward all 'hard and contrary things, nay even injuries', a question of christian willingness to suffer and endure and to bear the cross.

*The fourth degree of humility is, that if in this very obedience hard and contrary things, nay even injuries, are done to him, he should embrace them patiently with a quiet conscience, and not grow weary or give in, as the Scripture says: 'He that shall persevere to the end shall be saved'. And again: 'Let your heart take courage, and wait for the Lord'.*   Mt 10:22   Ps 27:14

In a life that puts the gospel of the Crucified and the Rule of St Benedict into practice, there is a great deal that is 'hard and contrary', that is difficult to bear and is at variance with one's own will and desire. Obedience and conformity with the monastic schedule (as with any fixed way of life) by their very nature stand in opposition to a person's will to freedom and independence. Often God intervenes in our life, either directly by his decrees and dispositions, or through the persons who are his representatives; he lets so much happen other than what we want, and shows us that 'his thoughts are not our thoughts, nor are his ways our ways' (Is 55:8). All this we should 'embrace patiently with a quiet conscience' as our Lord embraced his cross. We should, in humble docility toward God and his representative, 'persevere and not grow weary or give in' when confronted with the cross of obedience.

Among the hard and contrary things are all the painful tensions, experiences and disappointments caused by the contrast between ideal and reality, between intention and accomplishment, by the inadequacy of all creaturely power, and the wounding and weakening of human nature by original sin. The disparity between ideal and reality will remain as long as the course of earthly life continues. Not even the purest intention will find perfect fulfillment here on earth.

According to the explicit statement of our Lord, weeds will be allowed to grow alongside wheat in the field of the Church and the religious state until the end of the world. Until the return of our Lord, the growth and development of his kingdom within us will meet hindrance and opposition. We must recognize God's will and permission in this, too. We may not for that reason 'grow weary' in zeal, may not have doubts about the ideal of perfection to which God has called us, may not 'give in but must persevere to the end'. It is precisely for persons with high ideals, for persons full of fervor and zeal, for 'men of desires' (Dn 9:23) that it can become unspeakably difficult in the face of all these 'hard and contrary things to embrace them patiently with a quiet conscience,' to have to put up with so much without being able to change it, to 'persevere' until God's time has come.

St Benedict himself was just such a 'man of desires', zealous for God and his kingdom, with a choleric temperament even in striving for perfection. God took him into his own school in order to teach him patience. The failure at Vicovaro where the fiery young man of the spirit for the first time in his monastic life came face to face with the wretchedness and perversity of persons gone wrong, and where his idealistic efforts proved useless, was a painful lesson. And it was to be followed by many more such lessons.

He needed such sad experiences to acquire that marvelous, fully developed kindness and patience which makes itself felt throughout the Holy Rule. It is eloquent, for instance, in the description of the Good Shepherd's solicitude for the sick lamb that went astray, which is to serve as an example for the abbot in his care for erring brethren (RB 27); or in the exhortation to the abbot that he must 'prefer mercy to justice . . . and in his corrections must act with prudence, and not go too far, lest while he seeks too eagerly to scrape off the rust, the vessel be broken' (RB 64).

Benedict knew that regardless of how much individuals aim at ideals and superiors keep vigilance, in monasteries there will always be 'restless, undisciplined, negligent monks, despisers of the Rule, self-willed, intractable, haughty, disobedient persons, murmurers, such who though often corrected do not amend' (all expressions found in various passages of the Rule). He knew that there can also be superiors to whom the words apply, 'Do everything and observe everything they tell you, but do not follow their example' (RB 4; Mt 23:3), that there can be superiors of lower rank 'deeming themselves to be second abbots', that 'scandals and dissensions in the community' can occur (RB 65).

He knew all that, and we too should be aware of it. He definitely opposed disorder and sin, and took precautions lest his exhortation to patience and kindness be interpreted in such a way that the abbot 'allow vices to grow up' (RB 64). But his zeal never becomes 'an evil zeal of bitterness'. It always remains the 'good zeal' (RB 72) that grows out of the spirit of the fourth degree of humility.

Only this patient, loving zeal in humble service can vanquish evil interiorly and really gain mastery over human wretchedness. 'By patient endurance you will save your souls', your souls and the souls of others (Lk 21:19). 'Blest are the lowly; they shall inherit the land' (Mt 5:4). In true patience there is victorious power, the victorious power of him who by his endurance and suffering redeemed the world.

From all this it is clear that christian patience does not mean weary resignation, timorous non-interference, abandonment of effort to attain ideals. On the contrary; it concentrates all inner and outer strength, the strength of action and the strength of suffering, in order to sacrifice everything and to gain everything. 'Let your heart be comforted, and wait for the Lord!'

We must also have patience with ourselves. Certainly we have to engage in heroic battle to 'take the kingdom of God by force' for it 'suffers violence' (Mt 11:12). We have to 'resist to the point of shedding blood' in our 'fight against sin' (Heb 12:4). But we may never forget that by God's ordinance the development of the life of grace should be an organic growth the way natural life is. God could let us become holy all at once. It would be easier to offer oneself to

God when the soul is in a state of exaltation, on some feast day, at profession, before the altar during ordination, in an all-inclusive act of surrender, and in this act to bring everything to completion. Our way to God is otherwise, however. Just as the seed placed into the soil gradually evolves into fruit, just as our natural life develops over a period of time, so too, in accordance with inner laws, must we spiritually 'form that perfect man who in Christ comes to full stature' (Eph 4:13). 'There is an appointed time for everything, and a time for every affair under the heavens' (Qo 3:1).

That this is so, that it does not lie within our power to determine the manner and speed of our spiritual growth, reminds us again of the fundamental truth already dealt with in the Prologue, that in the last analysis it is not we who sanctify ourselves, but God who sanctifies us. As important as our cooperation with divine grace is, it is still more important that we give free play to what God wants to effect in us, that we allow ourselves to 'be sanctified' by him (Heb 10:14). 'May it be done to me as you say' (Lk 1:38).

Here the deepest significance and substance of the patience taught us by the fourth degree of humility is disclosed to us. 'Holy patience is an ultimate expression of self-surrender to God . . . . Inherent in patience is a final stage of dying to oneself' (Dietrich von Hildebrand). Inherent in it is unconditional acquiescence to all that God wants to do in us and with us, as also to the way he wants to do it and to guide us, an unrestricted willingness 'to let oneself be driven by the Holy Spirit'—*'divina pati'*, as the mystics express it, 'to suffer divine action'. One who is truly patient says: 'Lord, make me [and my fellowmen, my superiors, my brothers, my sisters] what you would have me [us] be!'

> *Let this or that be done as you will. Give what you will and when you will. Do with me in accordance with what you know and as best pleases you and as is most to your honor. Place me where you will, freely dispose of me in all*

> *things. I am in your hands; turn me this way and*
> *that as you choose. See, I am your servant, ready*
> *for all things (The Imitation of Christ, III.15).*

All the self-surrender embodied in the preceding degrees of humility is concentrated and perfected in patience.

In this complete docility lies our perfection. We give expression to this docility also when we humbly and patiently endure the weaknesses and faults and miseries which God allows to cling to us despite our good will and honest effort. In this way even our failures and imperfections contribute to our spiritual progress, even grave sins become a *felix culpa*— a 'happy fault'.

Lapses and frailties help us to make our striving for perfection entirely pure and sincere, to make us 'truly seek God' alone (RB 58), for even the desire to be perfect can arise from pride and vanity and self-seeking. Furthermore, they keep us from 'wishing to be called holy before we are so' (RB 4). They never let us forget that 'the good which is in us comes not from ourselves but from the Lord' (RB Prologue).

Is not this perhaps the reason why God let all his apostles become weak in the hour of his passion, why he permitted Peter, the Rock upon which he intended to establish his Church, even to deny him, lest the greatness of their vocation and election make them proud, so that in success and in wonderworking they would always say, 'Not unto us, O Lord, not unto us, but unto your name give the glory'?

Is not this perhaps the reason why God let his greatest apostle first become a persecutor of the Church just so he would never forget: 'By the grace of God I am what I am' (1 Cor 15:10; RB Prologue)? And later on, St Paul declared, 'In order that I might not become conceited I was given a thorn in the flesh' (2 Cor 12:7). Christian patience makes itself heard in the words of the apostle: 'I willingly boast of my weaknesses, that the power of Christ may rest upon me. Therefore I am content with weakness, with mistreatment, with distress, with persecutions and difficulties for the sake

of Christ; for when I am powerless, it is then that I am strong'
(2 Cor 12:9,10).

Let your heart be comforted, and wait for the Lord
(Ps 27:14).

Because St Benedict knew how important, but also how
difficult, this patience is in the face of all 'contrary things',
he showed us still more clearly the significance and substance
of this patience by appealing to the words of Holy Scripture,
and pointed out all the possibilities of putting it into practice.
Next to the 'fear of God', the first degree of humility, no
part of the ladder of humility is treated in such detail as
patience—indicating the importance St Benedict attached to
this degree. The words of the prayer which Benedict here
again places on our lips imply that we must thoroughly
assimilate, by renewed prayer and meditation, the thoughts
of this section.

*And showing how the faithful man ought to
bear all things, however contrary, for the
Lord, [Scripture] says in the person of the
afflicted: 'For you we suffer death all the
day long; we are esteemed as sheep for
the slaughter'.*                                    Rm 8:36

What was true of the Master must apply also to the disciple: 'Did not the Messiah have to undergo all this to enter
into his glory?' (Lk 24:26). To have to confront suffering
and death must be just as self-evident for us as it was for
Christ the Lord. After all, we are followers of him who as
the Lamb of God sacrificed himself for the sins of the world.
It is our vocation to be sacrificed together with him. This
way of sacrifice is the way to glory for the Lord as well as
for his faithful servant. 'By patience we must share in the
sufferings of Christ, that we may deserve to be partakers of
his kingdom' (the conclusion of the RB Prologue).

So it is that St Benedict continues to speak of 'sufferers':
*And secure in their hope of the divine reward,
they go on with joy, saying: 'But in all these*

*things we overcome, through him who has*
*loved us'.*                                        Rom 8:37

Why should we complain when 'hard and contrary things'
come our way? Should we not much rather rejoice? Do we
not have to accept the baptism of which Christ speaks, and
do not we too have to 'feel anguish till it is over' (Lk 12:50)?

This is why St Benedict repeatedly censured in very incisive language every manifestation of dissatisfaction and of
murmuring, even if only 'in the heart' (RB 5). 'Above all, let
not the evil of murmuring show itself by the slightest word
or sign on any account whatever' (RB 34). If he has to be
deprived of anything, the monk is to 'bless God and not
murmur. This above all we admonish, that there be no
murmuring among them' (RB 40). Murmuring is diametric-
ally opposed to the 'joyfulness' in suffering to which
Benedict, in the fourth degree of humility, wants to lead us,
to that triumphant power of faith and love whereby the
faithful disciple of Christ 'overcomes in all these [hard and
contrary] things, through him who has loved us'.

*And so in another place Scripture says: 'You*
*have proved us, O God; you have tried us as*
*silver is tried by fire'.*                          Ps 66:10

A precious metal must be purified by fire. We too need the
purifying and cleansing power of suffering in order 'to be
purged of sins and faults', to be wholly freed from our own
ego, from all earthly bonds.

*'You have led us into the snare'.*                  Ps 66:11

We may sometimes feel as though we have been trapped in
the coercion of obedience, in the hardships of community
life. Let us rejoice: we are 'prisoners for Jesus Christ'
(Eph 3:1).

*'You have laid tribulation on our backs.'*          Ibid.

Tribulations within and without, spiritual distress and temptation, anxiety and harshness of temperament in oneself and
in others, sickness and failure: all these falls under the great
law of suffering, of the cross.

It is in this light too that we must see the persecution of the kingdom of God by its enemies. Times of tribulation have always been times of blessing and of purification and of new fruitfulness for the Church of God. 'How blest are the poor . . . blest too are the sorrowing . . . . Blest are those persecuted for holiness' sake' (Mt 5).

*And in order to show that we ought to be*
*under a superior, [Scripture] goes on to say:*
*'You have placed men over our heads'.*        Ps 66:12

St Benedict deliberately lists every merely possible kind of 'hard and contrary thing' to make us understand what is at stake. Once again he explicitly mentions the special difficulties involved in obedience more strictly monastic. This has already been discussed.

It is indeed a cross that 'men are placed over our heads'. But how would we attain real self-surrender, literally 'imitating the Lord, who was made obedient even unto death', unless there were this human element which makes obedience so hard? It is then that faith and love have the function of penetrating beyond the veil of human frailty which hides the image of God in the superior, beyond the sound of the human voice and what it says, in order to hear the call of God, who does not hesitate to make use of a humanly weak, and indeed even an unworthy, instrument and mouthpiece. We have to see the similarity to the sacrament of faith and love in which we know that our Lord himself is present under the appearance of mere bread.

Moreover, it is a cross not only to have persons set over us, but also to have persons placed under us. Superiors too suffer from the human frailty of those they have to command. They have to take into account the human weakness of their subjects. The abbot 'must consider how difficult and arduous a task he has undertaken, of ruling souls and adapting himself to many dispositions' (RB 2). How often he finds no idealism where he looks for it! He finds only persons whose    thinking    is    purely    natural;    faint-hearted, dispirited persons.

In times of trial he gets no encouragement or comfort from his disciples. He must bear everything alone, like our Lord on the Mount of Olives. He must keep watch, in distress inwardly and outwardly, while his disciples sleep. That is why it is especially the superior, the priest, anyone responsible for others, who must make every effort to acquire the patience of the fourth degree.

'You have placed men over our heads.' There are many persons placed over us. If we call to mind Chapter 71 of the Holy Rule, actually everyone is above us: superiors with their human failings, as well as the brethren, whose 'infirmities of body and mind' we are to 'endure most patiently', with whom we are to 'vie in obedience. Let no one follow what he thinks good for himself, but rather what seems good for another' (RB 72). There is no limit to our self-surrender.

In its deepest roots this patience is really nothing else than that love which 'is patient and kind, is not self-seeking. There is no limit to love's forbearance, to its trust, its hope, its power to endure' (1 Cor 13:4-7). It is the imitation of the love of him who 'loved us to the end' (Jn 13:1) and who made it a commandment that we should 'love one another as he has loved us' (Jn 13:34). Disciples of Christ who have fully grasped this commandment of the Lord and who have set before their eyes the Master's love as the measure of their own love, no longer admit any measure, any limit to their self-sacrifice, their willingness to serve, their patience.

> *Moreover, fulfilling the precept of the Lord*
> *by patience in adversities and injuries, they*
> *who are struck on one cheek offer the other:*
> *to him who takes away their coat they leave*
> *also their cloak; and being forced to walk one*
> *mile, they go two. With Paul the Apostle,*
> *they bear with false brethren, and bless those*
> *that curse them.*                                    1 Cor 4:12

St Benedict must have considered this ultimate test of

patience extremely important, for of the four criteria of a
genuine monastic vocation he set down in Chapter 58, one,
in his judgment, is 'whether [the novice] is fervent in
humiliations'—a fervor like that in 'the work of God' and in
'obedience'. Therefore it is with eagerness, with inner joy,
that we should accept injustice and humiliations.

We should call to mind these words of our Lord: 'Blest are
you when they insult you and persecute you and utter every
kind of slander against you because of me. Be glad and
rejoice, for your reward is great in heaven' (Mt 5:11,12).
Have we ever experienced this fervor, this joy? Does not
everything in us rise in revolt against real or imagined
injustice?

Certainly, duty may demand a protest against an accusa-
tion, an insult, an injustice. It may be one's duty to justify
oneself and, especially when one is responsible for others, to
hold one's ground when conscience requires. Before the high
priest and before Pilate, our Lord too spoke out to assert his
divine mission and to defend his God-given rights. But anyone
who correctly understands Our Lord's example and the
meaning of the fourth degree of humility will do that only
when something higher than one's own self is at stake.

Where there is question of oneself only, the example to be
followed is still that of the Christ of whom it is written,
'Jesus remained silent' (Mt 26:63). He remained silent in the
face of all the injuries and insults and wrongs inflicted upon
him. Following his example we should, 'if hard and contrary
things, nay even injuries, are done to us, embrace them
patiently with a quiet conscience, and not grow weary or
give in . . . [persevering] to the end'. The world will of
course regard us as fools. But should we not become 'fools
on Christ's account' (1 Cor 4:10)?

We must think this fourth degree of humility through,
slowly, word for word. We must apply it concretely to our
circumstances, to all the 'hard and contrary things' we have
to endure, to the 'injuries' which burden our soul. We must

bring everything under the cross of him 'who has loved us', who for love of us 'obediently accepted even death, death on a cross'. He bore a thousand times more than we shall ever be able to bear. If we enter deeply into his self-surrender, there will of itself arise in our soul an ardent desire to love him in return as he has loved us, to do for him what he has done for us, to imitate him specifically in this 'obedience unto death on a cross' and, as St Paul says, to be 'united with him through likeness to his death in order to be so through a like resurrection' (Rom 6:5).

> *In all that we do we strive to present ourselves as ministers of God, acting with patient endurance amid trials . . . . We are called dead, yet we are alive; punished, but not put to death; sorrowful, though we are always rejoicing; poor, yet we enrich many. We seem to have nothing, yet every-thing is ours! (2 Cor 6:4,9-10).*

# DISCRETION

A SPECIAL FRUIT of this patience and the spiritual disposition resulting from it is the virtue which Bene-dict calls 'the mother of virtues': discretion (RB 64). The word's primary meaning is 'the ability to distinguish', and then 'moderation'.

This discretion must, according to St Benedict, be the special virtue of the abbot and of all who are charged with the guidance of others. It enables them to find the proper balance between what the ideal of perfection demands and the weakness of human nature allows, between 'the rigor of a master and the loving affection of a father' (RB 2). It teaches how to distinguish between the essential and the non-essential, between 'sin, which [the abbot] must hate, and the brothers, whom he must love' (RB 64). It makes superiors capable of assigning each person to his proper place, of marking off areas of responsibility suitably, and able 'so to arrange and dispose all things, that souls may be saved, and that the brothers may do what they have to do without just cause for murmuring' (RB 41).

Discretion helps him assess rightly the powers of each, 'to give assistance to the weak, that they may not do their work with sadness' (RB 35), 'to give to brothers who are weak or delicate such work or occupation as to prevent them either from being idle or from being so oppressed by excessive labor as to be driven away' (RB 48), 'in corrections to act with prudence, and not go too far, lest while [the abbot] seeks too eagerly to scrape off the rust, the vessel be broken . . . . In all his commands, whether concerning spiritual or temporal matters, let him be prudent and considerate. In the works which he imposes, let him be discreet and moderate, bearing in mind the discretion of holy Jacob, when he said: "If I cause my flocks to be overdriven, they will all perish in one day" (Gn 33:13). Taking then the testimonies borne by these and the like words to discretion, the mother of virtues, let him so temper all things that the strong may have something to strive after and the weak nothing at which to take alarm' (RB 64).

But all the other members of the monastic community should likewise be imbued with this virtue and it should permeate all areas of the mode of life Benedict prescribes. St Gregory specified precisely this as the chief characteristic of the Rule of Benedict, that it is 'pre-eminent for its discretion' (*Dialogues* II. 36), its wise moderation, the fine, considerate kindness behind all its prescriptions.

Everywhere in the Rule we find a clear distinction between what is essential for the attainment of perfection, and is therefore necessary, and what could well be otherwise. Where the fundamentals of the christian and monastic life are concerned, St Benedict is unequivocally clear and inflexibly stern. To the question 'Whether monks ought to have anything of their own' (RB 33) there is basically only one answer:

> *The vice of private ownership is above all to be*
> *cut off from the monastery by the roots. Let none*
> *presume to give or receive anything without leave*
> *of the abbot, nor to keep anything as their own,*
> *either book or writing-tablet or pen, or anything*
> *whatsoever; since they are permitted to have*
> *neither body nor will in their own power.*

At stake here is an essential interior disposition and docility, a radical decision as to 'whether monks may have anything as their own', that is, possess anything with right of free disposal. For one who by holy vows has totally surrendered himself to God in the monastic way of life there is no longer any right of free disposal, least of all over exterior goods, since monks 'are permitted to have neither body nor will in their own power'. The essential sacrifice does not consist of poverty and frugality as such:

> *But all that is necessary they may hope to receive*
> *from the father of the monastery: nor are they*
> *allowed to keep anything which the abbot has not*
> *given, or at least permitted them to have.*

St Benedict found the essence of poverty in the domain of the will where the determination to advance along the way to God resides. Hence in monastic profession he makes no provision at all for an explicit vow of poverty. It is contained in the vow of obedience, which is so extensive that it includes renunciation of all right of ownership. Chastity too, as renunciation of 'power over one's own body', is included in obedience. The total sacrifice which is the will's surrender by obedience is for St Benedict the innermost core of surrender to God. From this all-inclusive sacrifice everything else follows, as it were, automatically. And this total sacrifice—St Benedict recognized no exception and no concession—must be implemented all the way to its final consequence.

In the aforementioned distribution of necessities to the

members of the community, the abbot should, with wise discrimination and considerate kindness, regard individual requirements. By no means 'ought all alike to receive what is needful' (RB 34):

> As it is written, 'Distribution was made to
> every man, according as he had need'. Herein       Acts 4:35
> we say that there should be, not respecting of
> persons—God forbid—but consideration for
> infirmities.

The dangers which could arise from such consideration and discrimination are obviated by St Benedict in this fine passage:

> Let him, therefore, that has need of less give
> thanks to God, and not be grieved; and let him
> who requires more be humbled for his infirmity,
> and not made proud by the kindness shown to
> him: and so all the members of the family shall be
> at peace (RB 34).

Much the same is said regarding the sick, whose care is insistently enjoined upon the abbot:

> And let the sick themselves remember that they are
> served for the honor of God, and not grieve by
> unnecessary demands the brethren who serve
> them. Yet must they be patiently borne with,
> because from such as these is gained a more
> abundant reward.

St Benedict likewise devoted a special chapter to old monks and children, and ordered that 'their weakness be always taken into account . . . and a kind consideration be shown for them' (RB 37).

The same wise differentiation between what is essential and what nonessential is manifest in the directives for so highly important a feature of the monastic life as the celebration of the choir prayer. Insistently St Benedict calls his monks' attention to the sanctity and the dignity of 'the

Work of God, to which nothing may be preferred' (RB 43), 'their obligation to divine service which they may not neglect to fulfill' even when they are on a journey (RB 50).

In no fewer than eleven chapters of his Rule he devised, as the fruit of intensive study and long practical experience, a marvelous structure of liturgical prayer. And still the form he gave to the divine praise seems to him to be so far from essential and unalterable that he declares:

> *Above all, we recommend that if this arrangement*
> *of the psalms be displeasing to anyone, he should,*
> *if he think fit, order it otherwise.*

More essential than the form are the spirit in which the choir prayer is performed and the 'fervor in the Work of God' which is one of the chief criteria of a benedictine vocation (RB 58).

For personal prayer in general, Benedict assigns the basic norm, 'Our prayer ought to be short and pure, except it be perchance prolonged by the inspiration of divine grace' (RB 20). Beyond this he is content to give some exhortations: 'In the first place, whatever good work you begin to do, beg him with most earnest prayer to perfect' (Prologue). One should 'apply oneself frequently to prayer' (RB 4). If, when the Work of God is ended, 'a brother perchance wishes to pray by himself,' he should 'not be hindered by another's misconduct. If anyone desires to pray in private, let him go in quietly [into the oratory] and pray' (RB 52). Benedict knew that if a soul is truly receptive to the 'inspiration of divine grace'—and that is, of course, the fundamental interior disposition to which he wants to bring us—then 'frequent prayer' will of itself become the 'continuous prayer' of which our Lord speaks (Lk 18:1). Just as in matters basic to the spiritual life, so also in everything pertinent to the structuring of the practical life, 'the mother of virtues' must be the guide to proper discernment and moderation.

St Benedict goes into detail about the monks' clothing, listing every single article of apparel and remarking, 'The abbot should be careful about the size of the garments, that they be not too short for those who wear them, but of the proper length', and furthermore stipulates that 'in cold countries more is required, in warm countries less'. But 'let the monks not complain of the color or coarseness of these things, but let them be such as can be got in the country where they live, or can be bought most cheaply' (RB 55).

All external things like clothing, just because they are a part of human life, have their importance in the spiritual struggle, too. They can be the expression of a way of thinking, but they are not essential. The spiritual is not shackled to them. Still, they can get to be a danger and if they are too much in the foreground can divert attention from what is essential. There are many examples of this in monastic history. Hence St Benedict gives the capital admonition, 'Let not the monks complain about such things.' There are higher things to be concerned about.

As to food and drink, the Rule's directives have always been considered very moderate and lenient (RB 39, 40). Benedict wrote, 'It is with some misgiving that we appoint the measure of other men's living. For everyone has his proper gift from God, one after this manner, another after that.' Here too he wanted to 'consider the infirmity of the weak' and give what is 'sufficient'.

Yet he made the peremptory demand that 'above everything, all surfeiting is to be avoided. For there is nothing so adverse to a Christian as gluttony, according to the words of our Lord: "See that your hearts be not overcharged with surfeiting" (Lk 21:34)'. Self-control and moderation in food and drink as a matter of principle from which there may be no deviation was for St Benedict more important and more essential than any specific bodily austerities and mortifications. As for these, he was content with general exhortations among the instruments of good works: 'To chastise the body. To love fasting.' Only in Lent should the monk, 'with the blessing and permission of the abbot, withhold from his body beyond the measure appointed him something of his food, drink and sleep, and refrain from talking and mirth' (RB 49).

Of greater importance to St Benedict than any particular sacrifices and austerities are control of the body and all bodily activities and discipline emanating from an interior disposition of humility; about this he is more specific in the last degrees of humility. Characteristic of St Benedict's spirit, so preoccupied with the essential, is the counsel he sent, according to the account of St Gregory, to a hermit who had had himself shackled to his cave with an iron chain: 'If you are a servant of God, it is not a chain of iron that should hold you fast, but the chain of Christ' (*Dialogues* III.16).

In a monastic community persons differing in age and background, character traits and intellectual ability, are joined together. In the various tensions which inevitably result from this, it is again discretion that makes the adjustments. Benedict expressly refers to the relationship between seniors and juniors. There will always be a certain amount of opposition between the various age groups' views on life. A time of turmoil like the present intensifies such conflicts in the monastic and the christian life. St Benedict was aware of this. He himself was once a youthful enthusiast with an ardent heart. He had to fight his way to the self-possessed paternal maturity which produced his Rule. He knew how valuable and energizing this young exuberant vitality is. Without youth, without springtime, everything in the world would grow old and stay old.

St Benedict loved youth as the ever-bubbling fountain of new life, and out of this love came his exhortation to the elders 'to love the juniors'. Love youth! In loving kindness try to understand it. Do not automatically reject its thoughts, its impetuously urgent aspirations. 'It is often to the younger that the Lord reveals what is best', he admonishes the abbot. Therefore 'everyone should be called to council' (RB 3). And when a new abbot is to be elected he should 'be chosen for the merit of his life and the wisdom of his doctrine, even though he be the last in order in the community' (RB 64). In general, 'in no place whatsoever let age decide the order or be prejudicial to it; for Samuel and Daniel, when but children, judged the elders' (RB 3).

But Benedict knew too that youthful energy has to be tamed. He knew how readily and disrespectfully youth disdains what is old and venerable and tends to destroy what is precious. He knew how much youth needs to look up reverently, to recognize gratefully what their forefathers have created and fashioned. Parsifal, the young assailant of the castle of the Grail, would never have succeeded in his quest had not a venerable old man in a solitary cell cured him of his youthful folly. Out of such understanding came the Master's perceptive admonition to the juniors, 'Reverence the seniors' (RB 4), and his demand for mutual obedience wherein 'all the younger brethren are to obey their elders with all charity and vigilance' (RB 71; cf. RB 63).

This admonition, inspired by 'the mother of virtues', is applicable also to the hostility, today again keenly felt, between past and present. Benedict lived in a period of transition similar to ours, a time when an ancient world was collapsing and 'the Spirit of God was renewing the face of the earth' amid stress and strain. In his school of humility, of patience, of discretion, we learn to 'reverence', and reverently to preserve, what is good and valuable in the heritage from the past, and at the same time not simply to reject what is new just because it is new but to understand it lovingly. This is the attitude which accounts for that great breadth of vision which has become characteristic of the benedictine spirit which hears God's call in any period of history and can therefore always stand ready to serve, which follows the injunction of the apostle: 'Test everything; retain what is good' (1 Thess 5:21).

Discretion this way proves itself to be truly 'the mother of virtues'. It is itself, however, the fruit of that interior purification which the will undergoes by means of the patience treated in the fourth degree of humility. Patience gives us the inner freedom which raises us above human frailty and misery, above 'hard and contrary things, nay even injuries', which makes us independent of mood and caprice and self-will, which enables us to seek and find the right norms and decisions, no longer within the limitations of our own ego but in the wisdom of God. Patience opens our soul to the 'spirit of prudence' about which the apostle speaks in connection with the 'spirit of power and of love' (2 Tm 1:7), the 'holy prudence' of which the Fathers of eastern monasticism speak so insistently. It leads us to the true freedom of the children of God to whom the apostle's words apply: 'All is yours, and you are Christ's and Christ is God's' (1 Cor 3:22,23).

# Humble Confession

## THE FIFTH DEGREE OF HUMILITY

*The fifth degree of humility is, not to hide from one's abbot any of the evil thoughts that beset one's heart, or the sins committed in secret, but humbly to confess them. Concerning which the Scripture exhorts us, saying, 'Make known your way unto the Lord, and hope in him.' And again: 'Confess to the*     Ps 36:5 *Lord, for he is good, and his mercy endures forever.' So also the prophet says: 'I have*     Ps 105:1 *made known to you my offence, and my iniquities I have not hidden. I will confess against myself my iniquities to the Lord:*

*and you have forgiven the wickedness in my
heart.'*                                              *Ps 31:5*

T
HE GOAL of the degrees of humility we have thus far
considered is clear: to produce within us a fundamental
disposition in which our will's total capability of self-
surrender is concentrated, penetrating more and more into
the depths of our being, determining more and more our
every thought and deed. Fear of God, living according to the
will of God, obedience, and patience are the fruits and manifestation of this fundamental disposition. In the fifth degree
of humility there seems at first glance to be less a question of
a disposition of soul than of an act of 'humble confession to
the abbot'. But upon careful scrutiny of this act we find that
it too presupposes and fashions a spiritual attitude.

Benedict speaks of 'sins committed in secret'. It can
happen that someone leading the life of a perfect monk and
being a model of obedience, of patience, may nevertheless
in a moment of weakness fall victim again to the power of
evil and 'commit sin in secret'. No one has any inkling of it.
Then, says Benedict, reveal it to your abbot in humble confession.

Perhaps it does not even amount to doing something evil,
but 'evil thoughts beset one's heart'. No one suspects what
thoughts of self-seeking, of pride, of uncharitableness are still
alive in the soul, how 'the flesh lusts against the spirit' (Gal
5:17). It need not by any means be a matter of fully voluntary sinful thoughts and desires; '*any* evil thoughts', says
St Benedict. It may be that these thoughts are still no more
than a temptation, but does not every temptation imply the
possibility of sin? Every evil suggestion that comes into the
heart bears within itself the possibility of being actualized. It
reveals to us what wickedness we are actually capable of.
Otherwise the suggestion could not even come to us at all.
And who knows how swiftly consent would follow temptation if the grace of God did not hold us back.

Every temptation opens before us an abyss into which we can plunge even if we are already walking the heights of the spiritual life. Abysses, on the brink of which we must be seized with horror and dread, open up when we thus reflect on the occasions of sin which have already occurred in our lifetime because of evil thoughts coming into our heart.

See, says St Benedict, when evil thoughts such as these assail your heart, go to your abbot, to your 'spiritual father'. 'Make known your way to the Lord' in the person of his representative. Show him the abysses in your soul in order to humiliate yourself, to eradicate every 'kind of pride' within you. Tell him: 'Father, evil still has great power over me despite my outwardly blameless behavior. I would become wicked if God's mercy did not restrain me. I very much fear for my salvation. God has appointed you my guardian. Pray for me and watch over me!'

> *'Make known your way unto the Lord, and hope*
> *in him.'*

We may hope for a great deal of our spiritual growth from the exercise of the fifth degree of humility. There is a profound inner relationship between the fifth and the third, the 'most important degree of humility'. In the earlier degree the monk places his will into the hands of Christ's representative so that he may, in God's name, have disposal of it. Now, by disclosing the hidden evil and the secret thoughts of his heart he surrenders, in a voluntary act, what is for him innermost and ultimate. It is a spiritual dying, going still deeper than the sacrifice of the will in the preceding degrees.

But this dying at the same time means new life. By humble avowal before God's representative the monk brings into the brilliance of God's sight, before which all darkness must give way (cf. Jn 3:20,21), the evil that is in him or wants to get him into its power. He thereby takes its power away from evil, which can thrive only in darkness. 'He has brought the malignant evil one to naught, casting him out of his heart with all his suggestions, and has taken his bad thoughts, while they were yet young, and dashed them down upon the [Rock] Christ' (RB Prologue).

It is in this way that we 'die to sin' and to all the evil done or intended in secret in order to 'live for God' (Rom 6:11). The prayer of the psalmist is pertinent here: 'I have made known to you my offence, and my iniquities I have not hidden. I will confess against myself my iniquities to the Lord: and you have forgiven the wickedness of my heart' (Ps 32:5). Not only does God forgive the guilt of someone who humbly confesses, but the avowal prevents bad suggestions from being realized in evil deeds; it prevents the desire from growing and overpowering us.

But the effect of confession goes still deeper: this ultimate surrender of self by disclosing the evil and the possibility of sinning hidden within us gives us an unexpected insight into ourselves and our relationship to God. In all our reflections on the Holy Rule we have kept before us God's sacred word which speaks to us out of the depth of his love and grace and which we want to heed with all the docility of 'the ear of the heart'. In the fifth degree of humility we are dealing with a word that *we* speak and which too is a revelation: 'Make known your way unto the Lord'.

But what an appalling contrast! When God unveils his innermost being, radiant holiness and infinite goodness shine forth, and the more we are privileged to penetrate into his hidden depths, the more are fathomless treasures of glory revealed to us. When *we* disclose our innermost being, our 'hidden self', we make a revelation of sin and possibility of sinning.

St Bernard defined the essence of humility by saying:
*Humility is the virtue whereby a person, through utterly sincere knowledge of self, becomes vile— worthless, useless—in his own eyes.*†

By disclosing to another the evil hidden in us, formulating it

---

† Cf. *The Steps of Humility and Pride* 2; 14

in words through humble avowal (mere recognition of it is
not enough) we become aware of all the frightfulness of the
condition into which we have fallen as a result of original sin
and personal guilt. Confronted by this 'utterly sincere
knowledge of self', all human pride, all vain self-complacency
and false self-confidence must crumble.

We realize not only that we as creatures are nothing in the
presence of God's infinity, but that we are less than nothing;
unholy persons, as sinners, we stand before the radiant holiness of God. Even more abysmally than in the first degree of
humility does the cry of the prophet at the sight of the
Thrice-holy force its way to our lips: 'Woe is me, I am
doomed! For I am a man of unclean lips' (Is 6:5). The
anguished complaint of the apostle about the 'sin which
resides in me' becomes our own lament: 'I know that no
good dwells in me, that is, in my flesh . . . . What a wretched
man I am! Who can free me from this body under the power
of death? The grace of God, through Jesus Christ our Lord!'
(Rom 7:17,24,25).

The knowledge of ourselves which emerges from humble
self-revelation compels us to throw ourselves unreservedly
into the arms of the divine mercy with a self-surrender of
which we were previously incapable. 'Confess to the Lord, for
he is good, and his mercy endures forever.'

We feel how this fifth degree of humility reaches into the
depths of our being, how the act of humility it calls for can
be performed only as the expression and fruit of an interior
disposition which means a decisive step forward on the path
of humility and self-renunciation by which we attain God. In
this degree the decision is made whether we are going to set a
limit to the surrender of our own ego, and thereby also to
our quest for God, or whether we intend to take seriously,
down to its final consequence, the 'losing of one's life' and
thereby 'gain life.'

It was therefore of the greatest concern to St Benedict that
we put this degree of humility into practice. He speaks of it

in several places in the Holy Rule. In Chapter 4 he has already given the beginner this admonition as an instrument of the spiritual life: 'To dash down on the [Rock] Christ one's evil thoughts the instant that they come into the heart, and to lay them open to one's spiritual father.' In Chapter 46 he lays down as law for the monastic community that all external transgressions must be voluntarily confessed 'before the abbot and community' and satisfaction made. 'If, however, the guilt of [the monk's] offence be hidden in his own soul, let him manifest it to the abbot only, or to his spiritual seniors, who know how to heal their own wounds, and will not disclose or publish those of others.'

Whether the monk can actually put this degree of humility into practice exactly as St Benedict wished depends, more than is the case in any other detail of the monastic life, not on himself alone but also on his superiors. Precisely this point of the Rule shows clearly that a benedictine abbot must be primarily a 'spiritual father', as St Benedict calls him (RB 49), the 'director of souls' of the monastic family, the 'good shepherd' who is the representative of the divine Shepherd (RB 27). This fifth degree of humility forcefully reminds the abbot 'how difficult and arduous a task he has undertaken, of ruling souls' (RB 2), 'that he has undertaken the charge of weakly souls, and not a tyranny over the strong' (RB 27).†

---

† In order to prevent unwarranted encroachments in the area of conscience, the Code of Canon Law (Canon 530) emphatically forbids religious superiors 'to induce their subjects in any manner whatever to make a manifestation of conscience to them'. But it explicitly added that 'subjects are not forbidden to open their minds freely and spontaneously to their superiors; nay more, it is desirable that they approach their superiors with filial confidence and, if the superiors be priests, expose to them their doubts and troubles of conscience also.' This directive of Canon Law is in full agreement with the wording and the meaning of the fifth degree of humility of St Benedict's Rule. St Benedict too stated clearly that this manifestation of conscience may not be demanded by the superior, but the initiative must come from the subject, who does this as a voluntary act of humility.

In Chapter 46 St Benedict mentions 'spiritual seniors' to
whom, besides the abbot, this act of humble confession may
be made. He thus points out the possibility that here too the
abbot may 'share his burdens' (RB 21). According to the
general practice of the religious life it is certainly warranted
to see these 'spiritual seniors' above all in the fathers-con-
fessor and to derive from the fifth degree of humility a suggestion as to the way the reception of the sacrament of
reconciliation can be given a form corresponding to this
degree.

The confession should be an act of self-surrender whereby
we place our sinful soul into the hands of Christ's representative so that through absolution it may be cleansed and purified 'in the blood of the Lamb' (Rv 7:14). We should not
make our confession according to some fixed scheme more
or less repeated in every confession, then, but should try to
to disclose all 'the evil thoughts that beset one's heart, or the
sins committed in secret'. We should not merely tell the con-
fessor a few exterior faults but endeavor to expose the root
of our lapses and our perversity of heart. In 'humbly confessing' we should say things about which we have reason to
be ashamed and whose avowal is humiliating for us. Anyone
who earnestly strives in the spirit of St Benedict to make
progress on the path of humility cannot but come to an ever
more profound self-knowledge, to a growing refinement and
delicacy of conscience, to an ever greater repugnance for the
least offence against the holiness and perfection of God.†
Anyone who confesses in this spirit of humble self-surrender
avoids the danger of a routine, mechanical, superficial performance to which this sacrament is too easily reduced. Then
repentance and contrition and purpose of amendment will
spontaneously, from one confession to another, become

---

† By confessing in this manner, secular oblates of St Benedict too, and
all who want to live according to his spirit, can practice the fifth degree
of humility.

more resolute and sincere.

When the father-confessor, like the abbot, is 'believed to hold the place of Christ' (RB 2), God unquestionably gives him special graces to lead and guide on the way to God the soul which in such humble docility entrusts itself to him.†
Thus the sacrament of penance will become what in accordance with God's will it ought to be: the sacrament of spiritual regeneration which opens the soul completely to the life of Christ. 'Confess to the Lord, for he is good, and his mercy endures forever!'

# Brought to Nothing
## THE SIXTH DEGREE OF HUMILITY

FROM THE VERY OUTSET St Benedict's program of education in his 'school of the Lord's service' is governed by the basic principle that only 'by our good deeds' shall we attain to God, that in the spiritual life all knowledge remains sterile unless it finds fulfillment in 'the performance of good works'. This basic principle is doubly applicable to the core of the spiritual life: humility.

A humble disposition and attitude grows only out of practical humiliation either sent by God (we are thinking of the fourth degree of humility) or sought by oneself (as the fifth degree of humility teaches) and it occurs over and

---

† However it is not this spiritual direction which is really the essence of the fifth degree of humility (or the purpose of sacramental confession), but the 'humble confession' itself—interior self-surrender to God through his representative—whose salutary effects upon our self-knowledge and spiritual growth flow from this self-surrender as such. Corresponding spiritual direction will of course be able to make these results still more fruitful.

over in a humble life. Hence:

*The sixth degree of humility is for a monk to be contented with the meanest and worst of everything, and in all that is enjoined him to esteem himself a bad and worthless laborer, saying with the prophet: 'I have been brought to nothing, and I knew it not. I am become as a beast before you, yet I am always with you.'*						Ps 73:22

Anyone who 'has, through utterly sincere knowledge of self, become vile in his own eyes', who in the light of God's holiness and perfection has understood and made his own the cry of the psalmist, 'I have been brought to nothing, and knew it not', must necessarily also be content with the meanest and worst of everything. He will simply take it for granted when others consider him of no account, when he is ignored, when he receives the worst living quarters, clothing, and food, when he occupies the last place in the community.

He does not merely acquiesce in weary resignation; he is really 'content'. His soul is 'at peace', the peace of God. He realizes that the more he is deprived and free of all that is not God, the more securely hidden in God he is. He experiences something of that 'perfect joy' St Francis felt at the thought of extreme privation and renunciation. He discovers that there really is 'blessedness' in being 'poor in spirit', in being able to say, 'I have been brought to nothing, and I knew it not: I am become as a beast before you'.

*Ministers of God in all that we do . . . amid trials, difficulties, distresses, beatings, imprisonments . . . conducting ourselves with innocence, knowledge and patience, in the Holy Spirit, in sincere love . . . with the power of God . . . whether honored or dishonored, spoken of well or ill. We are called sorrowful, though we are always rejoicing; poor, yet we enrich many. We seem to have nothing, yet everything is ours! (2 Cor 6:4-10).*

It may be that one does not occupy the last place, that he does not have only 'the meanest and worst of everything', but instead God places him ahead of others, makes him 'his own workman in the multitude of the people' (RB Prologue), grants blessing and success to what he does. Still 'our sole credit is from God' (2 Cor 3:5). We labor with only borrowed strength, with talents entrusted to us. 'They know that the good which is in them comes not from themselves but from the Lord . . . who works in them' (RB Prologue).

Therefore no one can make any demands on God: 'When you have done all you have been commanded to do, say, "We are useless servants. We have done no more than our duty" ' (Lk 17:10). Anyone who toils the whole day in the Lord's vineyard can claim nothing more than someone who toils only one hour in it. All receive wages not because they earn them but because the Lord of the vineyard is 'generous' (Mt 20:15).

But if we insist on distinguishing between God's role and our role in the wonderful collaboration of divine grace and God-given human strength, this distinction can be made only in conformity with the basic principles of the Holy Rule: 'To attribute any good that one sees in oneself to God, and not to oneself. But to recognize and always impute to oneself the evil that one does' (RB 4). Does not our wretchedness and frailty put the stamp of imperfection on everything that God wants to accomplish through us? Is there a single work of ours we can point to that in every regard measures up to the mind and will of God?

Regent Wagner of Dillingen used to pray, 'Lord, forgive me my good works'. How much more clearly God's power would manifest itself in us if we did not fail again and again! Does this not fully justify St Benedict's demand that 'in all that is enjoined on him he esteem himself a bad and worthless laborer'? This admission is humiliating. But it accords with the truth. 'And the truth will set you free' (Jn 8:32).

The interior disposition treated in the sixth degree of

humility sets us free from everything that is not God. It makes us interiorly independent and detaches us from the things around us, from possessions and the comforts of life, from position and dignity, from success and failure, from recognition and disregard. It sets us free for God, entirely open to his call, entirely ready for his service.

'I am become as a beast before you.' A beast of burden, which accepts and bears whatever is placed on it, is a symbol of this humble docility, this untrammeled freedom for God, which found its most perfect realization in him who as the Lamb of God bore the world's burden of sin. With him we say in the sixth degree of humility: Father, you may take from me what you will. You may give me what you will. I want only one thing: to be with you always.

# Fools for Christ's Sake

## *THE SEVENTH DEGREE OF HUMILITY*

HAVE WE NOW reached the 'highest point of humility'? Is there still something of one's own life to lose? Is there still room in our heart for the stirring of pride, of self-seeking? Is there still an area in our soul that is not open to God, to which the call of God does not yet have full access?

It is quite possible that someone practising the fifth degree of humility by revealing to his spiritual father all the evil he has done in secret may think to himself: 'Others are still worse; others perhaps do still more evil in secret'. It is quite possible that someone who is 'content with the meanest and worst of everything' and ascribes to God all that results from his efforts, may consider himself better than others in this very contentment and humble disposition.

So a final step in the process of becoming humble, a final
act of dying to one's own ego, comes in the seventh degree
of humility which consists in this, that one 'should not only
call himself with his tongue lower and viler than all'—which
could still be empty talk or even an expression of pride—'but
also believe in his inmost heart' that he is more wretched and
contemptible than others.

> *The seventh degree of humility is, that he*
> *should not only call himself with his tongue*
> *lower and viler than all, but also believe him-*
> *self in his inmost heart to be so, humbling*
> *himself, and saying with the prophet: 'I am*
> *a worm and no man, the shame of men and*
> *the outcast of the people'. 'I have been*    Ps 22:7
> *exalted, and cast down, and confounded.'*    Ps 88:16
> *And again: 'It is good for me that you have*
> *humbled me, that I may learn your com-*
> *mandments.'*    Ps 119:71

But can a person really have a profound conviction of this
kind? Does not Benedict, the master of discretion, here
depart from the 'mother of virtues', wise moderation? Does
he not here strike out on a path that no longer accords with
truth and therefore cannot be right? Ought a person who till
now has been faithfully following this leader on his way to
God not feel in himself that he is coming closer to God?

It is exactly when he does feel that way that he will understand what St Benedict is driving at here. It is precisely the
approach to God that produces this profound conviction of
one's own wretchedness and nothingness. The closer man
comes to God, the more his soul is struck by light from God,
the clearer becomes his spiritual vision for all sin and imperfection. As long as there is no sunshine in a room, one does
not notice the dust in it. But if a ray of sunlight streams into
it, one sees countless dust particles filling the room.

A person who is very earnestly striving for holiness feels,
in the light of God, ever more painfully his manifold failures

and all his shortcomings in contrast to the loving guidance of divine grace, and he 'confesses' ever more sincerely his 'past sins with tears and sighs to God in prayer' (RB 4). With increasing clarity he sees the gap between God's spotless holiness and his own human imperfection and sinfulness. He understands more and more fully Benedict's admonition, 'Not to wish to be called holy before one is so: but first to be holy, that one may be truly so called' (RB 4).

Above all, it is the growing insight into the mystery of divine favor and election that more and more lowers him in his own esteem. The higher he is elevated by the call of God and the power of God's grace, the greater becomes the responsibility of the person thus favored. The more too must he, 'keeping his own frailty ever before his eyes' (RB 64), tremble at the possibility of not measuring up to God's call. On a low-lying path one cannot fall far. The higher one climbs, the greater the depths into which he can plunge.

If great saints, like St Francis of Assisi, considered themselves great sinners, and if St Benedict, who Gregory the Great says 'could not have taught otherwise than he lived', considered himself 'lower and viler than all', this is no pious exaggeration. Such persons close to God well know that if it were not for standing in such high favor they would actually be greater sinners than others. If St Francis of Assisi had not become the great saint he was, he would not have remained just an average person; he would have wandered away from God to the extent that with the help of grace he came close to him.

Lucifer was the angel most richly endowed by God and was called 'Light-bearer' because of the perfection bestowed on him. The quintessence of light became the abhorrent dragon. As great and glorious as he should have been according to God's plan, so reprobate and accursed did he of necessity become in his downfall, more miserable and wretched than all others, 'exalted and cast down and confounded'. Thus it is precisely the growing measure of grace given to the person striving for sanctity, and the perfection attained, that give reason to abase self and really consider oneself 'lower and viler than all'.

We stand between heaven and hell, between eternal happiness and eternal torment. Not without reason does St Benedict repeatedly call attention to this twofold prospect. We stand between a full measure of grace and an abyss of depravity. We stand between the possibility of becoming saints and of being the greatest sinners. Why does the first possibility and not the other become reality? Who would presume to ascribe it to his own merits?

The fifth degree of humility made us shudder at the thought of the possibilities of sin in our life. In every human life there are moments when, on looking back, a person sees clearly that at a certain point his life could have taken a different direction than it did. At that juncture there was the possibility of straying into 'ways which to men seem right, but the ends thereof lead to the depths of hell'. What kept us from 'becoming corrupt and abominable in our pleasures' (the first degree of humility)?

The mystery of divine favor and election, of predestination, is covered with a darkness which no human mind on earth can penetrate. How St Paul in his Epistle to the Romans (Ch. 9-11) wrestled with this mystery! He could not understand how his people, who had been called and favored and predestined first, were now rejected, while 'the Gentiles, who were not seeking justice, attained it' (Rom 9:30). He could only bow humbly before 'the wisdom and the knowledge of God. How inscrutable his judgments, how unsearchable his way!' (Rom 11:33). 'Friend, who are you to answer God back?' (Rom 9:20).

But one thing was clear to the apostle: the Gentiles, now favored, may not proudly look down on the disfavored Jews. They attained salvation before the Jews not because they were possibly more worthy of it but because the Jews rejected grace. The sin and hardheartedness of the Jews was the reason preference was given to the Gentiles. 'By their transgression salvation has come to the Gentiles' (Rom 11:11).

God wants all his grace to be effective. If those who first receive his call to grace refuse it, it goes out to others. When Judas rejected his apostolic office, Matthias took his place. The heavenly Father prepared his banquet. Because those invited first did not come, he sent his servant out 'quickly into the streets and alleys of the town to bring in the poor and the crippled, the blind and the lame' to the banquet (Lk 14:21). Perhaps we too have come to the Lord's table in this way, as 'lower and viler than all'. Can we still find reason to boast? Does not the apostle's warning to the favored Gentiles apply to everyone: 'Do not be haughty, but fearful' (Rom 11:20)?

We feel how this seventh degree of humility really reaches down into the uttermost depths of our being and our self-awareness. It forces our proud ego out of the last stronghold to which it could flee, removes the last possibility of self-righteous arrogance and makes us humble down to the very roots of our being.

The 'natural man' in us will of course rebel against 'believing in his inmost heart that he is lower and viler than all'. 'For him that is absurdity. He cannot understand it' (1 Cor 2:14). It is indeed foolishness. It is 'God's folly' which is 'wiser than men' (1 Cor 1:25). It is the folly of him who out of love for us made himself 'lower and viler than all . . . a worm, the shame of men and the outcast of the people,' who from the height of the cross could cry out the prophet's words which St Benedict in this degree of humility puts on our lips: 'I am a worm and no man, the shame of men and the outcast of the people'.

'We are fools on Christ's account' (1 Cor 4:10). When we contemplate our Lord as he hangs on the cross, literally trampelled and crushed like a worm, 'exalted, and cast down, and confounded' for our sake, must we not then believe ourselves truly 'lower and viler than all'? Can we still even make comparisons with others? He hangs before us in his unfathomable love. We stand before him in our sinfulness and ingratitude, in our continual resistance to the call of his grace. 'Upon him was the chastisement that makes us whole' (Is 53:5). He suffered what we deserved. This makes our sins colossal, whether we call them light or grave.

There are others who did not know him. Of his enemies he could say, 'They do not know what they are doing' (Lk 23:34). But we know him. We know what sin is. What has he not done for us? And what have we so far really done for him? Must we not admit that we are 'bad and worthless laborers'? If we truly loved him, if we really 'preferred nothing to the love of Christ' (RB 4), how very different our 'service of the Lord' would have to be! How shall we survive when one day we come into his presence for the judgment of which Benedict so often reminds us?

When we think about these things, must we not be overwhelmed with sorrow in the depths of our being and filled with remorse? Do not the words of the seventh degree of humility spontaneously force their way to our lips:

> I am a worm and no man, the shame of men and the outcast of the people: I have been exalted, and cast down, and confounded. Lord, now I believe myself in my inmost heart to be lower and viler than all. Now I understand: you are all, I am nothing! It is good for me that you have humbled me, that I may learn your commandments.

# Simplicity

## THE EIGHTH DEGREE OF HUMILITY

T HE WAY OF THE SPIRITUAL life and of interior aspirations embodied in the degrees of humility so far considered is summarized by St Thomas Aquinas, who treats of St Benedict's degrees of humility in his *Summa Theologica* (II.II,q.161, a.6), as follows: the first degree is concerned with the root of humility, with establishing its basis; the second to fourth degrees have to do with the will; the fifth to seventh degrees deal with the self-appraisal of a person who acknowledges his own weakness.

Because of the danger done to human nature by original sin, the human will has been set on a wrong course. The focal point of human endeavor is no longer the Creator and his plan, but one's own ego. That is why Benedict, once the first degree of humility has brought about a fundamental renunciation of sin, seeks in the second to fourth degrees to free our human will from perverse self-centeredness and direct it wholly to the divine will, which alone can be the true final end of human endeavor.

As a result of original sin, man's ego is the focal point not only of his will but also of his intellect, the spiritual faculty which determines the act of willing. All our thinking revolves primarily around our own ego. It is from the narrow perspective of self that we judge ourselves and the things around us: people, the world, ultimately even God.

So in the fifth to seventh degrees of humility St Benedict shows us how to rid ourselves of 'self-conceit' in order to come to an 'utterly sincere knowledge of self', to remove all obstacles impeding the absolute supremacy of God's design. Whatever is misdirected in our thinking must be set aright. 'The wisdom of this world must come to nought so that we may be filled with the mysterious hidden wisdom of God' (cf. 1 Cor 2:6-8).

In his introduction to the chapter on humility (RB 7) St Benedict says that the ladder of humility has two sides or uprights 'in which our divine vocation has placed various rungs which we must ascend. The sides of the same ladder we understand to be our body and soul.' The entire man must be directed to God and made responsive to his call. 'Our hearts and our bodies must be made ready to fight under the holy obedience of his commands' (RB Prologue). Because of the close union of body and soul, man's inner self cannot be surrendered to God at all without the body being included in this surrender, this humility.

The last five degrees of humility teach this externalization of the internal disposition of humility. 'They refer to the exterior signs of humility', says Thomas Aquinas; that is, in the everyday life of the community (eighth degree), in control of speech (ninth degree), feelings and emotions (tenth degree), in conversation and social communication (eleventh degree), in bodily demeanor (twelfth degree). 'By means of these exterior signs which proceed from the inner disposition of humility, that which is hidden within becomes manifest' (Aquinas). They 'always show a person's humility to all who see him' (the twelfth degree).

These degrees of humility show how the soul is the *forma corporis,* the formative principle of the body, how 'the new man' we become on the path of humility is exteriorly manifested by the way he conducts himself. This is why these manifestations of humility are placed not at the beginning but at the end of the spiritual path marked out for us by Benedict. In virtue of the interaction of body and soul, the outward expressions of humility, like all activity, in turn react inwardly, strengthening the interior disposition and giving it its final perfection.

The first of the degrees regulating the external life of a person is, according to Thomas, 'that one in his conduct not depart from the path of obedience'. Benedict says it this way:

> *The eighth degree of humility is for a monk to do nothing except what is authorized by the common rule of the monastery or the example of his seniors.*

The truly humble person does not see the divinely-willed

external manner of life in any sort of extraordinary and self-chosen works and exercises. He does not presume to think that he can discover a better way of living than has been tested and taught by the divinely appointed masters of the spiritual life and the venerable fathers of the monastic tradition, which has found its expression in the 'common rule of the monastery'. He does not consider himself better but 'lower and viler than all'.

For him this norm is, as St Gertrude once heard our Lord say, the 'articulation of the divine will', and it is wholly adequate for developing and perfecting his interior surrender to God. It is precisely the simple, ordinary, externally inconspicuous way of the common rule that he needs and is seeking. In the morning he gets up and begins the day's activities when and because God is calling him, in the sense intended by the words of the Prologue, 'It is time now for us to rise from sleep'. He 'opens his eyes to the deifying light' (Rm 13:11) which shines forth for him every day anew. He 'hears with wondering ears what the divine voice admonishes us, daily crying out'. He consciously enters upon the day 'not to do his own will, but the will of him who sends him' and shows the way through this new day precisely by means of 'the common rule of the monastery', by means of everything that obedience requires, by means of the various duties that come his way, by means of the regulations and arrangements and encounters that by God's providence this particular day will bring. In this enlarged sense, everything here said about 'the common rule of the monastery' is applicable also to the Christian in the world who wants to live in the spirit of Benedict. He responds to everything as our Lord did in the morning of his life, according to St Paul's testimony: 'I have come to do your will, O God' (Heb 10:7; Ps 39:8 Vulg, 40:7 AV).

In this spirit we go to prayer, to work, to meals, to recreation when and because God is calling us. We do what God bids us through his representatives on earth, through superiors of whom it is said, 'He who hears you hears me' (Lk 10:16; RB 5), and ultimately through anyone God sends to us. Everyone who meets us, who enters our life, is for us in some way or other God's call. *'Vidisti fratrem tuum, vidisti Dominum tuum'*, said the faith of christian antiquity: 'When you see your brother you see your Lord' (Tertullian). From faith such as this comes Benedict's admonition to see Christ always and everywhere, in the abbot, in the brothers, in the sick, in guests, and to keep Christ's words in mind, 'What you have done unto one of these little ones, you have done unto me' (Mt 25:40; RB 2, 36, 53).

Everything that comes our way during the day (especially everything unusual, unforeseen) we can regard and accept in the manner St Benedict directs the porter to receive everyone who comes:

> As soon as anyone shall knock, or a poor man call to him, let him answer, 'Thanks be to God', or bid God bless him, and then with all mildness and the fear of God let him give reply without delay, in the fervor of charity.

Accordingly, we should always be ready to thank God when he calls to us through someone who comes to us, who needs our help, whom we have to serve; and we should also be thankful for the trouble this person makes for us, for his disturbing us. We should always, at least inwardly, say words of blessing. We should believe that every person and every occurrence, every task, every duty brings us God's blessing. 'Now we know that for those who love God all things work together unto good' (Rom 8:28).

This is how we should go through our day. And at the end of it we should lie down to sleep when and because God so wills, after having once more opened ourselves to the word of God in the evening reading (RB 42). In sleeping we should put ourselves wholly into God's hands, in holy silence (RB 42) letting our mind, will, and activity sink deeply into God, so we may receive our being anew from his hands the next day.

How simple all this is! '*Simplex sigillum veri:* Simplicity is a criterion of truth'. Everything truly great is simple. The Old Testament prophet prays: 'O Lord God, in the simplicity of my heart I have joyfully offered all these things' (1 Chron 29:17, Douai translation). When a person offers everything, when he has only one more desire—to be wholly surrendered to God, wholly humble—his heart becomes *simplex,* simple, uncomplicated; there is no longer any complexity, any dual tendency in him. He is totally open to God, consistently oriented to him. By faithfully complying with the 'common rule', with the whole extent of his daily duties, in this 'simplicity of heart', he integrates his surrender to God into everything that this rule and this aggregate of duties require him to do.

It no longer matters then what we do, whether we pray or work, whether we recreate or endure sorrow and suffering, whether we are in quiet solitude or in the midst of people. It no longer matters where and in what circumstances we find ourselves. 'For in every place we serve one God, and fight under one King' (RB 61). No longer are things and activities the real goal of our endeavor; God is, that he 'may be glorified in all things' (RB 57). Our life is no longer split up into a variety of mutually exclusive activities, but our whole day, our whole life, is simply 'service of the Lord'. All 'the many things' which otherwise cause us so much worry and unrest are gathered together in 'the one thing required' (Lk 10: 41,42).

Everything truly great is simple, yet profound. God himself is supreme simplicity and infinite profundity, and everything he does is truly divine. By his almighty power he fashions the universe. He assigns the stars their orbit and causes immeasurable suns to burst into brilliance in cosmic space. The same creative power and creative love clothes the lilies of the field, cares for sparrows, and keeps count of the hairs of our head. Indeed the wonders of the microcosm would seem to us almost greater than the wonders of the

macrocosm. Similarly, everything in life of the humble monk
and the real Christian, even what is least and most insignificant, can be the expression of supreme self-surrender to God,
the kindling of most ardent love.

It may seem petty of St Benedict to forbid 'going anywhere, or doing anything, however trifling, without permission of the abbot' (RB 67), or 'keeping anything as one's
own, either book or writing-tablet or pen, or anything
whatsoever' (RB 33), or 'receiving, either from parents or
anyone else, or from the brothers, letters, tokens or any gifts
whatsoever, or giving them to others, without permission of
the abbot' (RB 54). But anyone whose mind and heart are
filled with generous self-surrender to God understands
St Benedict's reason for these regulations: 'For monks are
permitted to have neither body nor will in their own power'
(RB 33). For him all things, even the most insignificant, are a
practical opportunity for and an expression of self-surrender
to God, and if they are not that, he considers them worthless
and meaningless.

Later we shall look at various other specific areas of our
everyday life in the light of the Rule. What we intended here
was merely to give a quick glimpse in order to note the consistency and simplicity of the spiritual way Benedict sets
before us.

For many people striving for perfection it was a profound
relief and joy to discover in the lives of such saints as
Brother Konrad and Thérèse of the Child Jesus a 'little way'
leading to God, to hear that perfection does not consist of
extraordinary achievements, that there is an 'everyday' kind
of sanctity. In persons endowed with grace, like St Thérèse or
Charles de Foucauld, we discerned anew what St Benedict
had already pointed out in his chapter on humility, especially
in the eighth degree. 'Lord, I have not walked in great things,
nor in wonders above me' (Ps 131:1; Vulg. 130:1; RB 7,
introduction). Benedict's great contribution to asceticism
was to shift the essence of christian and monastic perfection

unmistakably to a person's spiritual disposition. All external works and achievements have value only as the outlet for internal purpose, or as 'instruments of good works' to strengthen and safeguard the inward disposition.

In the extraordinary, in conspicuous works of penance and austerities which depart from the ordinary way, Benedict—in contrast to monasticism before him—saw a danger to perfection rather than an aid to it, because these things blur one's vision for what is essential and give occasion for pride. The safest and shortest way to holiness is the way of the 'common rule', the way everyone can and should go. We already know the admonition he sent to a hermit who had himself shackled to his cave with an iron chain: 'If you are a servant of God, it is not a chain of iron that should hold you fast, but the chain of Christ'.

The way of the 'common rule' is the way of inner freedom. Because fidelity to this rule, like all external activity, has its source in a generous interior disposition, in unreserved self-surrender to God, it is free of any narrowness or rigidity. It has as its guide not the letter which kills, but the spirit which gives life (cf. 2 Cor 3:6).

There are also 'exceptions' to the common rule, not those, of course, which originate in human caprice and whimsy and shirking sacrifice, but only those required specifically by submission to the will of God. When duties imposed by fraternal charity, by concern for souls, necessitate an interruption of ordinary routine, it is precisely in the incidence of such duties that God's will expresses itself and sets a higher objective in place of the 'common rule'. When sickness and afflictions intrude upon the normal course of life, then it is God's will that this sickness, these afflictions, and everything connected with them be endured with humility and patience. In this way is the spirit of the eighth degree of humility always preserved in principle and the common rule remains the guide that 'all must in all things follow and no man may rashly depart from it' (RB 3).

A way of superb simplicity and consistency St Benedict sets before us. Great security and constancy must of necessity come into our life if 'in the simplicity of our heart' we go the way of the divine will. Exterior activities and duties may change, but no matter what may occur outside us, we face everything with the same inward attitude. We need have only one concern, need ask only one question over and over: am I firmly rooted in the will of God? Is what I am now doing, and the manner in which I am doing it, in conformity with the 'common rule', namely, the will of God as it is manifesting itself to me today and at this very hour? Is there anything in me, in my thinking and willing and acting, that is not in harmony with it? It is thus that we must 'keep guard at all times over the actions of our life' (RB 4) to see whether its direction is Godward, just as the sailor or the aviator repeatedly checks direction by the compass.

Perhaps the secret of the powerful and pervasive influence that once emanated from the sons of Benedict in the golden age of the Order is precisely this simple, uncomplicated, unquestioning living according to the 'common rule', which is in fact nothing else than a compendium of, and concrete form of life according to, the gospel. This holy simplicity is the source of what Cardinal Newman once designated as the most outstanding characteristic of St Benedict and his spirit: '*Summa quies*—the most perfect quietness', and what the motto of our Order expresses in the word '*Pax*—peace'! If we lay ourselves completely open to the secret of holy simplicity, great peace will come into our life, that peace which 'the world cannot give', nor take away, that peace which radiates so wondrously from the life and death of St Benedict and so many other saints of God who 'in the simplicity of their heart joyfully offered all these things'.

We must not overlook a little addition which in the text of the eighth degree of humility stands next to the 'common rule of the monastery': the monk may 'do nothing except what is authorized by the common rule of the monastery, or the example of his seniors'. Just as the teaching of the Church and sacred tradition interpret and explain the words of Holy Scripture, so the '*exempla majorum,*' the living example and the tradition of the superiors and senior brothers, supplement the words of the Holy Rule. All who because of their office or their age and experience stand on a higher level in the spiritual life give by their very life a perceptible, a graphic exemplification of the text of the Rule, and 'set forth the divine precepts by the example of their deeds' (RB 2). And their subordinates and the juniors should be able to see, actually see, in the *majores,* the seniors, their God-given guides and exemplars on the way to God.

It is then on the ground of the 'common rule of the monastery' that the existent monastic community is built, 'the fraternal battle array' which for the individual becomes the effective means of forming and fashioning himself in the spirit of the common rule. The definition of cenobitical monasticism given in the first chapter of the Rule thereby acquires its full meaning. It is truly 'the strongest kind of monks, who, living in community, engage in combat under a rule and an abbot'. Each individual lives and strives by drawing upon the strength of the community, in which 'we are all one in Christ' (RB 2).

In this way 'the whole body', the *corpus monasterii,* the monastic body (RB 61), 'grows . . . and builds itself up in love' (Eph 4:16). The 'communion of saints' grows; the monastic community within it becomes a replica of the ecclesiastical community and at the same time a model for it. Its external life is determined by the daily order of the Rule, and it is inwardly animated by the spirit which brought this Rule into being, the spirit of humility as it lived and still lives in all who have fashioned their life according to this Rule and out of this spirit.

'The example of the seniors' expands into benedictine tradition. The plain and simple practical norm of fidelity to the common rule of the monastery becomes filled with the ardor of self-sacrificing love and docility, just as throughout the fourteen-hundred year benedictine past it has lived in thousands upon thousands of persons 'truly seeking God' in monasteries and in the world. And the words the 'examples of the seniors' bring to mind all those illustrious figures in whom we see the ideal of the Holy Rule realized: first of all, the founder of the Order, St Benedict himself, with his first disciples Maurus and Placidus, St Gregory and St Bernard, St Anselm and St Boniface, St Gertrude and St Hildegard, all the great benedictine missionaries, men and women of contemplation and absorption in God and of the apostolic life, luminaries of learning and bearers of culture, as manifold in character and period and circumstances of life and national traits as the stars of heaven, yet united in faithful fulfillment of the common rule of the monastery, in the simplicity and oneness of the eighth degree of humility. 'See that you make them according to the pattern shown you on the mountain' (Ex 25:40).

# Religious Gravity

## THE NINTH TO ELEVENTH DEGREES OF HUMILITY

A S IN THE DEGREES of humility which concern the interior life Benedict consistently followed through to the ultimate consequence and aimed at taking total possession of intellect and will, so now he laid hold of the entire area of the 'externalizations' of life in order to shape them from within in the spirit of humility and thus 'make our hearts and our bodies ready to fight under the holy obedience of his commands' (RB Prologue).

*The ninth degree of humility is, that a monk
refrain his tongue from speaking, keeping
silence until a question be asked him, as the
Scripture shows: 'In much talking you shall
not avoid sin': and, 'The talkative man shall*      Pr 10:19
*not be directed upon the earth'.*                   Ps 140:11

To anyone who in all seriousness wants to ennoble his
intellect and will fully in the school of Benedict and direct
them unreservedly to God it is self-evident that he must
resolutely try to gain control of his tongue, through which
the intellect and will manifest themselves outwardly. As
Benedict was writing the ninth degree of humility he was
undoubtedly thinking of the incisive words of the Apostle
James about self-discipline in speech:

*The tongue is a small member, yet it makes
great pretensions. See how tiny the spark is
that sets a huge forest ablaze! The tongue is
such a flame. It exists among our members as
a whole universe of malice. The tongue defiles
the entire body. Its flames encircle our course
from birth, and its fire is kindled by hell . . . .
It is a restless evil, full of deadly poison. We
use it to say, 'Praised be the Lord and Father';
then we use it to curse men, though they are
made in the likeness of God. Blessing and
curse come out of the same mouth. This
ought not to be, my brothers!*                       Jm 3:5-10

Anyone who is conscious of his responsibility and has
thoughts like these about the tongue's power and the gift of
speech must of necessity 'refrain his tongue from speaking'.
He knows what the Lord himself said: 'I assure you, on
judgment day people will be held accountable for every
unguarded word they speak. By your words you will be
acquitted, and by your words you will be condemned'
(Mt 12:36,37).

At the outset of the spiritual life St Benedict spoke at

length about *taciturnitas,* the practice of silence, as a necessary prerequisite for spiritual progress. To anyone who has followed St Benedict in the school of the Lord's service this far, what was at first a precept 'which he had hitherto observed through fear' (RB 7) becomes more and more a familiar and cherished 'custom', taken for granted as the atmosphere in which his interior life of union with God attains ever fuller development.

In conformity with the example of his master Benedict, he dwells in holy tranquillity in what Gregory the Great called 'his beloved solitude' until he is summoned, until a call from God, a call of obedience, a call of love bids him speak and act. Speech and action like this, emanating from genuine inwardness, do not at all mean abandonment of the practice of silence. The soul in quiet prayer and contemplation is in fact always listening for God's call, to which in humble docility it responds also by outward speech and action.

So what St Benedict requires in the ninth degree of humility is more than mere control of the tongue and avoidance of sins of the tongue. The practice of silence in the ninth degree is the fruit and climax of the spiritual effort a person has made in the preceding degrees. It means the concentration of all the interior and exterior faculties in an inwardness filled with God, and it brings about the tranquillity of a spiritual security which is granted a person when he hands over his whole intellect and will and being to God as unreservedly as Benedict tells us should be done.

Sin, which 'in much talking you shall not avoid', scarcely has a point of contact any more in a soul thus anchored in God. The uncertainty and insecurity to which 'the talkative man' is prey have been replaced by a firm confidence and quiet serenity. 'If a person is without fault in speech he is a man in the fullest sense, because he can control his entire body' (Jm 3:2).

As in speech, so too in the expression of his feelings, especially of joy, the truly humble person is discreet and

restrained. Someone who in St Benedict's school of humility
has been awed by the majesty and grandeur of God and has
recognized his own nothingness and the futility of everything
earthly takes for granted what Benedict has already said in
Chapter 6 about 'buffoonery or idle words, such as move to
laughter' and here enjoins in a specific degree of humility:

> *The tenth degree of humility is that he be not*
> *easily moved and prompt to laughter; because*
> *it is written: 'The fool lifts up his voice in*
> *laughter'.*                                    Sir 21:23

Benedict never intended to banish joy from the monastery
with this degree. On the contrary. Throughout the Holy Rule
there is an echo of the christian joy which the apostle wanted
to see in those redeemed by Christ, crying out to his converts: 'Rejoice in the Lord always! I say it again. Rejoice!'
(Phil 4:4). Already in the Prologue Benedict spoke of the
'unspeakable sweetness of love with which we run in the way
of God's commandments'. In regard to obedience he em-
phasized that 'it ought to be given by disciples with a good
will, because "God loves a cheerful giver" ' (RB 5). About
lenten sacrifices and works of penance he said that we ought
to offer them to God 'with joy of the Holy Spirit . . . with
the joy of spiritual longing' (RB 49). He wanted monastic
life in its entirety to be regulated in such a way 'that no one
may be troubled or grieved in the house of God' (RB 31).

He is not contradicting this when in the tenth degree of
humility he specifies religious gravity as an essential element
of the interior and exterior attitude of his monks, and when
elsewhere he speaks of 'compunction of heart' (RB 49) and
of the 'tears and sighs' with which we should invoke God in
prayer and daily confess before God our past sins (RB 4,20,
52). Truly christian joy comes precisely from the 'holy
sorrow' which our Lord himself indicated as a source of
blessedness (Mt 5:5); it comes from that inner clarity and
spiritual freedom which we attain by means of the religious
gravity of humility.

There is deep insight in the statement that 'laughing must be done in humility; otherwise it is diabolical . . . . There is something terrifying about evil laughter.' It is 'the opposite of christian cheerfulness'.† It is this 'evil, diabolical laughter' and everything that leads to it, every kind of 'frivolity' (RB 6, 43, 49), of unrestrained exuberance, of sheer earthly merriment without deeper content, that the tenth degree of humility means 'utterly to condemn in every place' (RB 6). Thereby we are set free for 'laughter in humility', for genuine 'cheerfulness' in obedience, for the 'joy of the Holy Spirit' which derives from 'childlike security' in God, 'from awareness of being sustained by God', and is a foretaste of the never-ending bliss of eternal life.

> *This joyous simplicity is of course not easily achieved . . . . These are things which result from long development and effort and only by the grace of God.*

The Holy Rule's degrees of humility embody this long way of development and effort whereby with the help of grace we attain genuine Christian joyfulness.

The ninth and tenth degrees of humility show us that the practice of silence and a sober reserve are characteristic of a humble soul. The eleventh degree shows the humble person by the use he makes of speech, how he communicates with people.

> *The eleventh degree of humility is, that when a monk speaks, he do so gently and without laughter, humbly, gravely, with few and reasonable words, and that he be not noisy in his speech, as it is written: 'A wise man is known by the fewness of his words'* (Pr 17:27).

Repeatedly we have spoken of the 'Word', the Word of God, the One, the Eternal, for which we listen with spiritual

---

† Hans Eduard Hengstenberg, *Christliche Grundhaltungen* (Paderborn, 1938) 157-8.

longing, which is the essence of divine wisdom and divine life. Over and over in the Holy Rule we hear as well about human words, the all too many (*multiloquium:* RB 20), often useless (*verba otiosa:* RB 6) human words which, just because there are so many of them, no longer have any force or meaning.

That is why it is so necessary to gain the mastery over the word by deliberate self-control, to free oneself from all frivolity and talkativeness. In this self-discipline and silence the 'reasonable words' then flower, words which are filled with meaning and thought-content, words which issue from the depths of intelligence and from true life of the spirit, words in which something of the wisdom and power of God's eternal Word comes to life, for God's Word reveals itself not in loud noise but in sacred silence.

A good illustration of this degree of humility is given by St Gregory in his biography of St Benedict when he says of him: 'Not even his ordinary speech was lacking power, for, as his heart always dwelt upon heavenly things, he never uttered a word that was not to the purpose' (1 *Dialogues* II.13, translated by Alexius Hoffman, OSB). We feel this power and purposefulness in the words of his Rule, in those relatively few words which have become an inexhaustible font of divinely enlightened wisdom for countless persons.

What St Benedict meant in all these degrees of humility is perfectly exemplified by the appearance of the eternal Word in human form in Jesus Christ. Our Lord during his earthly sojourn must have been 'quiet' and absorbed in God, till 'his hour came'; and when he did speak, he proclaimed words of life and wisdom 'gently, earnestly, humbly and with dignity', speaking as 'one with authority' (Mt 7:29).

Over the ninth to eleventh degrees of humility we can write the word Benedict uses in the eleventh degree and elsewhere in his Rule (RB 22, 42, 47): the word *gravitas*. *Gravitas* means seriousness, dignity, nobleness. It says that there is something dignified, something demanding respect, about someone who possesses this *gravitas*. Something of the brightness of the divine majesty to which his gaze is unceasingly directed must of necessity rest upon anyone who seeks to fashion his life in keeping with the radical self-surrender to God called for by St. Benedict's teaching on humility, as it once did upon Moses when he sojourned on the mountain of God. A reflection of the glory of the Infinite, before whom the soul constantly humbles itself, flows over upon man's being and action, and transmits a consecration to him.

That is why Benedict speaks about this *gravitas* above all in connection with the choir prayer. 'Let everyone hasten to the oratory with all speed, and yet with seriousness' (RB 43). Whoever has to sing or read should do so 'with humility, gravity, and awe' (RB 47). If something must be said or done in the especially sacred time of nightly silence, 'let it be done with the utmost gravity and moderation' (RB 42).

A sort of aristocratic or noble air has been attributed to the Order of St Benedict. If there actually is something of the kind inherent in it, then it is due to this *gravitas*, this holy seriousness, this dignity and consecration which have their source in humility. This does not contradict humility, which according to the Holy Rule must govern life in its entirety; on the contrary, it is the fruit of humility, the expression of *gravitas*. In fact, only as the fruit of humility can this 'dignity' endure. It must grow, as it were, naturally (*quasi naturaliter*) out of humility. We must not seek it, nor intend to produce it artificially. If we do, it becomes a hollow, exterior mold, a mask behind which only boastful pride and cold arrogance hide themselves.

There is something else contained in the word *gravitas:* it means weight, power, and might. In true christian humility there is no room for anything flabby or unmanly. Humility has nothing in common with abject submissiveness and servility, with fearfulness, timidity, and irresolution. Christian humility demands supreme courage, the radicalism and the heroism of total self-surrender down to its last consequence. Christian humility is the crown of true humanity, the perfection of the person unto 'that perfect man who is Christ come to full stature' (Eph 4:13).

The way of humility is the way of Christ, the son of God, who 'emptied himself and took the form of a slave, being born in the likeness of men. He was known to be of human estate, and it was thus that he humbled himself, obediently accepting even death, death on a cross' (Phil 2:7,8). Because Christ went this way of humility, 'God highly exalted him and bestowed on him the name above every other name, so that at Jesus' name every knee must bend, in the heavens, on the earth, and under the earth, and every tongue proclaim to the glory of God the Father: Jesus Christ Is Lord!' (Phil 2:9-11). The Christian 'whose attitude is that of Christ' (Phil 2:5), who with Christ goes the way of humility, also shares in the dignity, in the exaltation, in the glory of Christ.

The proud person is not really great. 'Every one that exalts himself shall be humbled, and he who humbles himself shall be exalted' (Lk 14:11; 18:14). There is nothing mightier, nothing nobler than christian humility. 'The least one among you is the greatest' (Lk 9:48). 'Whoever wants to rank first among you must serve the needs of all. The Son of Man has not come to be served but to serve' (Mk 10:44,45).

# Before the Judgment Seat of God

## THE TWELFTH DEGREE OF HUMILITY

W E COME to the summit of the ladder of humility, the final rung.

*The twelfth degree of humility is, that the monk, not only in his heart, but also in his very exterior, always show his humility to all who see him: that is, in the work of God, in the oratory, in the monastery, in the garden, on the road, in the field or wherever he may be, whether sitting, walking or standing, with head always bent down, and eyes fixed on the earth, that he ever think of the guilt of his sins, and imagine himself already present before the terrible judgment-seat of God: always saying in his heart what the publican in the Gospel said with his eyes fixed on the earth: 'Lord, I a sinner am not worthy to raise my eyes to heaven'. And again, with the* Cf. Lk 18:13 *prophet: 'I am bowed down and humbled on every side'.* Ps 119:107

Benedict is referring to bodily carriage, which should 'always show our humility to all who see us' having 'our head always bent down and our eyes fixed on the earth'. What has already been said about all other externalizations of humility applies more than ever to this ultimate one: it must *quasi naturaliter,* as it were naturally, proceed from the inward spiritual disposition of humility. St Benedict carefully portrays the interior spiritual process which leads to this corporal expression of humility.

A monk should 'ever think of the guilt of his sins and imagine himself already present before the terrible judgment-seat of God'. Let us ponder this thought. Let us place ourselves 'before the terrible judgment-seat of God' where the final settlement between God and ourselves will be made. God's all-knowing perception will illuminate the most hidden recesses of our life and our conscience; the final decisive verdict on our life will be pronounced, the verdict of blessedness or the verdict of damnation. Is not this the most important and fateful moment of our life? Does not our eternal destiny depend on it? Is it not therefore right and proper for us to be 'always, at every hour' oriented to this moment?

And should not the prospect of this moment make us tremble? Now that we have gone through the first, the fifth, the seventh degrees of humility we know what sin is all about. We know about the frightful possibilities of sin in our life. We know about all our weakness and frailty. We have some idea of how far what we have accomplished in life falls short of what God really wanted to make of us, how little our response has measured up to God's call. How will God judge our life? What will become of us?

St Benedict reminds us of a judgment scene in which two persons stand before God: the Pharisee and the tax collector. God himself pronounces the verdict on each of them: 'Believe me, this man went home from the temple justified but the other did not' (Lk 18:14). The one who was justified before God was not the Pharisee, 'who believed in his own self-righteousness', but the tax collector, who 'did not even dare to raise his eyes to heaven' (Lk 18:9). Instead, because he felt guilty on account of his sins, 'all he did was beat his breast and say, "O God, be merciful to me, a sinner".' At the twelfth degree of humility, the compendium of all the other degrees, we keep this scene ever before our eyes and we find ourselves 'at all times' as humbly disposed as was the tax collector.

We know the words of the Pharisee, who in his conceit and self-righteousness stood apart and prayed: 'I give you thanks, O God, that I am not like the rest of men, grasping, crooked, adulterous, or even like this tax collector. I fast twice a week. I pay tithes on all I possess.' In the Prologue St Benedict has warned us about being self-righteous, 'puffed up with our own good works', and forgetful that every good work is a grace.

That is why in the seventh degree of humility he so urgently insisted that we consider ourselves 'lower and viler than all'. All striving for virtue, all 'employment of the tools of the spiritual craft day and night', all struggling for perfect humility will do us no good if we 'give the glory to ourselves and not to God's name', if we are not humble down to the roots of our being and do not 'attribute any good that we see in ourselves to God, and not to ourselves' (RB 4). It is not works and our efforts that justify us, but solely God's grace. 'It is not a question of man's willing or doing but of God's mercy' (Rom 9:16).

At the 'terrible judgment-seat' there will be huge surprises. 'Those who believe in their own self-righteousness' will 'not go home justified.' Holy Scripture contains verdicts of frightful severity:

> *I know your conduct; I know the reputation you have of being alive, when in fact you are dead! . . . I find that the sum of your deeds is less than complete in the sight of God . . . . You keep saying, 'I am so rich and secure that I want for nothing.' Little do you realize how wretched you are,*

*how pitiable and poor, how blind and naked
(Rv 3:1,2,17).*

We know the dread words of our Lord that 'it will go easier'
for Tyre and Sidon and Sodom on the day of judgment than
for 'the towns where most of his miracles had been worked'
(Mt 11:20-22), and that 'many will come from the east and
the west and will find a place at the banquet in the kingdom
of God with Abraham, Isaac, and Jacob, while the natural
heirs of the kingdom will be driven out into the dark. Wailing
will be heard there, and the grinding of teeth' (Mt 8:11,12).

Away with all pharisaical self-complacency and self-
righteousness, with all lofty disdain of others, whether they
are tax collectors, sinners or pagans! We are so irresponsible
in our judgment of others. 'If you want to avoid judgment,
stop passing judgment' (Mt 7:1). How thoughtlessly we talk
like the Pharisee, if not in so many words then at least in
intent: 'I give you thanks, O God, that I am not like the rest
of humanity'. Away with all sham, with all self-deception,
with all extolling of our own merits, or at the 'terrible judgment' to come God will have to remove the blindfold from
our eyes. Woe to us should we be in the position of the
Pharisee, who our Lord says was not justified.

Away with all pharisaical self-assurance, as if there were
no longer any danger for us. The Holy Rule prescribes that at
profession the secular garments of a 'newly-received brother'
must be 'laid by and kept in the wardrobe' so that they may
again be exchanged for the garments of the monastery 'if
ever, by the persuasion of the devil, he consent (which God
forbid) to leave the monastery' (RB 58). There is no absolute
certainty of salvation. As long as we are in the flesh on earth,
the terrible possibility remains that we may become unfaith-
ful to our vocation and be lost.

In his high priestly prayer our Lord prayed for his disciples
and said that not one of those that the Father had given him
had been lost 'but him who was destined to be lost' (Jn 17:
12). So one of them actually was lost even though he had

been given to Our Lord by the Father, even though Our Lord had watched over him and given him grace like the others. And the others too could all have been lost had the 'terrible judgment' come upon Peter after he denied his Lord, and upon all the others after they disloyally deserted him. Must we not shudder and lower our eyes to the ground when we think of these awful possibilities?

There is only one escape: humility, humility! There is only one possibility of surviving the terrible judgment, to be like the tax collector, to say what he did in humble avowal of guilt: 'Lord, I a sinner am not worthy to raise my eyes to heaven,' or with the psalmist, 'I am bowed down and humbled on every side'.

We begin to see how this last degree recapitulates everything we have up to now reflected upon and thought out, how it leads soul and body to an ultimate inward and outward attitude which is, so to say, the sum total of our life, to that attitude in which we shall one day have to stand before God at the terrible judgment if we want to be saved: 'I am bowed down and humbled on every side'.

We are to have this interior and exterior attitude *semper, omni hora,* always, everywhere, whatever we do: at choir prayer, at personal prayer, in the monastery, in the garden, on the road, in the field, at work, wherever we may be, whether sitting, walking, or standing. Actually we may be called at any time to the terrible judgment-seat of God. We are told that the judgment will break in suddenly like 'a thief in the night . . . at the time you least expect' (Mt 24:43,44; Lk 12:39,40).

The twelfth degree of humility brings us then to that pristine christian disposition of preparedness for the day of final decision, the continuous expectation of the Lord's coming to judge for all eternity. It 'trains us . . . to live temperately, justly, and devoutly in this age as we await our blessed hope, the appearing of the glory of the great God and of our Saviour Jesus Christ. It was he who sacrificed himself for us to redeem us from all unrighteousness and to cleanse for himself a people of his own, eager to do what is right' (Ti 2:12-14).

This is the 'highest point of humility' to which Benedict wanted to bring us. Anyone who has climbed to this summit with him has committed his total being and existence unreservedly to God, has placed his temporal and eternal destiny, his life and death, into God's hands. He has become completely open and ready for God's call, ready also for the word of God that summarizes for us all the words of God: his word of judgment at the end of our earthly life, directing us to heaven if our heart has humbled itself.

Now we know why whenever an opportunity presented itself Benedict reminded the abbot of the monastery 'that he will have to give an account to God of all his judgments and all his deeds' (RB 63. Cf. RB 2, 3, 55, 64, 65). Whoever is to be teacher and guide for others in the school of humility must himself have climbed to the 'highest point of humility'. It is this twelfth degree of humility that comes into play when the abbot is admonished to keep his eyes constantly fixed on the day of judgment on which, 'whatever may be the number of brothers under his care, let him be certainly assured that he will have to give an account to the Lord of all these souls, as well as of his own'.

For an abbot who 'does everything with the fear of God and in observance of the Rule, knowing that he will have without a doubt to render to God, the most just Judge, an account of all his judgments', the fullness of authority given him will not become a danger.

> Being ever fearful of the coming inquiry which the Shepherd will make into the state of the flock committed to him, while he is careful on other men's account he will be solicitous also on his own. And so, while correcting others by his admonitions, he will be himself cured of his own defects (RB 2,3).

# Pharisee and

# Tax Collector

THE PORTRAIT of the tax collector at the end of St Benedict's treatise on humility takes us back to the beginning of the chapter, which opened with the scriptural text, 'Every one that exalts himself shall be humbled, and he who humbles himself shall be exalted'. These are the words that conclude the parable of the Pharisee and the tax collector in the Gospel (Lk 18:14). The contrast of these two men shows us plainly what is at the heart of St Benedict's teaching on humility. In the tax collector is embodied the mystery of humble self-abasement which leads to 'heavenly exaltation'. In the Pharisee is shown its opposite, 'self-exaltation', *superbia,* pride, 'against which the prophet shows himself to be on his guard when he says, "Lord, my heart is not exalted nor my eyes lifted up".' Insights gained are deepened also when we ponder this opposite of humility—pride, the interior and exterior attitude of the Pharisee, in which Benedict evidently sees the crucial danger for our spiritual progress.

In recounting the parable of the Pharisee and the tax collector the evangelist expressly states that our Lord 'addressed it to those who believed in their own self-righteousness while holding everyone else in contempt' (Lk 18:9). In the other two passages in which our Lord uses these same terms of self-exaltation and self-abasement, the attitude and thinking of the Pharisees is portrayed in still greater detail: 'All their works are performed to be seen. They widen their phylacteries and wear huge tassels. They are fond of places of honor at banquets and the front seats in synagogues' (Mt 23:5; Lk 14:7).

If we trace this pharisaical attitude and thinking back to its root cause, we find it is just what Benedict attacked in his degrees of humility: one's own ego occupies the center of one's thinking and willing, man persists and hardens himself in his self-seeking self-centeredness resulting from original sin and personal guilt. There is no longer any submission to God, any openness to his call. 'The eyes' are not 'open to the deifying light', 'the ear of the heart' does not 'hear what the divine voice admonishes us, daily crying out.' But where this submission and openness are lacking, the eye of the soul little by little becomes blind and the ear of the heart dull. Docility to the guidance of the Holy Spirit (Rom 8:14) is gradually replaced by spiritual callousness and hardheartedness, which in its ultimate consequence leads to 'blasphemy against the Spirit' (Mt 12:31). To the extent that this pharisaical spirit dominates a person, his receptivity to divine grace disappears. In fact, if any grace from God draws near his soul, it becomes for him the occasion to fix himself still more in his perverse disposition, just as, on the contrary, the person who is docile to the action of the Holy Spirit becomes ever more widely open and receptive to his inspiration.

The Pharisees, conspicuous as the guardians and most faithful observers of the law given by God, the champions of the order willed by God and the heralds of the messianic expectation, committed the most frightful sacrilege against the divine law, frustrated divine revelation, and rejected the living Word of God, bringing about his death. In this light we understand the terrible woes our Lord pronounced against the Pharisees in connection with what he said about self-exaltation and self-abasement. We too are in danger of everything with which Christ reproached the Pharisees. Indeed, this is very likely the greatest danger to being a real Christian and to genuine perfection, because there is nothing our Saviour attacks so categorically as this pharisaical spirit. It is assuredly for this reason too that in her prayers the Church constantly sets before us the fate of this people, and that Benedict saw in humility, the opposite of pharisaical pride, the most important lesson of his school of the Lord's service.

The possession of divine truth, the security which comes from faith, the plenitude of grace afforded by the sacramental order of the christian life, the predestination implied by the special vocation to the Lord's service, the 'following of Christ': all this becomes a danger if the possession of divine truth and grace is not considered and accepted and rendered fruitful in true humility and docile submission, as a freely bestowed mark of God's love and unmerited divine mercy, literally as 'grace'.

When this humility is lacking, when we 'attribute any good we see in ourselves to ourselves and no longer to God', when we give glory to ourselves and no longer to the Lord, when we, unlike St Paul, forget that 'by the grace of God we are what we are' (cf. RB Prologue), when we cease being humbly submissive and gratefully receptive, what is grace becomes danger, what is blessing becomes curse, what is dynamic life occasions hardheartedness. Then 'the good zeal which leads to God' becomes 'an evil zeal of bitterness, which separates from God, and leads to hell' (RB 72). Self-surrender to God is replaced by self-seeking, we are persons 'shut up, not in the Lord's sheepfold, but in their own' (RB 1).

The result is self-deception and spiritual blindness in which 'whatever one thinks fit or chooses to do he calls holy, and what he does not like he considers unlawful' (RB 1). In false self-assurance 'one believes in his own self-righteousness while holding everyone else in contempt'. He thinks that he has 'already arrived and has already been made perfect' (cf. Phil 3:12), that he has nothing more to learn and to heed (Jn 6:45), that he no longer needs 'conversion of life' (RB 58), that he does not need to 'fear

the day of judgment and to be in dread of hell', 'daily to
confess his past sins with tears and sighs to God, and to
amend them for the time to come' (RB 4).

This pharisaical self-assurance and self-righteousness is
death to any real spiritual progress. It robs the soul of openness to the impulse and influence of divine grace. It robs the
soul of willingness to change, which is the classic criterion of
where we stand in religion. It is to blame for the spiritual
narrowness and lack of freedom often found in pious
persons, for the lack of openness to new calls from God and
to new tasks demanded by a new age. It is to blame when
damage in one's own spiritual life or in the life of the
ecclesiastical community is not recognized and necessary
reforms are not promptly put into effect. The spirit of the
Pharisees is in very truth the supreme danger for the realization of the christian and the monastic ideal.

That is why in his way of humility St Benedict waged such
unrelenting and radical warfare against this spirit. That is
why he, who was filled with the gentleness of the Good
Shepherd in regard to faults committed out of weakness and
ignorance, was inexorable in his severity when he encoun-
tered *contumacia,* stubbornness and obstinacy (RB 23, 62,
71), when someone 'puffed up with pride, even wishes to
defend his deeds' (RB 28).

Those who because of their office or ordination have been
raised above others are especially exposed to the dangers to
which the Pharisees, the chosen guardians of the law and
leaders of the people, once succumbed. With our knowledge
of these dangers, we understand the exceptionally sharp
words St Benedict uses in Chapter 65, 'Of the Prior of the
Monastery', about priors 'who, puffed up by the evil spirit of
pride, and deeming themselves to be second abbots, take
upon themselves to tyrannize over others, and so foster
scandals and cause dissensions in the community'. In the
same way he says about a priest who does not want to conform humbly to the monastic routine: 'He shall be judged,

not as a priest, but as a rebel; and if after frequent warning he does not correct himself, let recourse be had to the intervention of the bishop. If even then he will not amend, and his guilt is clearly shown, let him be cast forth from the monastery, provided his contumacy be such that he will not submit nor obey the Rule' (RB 62).

When the spirit of pharisaical pride takes hold of someone who has a responsible office, the higher his position the more terrible will the result necessarily be for him and for those entrusted to him. So it is the priest must 'rather give an example of humility to all' (RB 60).

> *Let him who is ordained beware of arrogance and pride . . . knowing that he is now all the more subject to regular discipline. Let him not, by reason of his priesthood, become forgetful of the obedience and discipline of the Rule, but advance ever more and more in godliness (RB 62).*

The Pharisee and the tax collector stand before us as graphic illustrations of the text placed at the head of the Holy Rule's chapter on humility: 'Everyone who exalts himself shall be humbled, and he who humbles himself shall be exalted'. The way taken by the Pharisee in his self-assurance and callousness shows us the frightful danger in which we ourselves stand. There is only one possibility of being 'justified': like the tax collector to stand before God in humility. Here there is nothing of self-righteousness and boasting about one's own good works. Nor is there anything opposed to the action of the Holy Spirit. All the doors of the soul are open for the call of God, for the influx of divine grace.

A person who in this way is conscious of his own powerlessness and, 'ever thinking of the guilt of his sins, imagines himself already present before the terrible judgment-seat of God', cannot help but throw himself into the arms of divine love in boundless trust, giving himself to God wholly in unconditional surrender. 'I have been brought to nothing, and I knew it not . . . lower and viler than all . . . a worm and no man . . . not worthy to raise my eyes to heaven . . . bowed down and humbled on every side . . . yet I am always with you.'

# Perfect Love

*Having, therefore, ascended all these degrees of humility, the monk will presently arrive at that love of God which, being perfect, casts out fear: whereby he shall begin to keep, without labor, and as it were naturally and by custom, all those precepts which he had hitherto observed through fear: no longer through dread of hell, but for the love of Christ, and of a good habit and a delight in virtue.*

I T SEEMS as though St Benedict is now speaking a different language. There is complete relaxation as if after terrific tension. It is as though the summit aimed at has, after a laborious climb, been attained. The earth lies at our feet. Above us the view is unobstructed. We are standing in the full light of the sun. Here we are on 'the highest point of humility'. Every downward pull has been overcome. We are free and responsive to everything divine. All the doors of the soul stand open to receive God's call and the action of his grace. Now the love of God can be 'poured out in our hearts through the Holy Spirit who has been given to us' (Rom 5:5).

The love of God! If we want to know what the 'perfect love of God' is, we have to look into God himself, into his inner trinitarian life there where 'the Word is present to God', where Father and Son are 'perfectly one' (Jn 1:1, 10:30). So boundless is the love with which the Father and the Son love each other that this love is itself a Divine Person, the Holy Spirit, and so perfectly are the three Divine Persons one in this love that St John saw the very nature of God summed up in it: 'God is love' (1 Jn 4:16).

From the depths of the Most Holy Trinity this love overflows upon human beings in order to enfold them as well and to draw them into the triune God's communion of love, that they 'might become sharers of the divine nature' (2 Pt 1:4), of the substantial love of God. The love of God that unites the Divine Persons with one another and that is God's gracious gift to man is in reality one and the same. In his last prayer Our Lord says explicitly to the Father: 'So that your love for me may live in them, and I may live in them' (Jn 17:26).

But the way by which this perfect love of God came to man was the way of humility described by the apostle in chapter two of the Letter to the Philippians. This way did not merely bring down the Son of God, who 'emptied himself and took the form of a slave', into the nothingness of a created nature. It brought him, through obedience, to death on the cross, to the fulfillment of the prophecy: 'I am a worm and no man, the shame of men and the outcast of the people' (Ps 22:6). It was a way of incredible humility and abasement.

In this humility and abasement, however, the love of God manifested itself more marvelously than in all the works of creation, than in all the revelations of divine glory. By contemplating this way of humility we begin to realize that humility itself at its innermost depth is love, love of a kind so incredibly great that it 'surpasses all knowledge' (Eph 3:19).

'God is the humbly loving One . . . . Humility begins not with men, but with God'.† Incomprehensible love, as only

---

† Romano Guardini, *The Lord*. See Part Five, Ch. III, 'God's Humility', and Ch. IX, 'The Footwashing'.

infinite God can have, 'love to the end', prompted the mysterious decision for that *kenosis,* that 'self-emptying' or 'self-renunciation' of which St Paul wrote; in such love, surrendering self to the point of 'annihilation', the redemptive sacrifice of Our Lord reaches its climax. To make this clearly understood was the purpose of the startling act of humility with which Our Lord opened 'the hour for him to pass from this world to the Father' (Jn 13:1). 'Jesus, fully aware that he had come from God and was going to God, the Father who had handed everything over to him'—like Paul in Phil 2:6, John emphasizes here the Lord's divine dignity in order to make us aware of how incredible his conduct was—'rose from the meal and took off his cloak. He picked up a towel and tied it around himself. Then he poured water into a basin and began to wash his disciples' feet and dry them with the towel he had around him' (Jn 13:3-5).

*No wonder the disciples were perplexed! Everything was really upside-down! The earnestness of Jesus' act is perhaps best measured by his remark to Peter: 'What I am doing you do not know now . . . if I do not wash you, you have no part with me.' Peter had to participate in the mystery of divine surrender if he was to share in the life of Christ, for it is the kernel of Christianity. That is why the Lord adds: ' . . . as I have done to you, so you also should do.' The disciples were not only to learn humility and fraternal love, they actually had to participate in the mystery.*

*Every Christian one day reaches the point where he too must be ready to accompany the Master into destruction and oblivion: into that which the world considers folly, that which for his own understanding is incomprehensible, for his own feeling intolerable. Whatever it is to be: suffering, dishonor, the loss of loved ones or the shattering of the work of a lifetime, this is the decisive test of his Christianity. Will he shrink back before the ultimate depths, or will he be able to go all the way and thus win his share of the life of Christ?*†

Only now do we fully understand why for St Benedict humility, self-abasement, is at the 'heart' of the spiritual life, and why he took over into his monastic routine the venerable custom of foot-washing as a sacred heritage from christian antiquity. When the weekly servers in the kitchen are changed at the end of the week, 'let both him who goes out and him who is coming in wash the feet of all' (RB 35). 'Let the abbot as well as the whole community wash the feet of the guests; after which let them say this verse: "We have received your mercy, O God, in the midst of your temple" ' (RB 53).

Proud persons cannot of course understand this humility. 'In truth, this God destroys everything that man in the pride of his revolt constructs of his own inspiration. Here ultimate temptation lifts its head: the impulse to say: "I will not bend the knee to such a God!" ' (Guardini, p. 328). But proud persons cannot really love either. Humility is not only truth; it is love, God's love as revealed in Jesus Christ, and love for God 'as response to the incarnation of God in Jesus Christ'.

The mystery of this loving humility and humble love is disclosed only under the cross, to which Benedict has repeatedly brought us—in the third, fourth and seventh degrees of humility—and in the exercise of humility, in putting into practice the following of Christ, in having 'the attitude of Christ' (Phil 2:5) as taught by the degrees of humility. By 'imitating the Lord, of whom the apostle says, "He was made obedient even unto death",' by 'patience sharing in the sufferings of Christ', by descending with him through all the stages of 'self-emptying', 'bowed down and humbled on every side', a person is at the same time 'exalted' with him; he rises, or rather is raised to an ever more intense participation in the mystery of God's love

---

† Guardini, *The Lord*, p. 365.

revealed in Christ.

The metaphor used by Benedict at the beginning of his chapter on humility, that of 'a ladder such as Jacob beheld in his dream, by which the angels appeared to him ascending and descending', is now given its full application. It is not only God's angels that ascend and descend. God himself 'for our salvation came down from heaven' into our earthly lowliness, into 'self-emptying' and 'annihilation', to enable us to 'ascend into heaven' when our heart has become humble, to take us into the blessed communion of his own love within the Trinity. When our heart has become humble . . . . Just as God's love for us reveals and communicates itself in God's humility, so also does our love for God prove itself in following our humble Saviour, and the words of Our Lord are fulfilled: 'Anyone who loves me my Father will love, and we will come to him and make our dwelling place with him' (Jn 14:23).

Benedict did not go into further detail about the effect on our life this perfect love of God, has God's love for us and our love in return, kindled by the divine love. That belongs to 'the perfection of religion' which he merely suggests in the final chapter of his Rule. For it he refers us to 'the teachings of the holy Fathers, the following of which brings a man to the height of perfection', especially 'the divinely-inspired books of the Old and New Testaments, which are a most unerring rule for human life'. He intended to teach us only the *initium conversationis,* the beginning of the way of perfection. And this beginning of the spiritual life is humility— self-abasement and self-renunciation in that far-reaching breadth and depth Benedict has shown us 'by the guidance of the Gospel' exemplified by Jesus Christ.

When this beginning is accomplished, we arrive 'at the lofty summits of doctrine and virtue of which we have spoken above'. Without this humility we are denied access to the heights of love of God and union with God. 'Whoever would save his life will lose it, and whoever loses his life for my sake will save it' (Lk 9:24). Only when we can say, 'It is now no longer I that live'—this is perhaps the shortest possible formulation of the substance and import of Benedict's teaching on humility—may we also say, but 'Christ lives in me' (Gal 2:20).

Actually, this is just what frightens us about being a Christian. The natural man 'flies in dismay from the way of salvation, whose beginning cannot but be strait and difficult' (RB Prologue)' He is afraid to 'lose his life', to surrender and sacrifice his own self. Benedict wanted to help us overcome this fear by calling to our attention, as he did at the conclusion of the Prologue, that fear in fact decreases to the extent that love becomes effective in our life of humility; as the apostle of love says, 'Love has no room for fear; rather, perfect love casts out all fear. Fear has to do with punishment' (1 Jn 4:18).

What love urges upon us is done no longer from fear or force, from inner constraint and with inner resistance, but 'without labor, and as it were naturally and by custom'. The interior and exterior attitude of humility gradually becomes second nature. It blends with our very being, it gets to be a 'custom', the spontaneous disposition of the 'new man' in us who goes the way of humility 'no longer through dread of hell, but for the love of Christ', whose 'mind he has in him', 'who lives in him', 'and of a good habit and a delight in virtue'.

The more resolutely and unhesitatingly we go the way of humility, the more profoundly do we understand the essence of humility, its inner beauty, its godliness, its kinship with love. Everything is little by little transformed into this love. What at first caused us to shrink back in dread becomes for us a source of joy, of yearning. We begin to love what is 'strait and difficult'. We become 'fervent in humiliations' (RB 58). There will be for us 'more happiness in giving than receiving' (Acts 20:35), in 'serving' than in 'being served' (Mt 20:28). Times of more occasion for sacrifice, such as

Lent, become times of 'joy of the Holy Spirit, joy of spiritual longing' (RB 49). Even dread of the 'terrible judgement of God' is changed into joyous hope; 'our love is brought to perfection in this, that we should have confidence on the day of judgment; for our relation to this world is just like his' (1 Jn 4:17)—who was 'bowed down and humbled on every side'.

'We shall with hearts enlarged and unspeakable sweetness of love run in the way of God's commandments' (RB Prologue), the way of following our humble Saviour. Joyfully 'we suffer death all the day long for the sake of him who has loved us' (the fourth degree of humility), 'preferring nothing whatever to Christ. And may he bring us all alike to life everlasting' (RB 72).

> *God will vouchsafe to manifest this by the Holy Spirit in his laborer, now cleansed from vice and sin.*

# PART FOUR

# ONE WITH GOD IN PRAYER AND ALL OF LIFE

# LITURGICAL PRAYER

## CHAPTER 19: OF THE DISCIPLINE
## OF SAYING THE DIVINE OFFICE

IN THE TWELFTH DEGREE of humility Benedict clearly designates the goal of all ascetical endeavor: that humility should consistently determine and shape the monk's whole life, that humility should become his 'general attitude' from which flows everything he does and which gives uniform character to all his thoughts, words, and deeds.

> *The monk must, not only in his heart, but also outwardly, always show his humility to all who see him, that is, in the Work of God, in the oratory, in the monastery, in the garden, on the road, in the field or wherever he may be, whether sitting, walking or standing.*

The more humility in this way becomes a person's way of life, the more will 'perfect love' become the dominant and formative power, the person's essential disposition. In the routine of practical life that St Benedict erects on the ascetical principles considered so far (RB 8 ff.) he has shown how life in its entirety will as a result be permeated with the spirit of love and humility.

# Humility Expressed in Worship

A S THE FIRST major area in which humility is at work St Benedict designated the *Opus Dei*, praise of God in common, liturgical prayer. It is no mere external coincidence that the Rule's chapters on the monastic choir prayer immediately follow the chapter on humility. There is a very profound inter-relation between humility and the *Opus Dei*. Chapter 19, '*De disciplina psallendi*, Of the Discipline [interior and exterior] of saying the Divine Office' which concludes the liturgical directives of the Rule (RB 8–18), is in part a word for word repetition and recapitulation of the thoughts in the chapter on humility, especially in the fundamental first degree.

> We believe that the divine presence is every-where, and that the eyes of the Lord behold the good and the evil in every place. Especially should we believe this, without any doubt, when we are assisting at the Work of God. Let us, then, ever remember what the prophet says, 'Serve the Lord in fear'; and again, 'Sing wisely'; and, 'In the sight of the angels I will sing praises unto you'. Therefore let us consider how we ought to behave ourselves in the presence of God and of his angels, and so assist at the Divine Office, that our mind and our voice may accord together (*RB 19*).

*Ps 2:11*
*Ps 47:7*
*Ps 137:1*

The basic disposition of soul upon which Benedict, in the first degree of humility, builds up the entire spiritual life—belief in the omnipresence and omniscience of God, reverential awe in face of his infinite majesty and holiness—must be living and active especially in liturgical prayer. There we come before the throne of the Most High in order to offer him the 'duties of our service', the 'obligation of divine service' (RB 16, 50) which we owe him as his creatures and his children by grace. There we join in with 'the voices of many angels who surround his throne' (Rv 5:11) to give, together with the throngs of the blessed, in the name of 'every creature in heaven and on earth and under the earth and in the sea, to the One seated on the throne, and to the Lamb, praise and honor' (Rv 5:13). 'It is just such worshipers the Father seeks' (Jn 4:23).

### WHAT IS WORSHIP?

In Chapter 4 of the Book of Revelation St John describes the worship of God by the representatives of all creation, the living creatures and the twenty-four elders:

> They fall down before the One seated on the throne, and worship him who lives forever and ever. They throw down their crowns before the throne and sing: 'O Lord our God, you are worthy to receive glory and honor and power! For you have created all things; by your will they came to be and were made!'

Guardini comments on this passage as follows:

> In a powerful image the twenty-four elders, representatives of all humanity before God, clothed in festive garments and crowned with gold, rise, prostrate themselves, and place their crowns at the feet of the throning One . . . .
>
> The act of standing is a timeless human gesture. It says: I am. Here I stand, strong and determined to defend my rights—if necessary, by force. He

*who adores, sacrifices this independent attitude.
Originally, prostration was a vassal's expression of
self-obliteration before the power of his lord. Here
the same idea is transposed to the spiritual plane.
The worshiper's whole person says: Thine the
power, not mine! Rise and reign! There where the
worshiper stands, in the sphere of his personality,
God alone should rule, he who really is (*The Lord,
p. 489*).

Is it not indeed to the inner self-surrender to God achieved
here, and its externalization in the act of worship, that
humility wants to bring us? Surely it is the quintessence of
humility to give way to God within ourselves, so that his
power may 'rise and reign' and God may occupy the place
wrongfully held by our own ego. The act of worship, as well
as the humility which is its source, has 'plumbless depths.
This clearing the way for God, this will to see in him all
genuine being and power, can become increasingly pure,
complete, essential; the "space" allowed him ever freer and
more vast' (*ibid.*).

In the twelve degrees of humility we little by little empty
all the rooms of our soul, we open all the inner doors, we
surrender our will, our whole being to God ever more fully
and fervently, 'so that God may be all in all' (1 Cor 15:28).

'Having, therefore, ascended all these degrees of humility,
the monk will presently arrive at perfect love of God.' The
act of worship and the disposition of humility underlying it
do not come from superior physical power on the part of
God to which a person is forced to submit, but from
acknowledgement of the great creative power, holiness and
goodness of God, from the acknowledgement that God is
'worthy to receive glory and honor and power', that he 'is
worthy of omnipotence, worthy to be God—perhaps then we
too will discover great joy in this contemplation that has
inflamed so many saints' (Guardini, p. 492).

'Come!' bids Psalm 95,† with which Benedict so pro-

† Vulgate Psalm 94.

foundly and significantly has the daily choir prayer of his monks begin. 'Come, let us sing joyfully to the Lord; let us acclaim the Rock of our salvation. Let us greet him with thanksgiving; let us joyfully sing psalms to him . . . . Come, let us bow down in worship; let us kneel before the Lord who made us. For he is our God, and we are the people he shepherds, the flock he guides.'

Thus we 'perform the Work of God, in godly fear, and on bended knees' (RB 50). We are conscious of being 'in the presence of God and of his angels'. Faith tells us that the place where we are standing and praying is filled with the glory of God, as the temple of Jerusalem once was at its dedication, and we do what Scripture says the children of Israel did: they saw 'the glory of the Lord upon the house, and they fell down upon the pavement with their faces to the earth and adored' (2 Chr 7:3).

Now we understand why worship of God in the *Opus Dei*— choir prayer, liturgical services—is the focal point of the benedictine way of life, not for its own sake but as the most profound expression of self-surrender to God, of belonging to God, of humility as the 'service of devotion' (RB 18). Again we see that what Benedict asks of his monks is nothing but what belongs to being fully a Christian. Worship of God must be central in christian life.

In worship, the spirit of self-sacrifice which is at the heart of the christian attitude develops in the human soul. In worship we acclaim in mind and heart the absolute glory which is God's as our Creator and Lord, we acknowledge our dependence upon him and give ourselves to him in love. Like the elders in St John's Book of Revelation we prostrate ourselves with our whole being, body and soul, before God 'the Lord of all', and we anticipate what will ultimately be the culmination of our existence in eternity: worshiping God, surrendering self totally to him whom the seer of the Apocalypse beheld in that wondrous vision.

'Nothing is more important for man than to incline his

spirit before God', that is, to adore him, to give way to him, so that he may 'rise and reign'. To be of this mind, to conform to this in the depths of our being, to the fact that God is worthy of adoration because he is holy and true, infinite, absolute, is beautiful and grand and eminently salutary.

> *Even when we are tired, inert, definitely unmoved to worship, it is something to place ourselves in God's presence and to remain there for a while with a feeling of—to use the humblest word— respect. Such moments will work their way into our consciousness, bringing their truth with them; particularly if they are permitted to bear fruit in our daily lives, helping us to refrain from an untruth because God is Truth, or to act with justice towards another because God thrones in holiness (Guardini, p. 492).*

To anyone who has grasped this inner connection, this dictum of the Rule of St Benedict is self-evident: '*Operi Dei nihil praeponatur*—Let nothing be preferred to the Work [worship] of God' (RB 43). The context in which this sentence is placed is noteworthy. It occurs not in the specifically liturgical chapters of the Rule but in Chapter 43, 'Of those who come late to the Work of God, or to table':

> *At the hour of Divine Office, as soon as the signal is heard, let every one, leaving whatever he had in hand, hasten to the oratory with all speed, and yet with seriousness, so that no occasion be given for levity. Let nothing, then, be preferred to the Work of God.*

Benedict says this in a context of prompt obedience, of immediate availability for every call of God. Zeal for the Work of God, for worship, expresses a person's total readiness for the service of God. Worship of God in the liturgical office and sacrifice is humility at prayer. It is the most exquisite flower, the most precious fruit of humility. 'To find favor with you . . . with contrite heart and humble spirit let us be

received . . . . Let our sacrifice be in your presence today'
(Dn 3:38–40).

The way Benedict here makes the *Opus Dei,* liturgical
prayer, flow from an inner disposition, from the basic
christian spirit of humility, is of great importance in determining the place to be assigned liturgical prayer in the
spiritual life of the Christian, and gives direction to all work
in the field of liturgy. All liturgical formation must make its
goal the development of this inner disposition. It must instill
reverence before the Divine Majesty, an unquestioning conviction of God's presence, and humility in the comprehen-
sive sense taught by Chapter 7 of the Holy Rule.

Where liturgical prayer and action do not issue from this
inner disposition they are open to the danger of becoming
superficial and remaining sterile. But where 'our mind', our
inner disposition, 'and our voice accord together' liturgy
becomes truly 'Work of God' in the profound twofold meaning of this term.

# Liturgy. God's Work.

The *Opus Dei,* the Work of God, in the first instance
means (and so far we have been considering this meaning) a
work that man does for God. It denotes the 'service' of worship we give to God. But 'Work of God' can also mean work
that God does, a work that the almighty Creator, the
merciful Saviour and Sanctifier, performs on mankind.

'We believe that the divine presence is everywhere', wrote
Benedict. 'Especially should we believe this, without any
doubt, when we are assisting at the Work of God.' Where God
is present in a special way, he is also at work, there he performs special works of grace and mercy.

In his directives for liturgical prayer Benedict called for great reverence at the reading of the Gospel. All are to stand and listen 'in awe and reverence' to the Word of God, the 'good news' of our Lord and Saviour (RB 11). When the Word of God in the Gospel is read and heard in the liturgy, it is not mere human words being said and listened to. The Word of God is being proclaimed anew through the mouth of the Church. It comes alive again, and for those who accept his Word in faith Our Lord, who once proclaimed it, is as near as he was to his disciples who at that time heard him speak. 'I flee to the Gospel,' said Ignatius of Antioch, 'as if to Christ who is present' (To the Philadelphians, 5).

By extension this applies to the liturgy in its entirety, for most of its texts are taken directly from Holy Scripture. When we pronounce these sacred words in prayer, something similar to what God once said to the prophet occurs: 'See, I place my words in your mouth!' (Jer 1:9, Is 51:16). The words of God are 'words of eternal life' (Jn 6:68). Man lives 'on every utterance that comes from the mouth of God' (Mt 4:4). God reveals himself to us, communicates himself to us in his Word. God's thoughts pass over into our thinking. The Spirit of God unites himself with our spirit. 'The Spirit we have received is God's Spirit, helping us to recognize the gifts he has given us. We speak of these, not in words of human wisdom, but in words taught by the Spirit' (1 Cor 2:12,13).

This is that mysterious prayer of the Spirit who 'himself makes intercession for us with groanings that cannot be expressed in speech . . . . The Spirit intercedes for the saints as God himself wills' (Rom 8:26,27). It is the rejoicing and thanksgiving and praise described by St Paul in Colossians: 'Let the word of Christ, rich as it is, dwell in you. In wisdom made perfect, instruct and admonish one another. Sing gratefully to God from your hearts in psalms, hymns and inspired songs' (3:16). After prayer like this there occurred what is reported in the Acts of the Apostles (4:31): 'The

place where they were gathered shook as they prayed. They
were filled with the Holy Spirit and continued to speak God's
word with confidence.'

Do we begin to understand what such prayer must mean
not only for the spiritual growth of the individual but for the
growth of the entire kingdom of God?

The culmination and perfection of this union with the
Word of God, this grace-laden 'divine presence' in which 'we
should believe, without any doubt', is the celebration of the
Holy Eucharist. In the Eucharist we not only receive
spiritually in faith the living Word of God come down from
heaven, but consume it in the sacred sacrificial meal as 'real
food and real drink'. It is the fulfillment of what our Lord
said when he promised this sacrament: 'The man who feeds
on my flesh and drinks my blood remains in me, and I in
him' (Jn 6:56).

The Eucharist makes present Christ's sublime act of
obedience unto death—set before us in the third degree of
humility—, Our Lord's supreme self-renunciation and self-
abasement whereby we were redeemed. 'As often as this
memorial sacrifice is offered, the work of our redemption is
performed'†.

Here too is the deepest source of strength enabling us to
walk the path of humility, 'imitating the Lord, of whom the
apostle says: "He was made obedient even unto death".'
Here is the flowing font of that Christocentric spirit evident
throughout the Holy Rule, the font of that 'love of Christ to
which nothing may be preferred' (RB 4), of that ardent self-
surrender to the divine Master so beautifully portrayed in
St Benedict himself when at the point of death 'he had himself carried to the oratory by his disciples', to the place
where day after day he had sung the praises of God. There
    *he strengthened himself for his departure by*

---

† From the Prayer over the Gifts in the Maundy Thursday Mass of the
Lord's Supper.

*receiving the Body and Blood of the Lord, and resting his feeble body upon the arms of his brethren he stood with his hands raised toward heaven and breathed forth his soul in prayer (Gregory, Dialogues II.37, transl. by A. Hoffmann).*

# Continuous

# Spiritual Growth

'THE ACT OF WORSHIP has plumbless depths . . . . The "space" allowed God can become ever freer and more vast' (Guardini, p. 489). That is why liturgical worship means continuous spiritual growth, the ever renewed conferring of grace. The 'divine presence' at the liturgical Work of God has an ever greater effect upon us. Ever more truly does the praise of God become 'singing wisely', in 'God's wisdom . . . which God has revealed to us through the Spirit. The Spirit scrutinizes all matters, even the deep things of God' (1 Cor 2:7,10).

The daily Office as arranged by the Holy Rule begins with the thrice repeated petition, 'O Lord, open my lips, and my mouth shall declare your praise' (Psalm 51:17, AV; RB 9), and each separate time of prayer begins with the entreaty, 'O God, come to my assistance; O Lord, make haste to help me' (Ps 70:1, RB 18).

Nor does the praise of God ever cease. The Work of God in the liturgy is performed continuously (RB 16):

*As the prophet says: 'Seven times in the day have*

*I given praise to you.' And we shall observe*     Ps 119:164
*this sacred number of seven if, at the times of*
*Lauds, Prime, Tierce, Sext, None, Vespers and*
*Compline, we fulfil the duties of our service.*
*For it was of these hours of the day that he*
*said: 'Seven times in the day have I given*
*praise to you'; just as the same prophet says*
*of the night watches: 'At midnight I arose to*
*give you praise.' At these times, therefore, let*     Ps 119:62
*us sing the praises of our Creator for the*
*judgments of his justice: that is, at Lauds,*
*Prime, Tierce, Sext, None, Vespers and Com-*
*pline; and at night let us arise to praise him.*

Day follows day, joining to form a week, the time period
God himself sanctioned. It determines the rhythm of liturgical prayer by the regulations that the first day of the
week, 'the Lord's day', be marked by a longer and more
solemn Office (RB 11,12), and that 'the whole psalter of a
hundred and fifty psalms be recited every week, and always
begun afresh at the Night-Office on Sunday' (RB 18).

Occasions of special celebration similar to that of Sundays
are 'the festivals of saints, and all other solemnities'. On these
days the Office is to be 'ordered as we have prescribed for
Sundays: except that the psalms, antiphons and lessons
suitable to the day are to be said' (RB 14), so that in the
'Work of God', the *Opus Dei*, the 'work of our redemption'
may be venerated in worship and made present in grace in
accordance with the respective mystery of the various feast
days. The climax of all these feasts and of the entire liturgical
year is the holy feast of Easter, with its preparatory period of
Lent to which Benedict devotes a special chapter of his
Rule (RB 49). In the christian mystery of the lenten and
paschal season occurs that spiritual dying, that 'being crucified and buried' with Christ of which Paul speaks in the
Epistle to the Romans (6:4 ff) and to which Benedict wants
to bring us by his doctrine of humility. 'New life for God in

Christ Jesus' bursts forth, spiritual resurrection with the Lord enables us to say with the apostle, 'The life I live now is not my own; Christ is living in me' (Gal 2:20).

That is why during the forty days of Lent the monks are to focus their full strength on self-surrender and openness and try at least during this time to realize the ideal of the spiritual life as completely as possible. Chapter 49, 'Of the Observance of Lent,' is like a synopsis of the entire Rule:

> *Although the life of a monk ought at all times to have about it a lenten character, yet since few have strength enough for this, we exhort all, at least during the days of Lent, to keep themselves in all purity of life, and to wash away, during that holy season, the negligence of other times. This we shall worthily do, if we refrain from all sin, and give ourselves to prayer with tears, to holy reading, compunction of heart and abstinence. In these days, then, let us add something to our wonted service; as private prayers, and abstinence from food and drink, so that every one of his own will may offer to God, with joy of the Holy Spirit, something beyond the measure appointed him: withholding from his body somewhat of his food, drink and sleep, refraining from talking and mirth, and awaiting holy Easter with the joy of spiritual longing. Let each one, however, make known to his abbot what he offers, and let it be done with his blessing and permission: because what is done without leave of the spiritual father shall be imputed to presumption and vain-glory, and merit no reward. Everything, therefore, is to be done with the approval of the abbot.*

We cannot fail to discern the joyful note sounding throughout these words despite all their penitential seriousness— proof that the whole doctrine of humility, of sacrificing one's own ego, serves only joy, religious development, and spiritual resurrection. 'With joy in the Holy Spirit' should the monk (and the Christian) offer his life to God. 'The joy of spiritual longing' should constantly urge him onward on the way to God, his gaze fixed in joyful hope and holy expectation on 'holy Easter', spiritual resurrection, the new life with Christ.

Every liturgical celebration intensifies this life with Christ in us and brings us closer to its perfection in eternal bliss. That is why the sacred service of prayer is not a burden for the monk but a service of joy to which 'as soon as the signal is heard, let every one hasten with all speed' (RB 43). That is why throughout the choir prayer, especially on Sunday, *Alleluia* resounds again and again except during Lent. Above all 'from the holy feast of Easter, until Pentecost, without interruption, let *Alleluia* be said both with the psalms and the responsories' (RB 15).

*Alleluia* is the cry of joy of redeemed and glorified Christendom. John heard 'what sounded like the loud song of a great assembly in heaven. They were singing: "*Alleluia!* Salvation, glory and might belong to our God, for his judgments are true and just" ' (for which we sing his praises: RB 16). Then John saw how 'the four and twenty elders and the four living creatures fell down and worshiped God seated on the throne,' and heard how they sang, 'Amen! *Alleluia!*' (Rv 19:1-4).

This is humble self-surrender in worship transformed over and over into the exultation of perfect love. The holy 'fear in which we serve the Lord' turns into rejoicing in God's glory and loving mercy. 'Believing, without any doubt, in the divine presence,' we are aware of being 'in the sight of God and of his angels', placed among the throngs of the blessed in heaven, with them to 'worship the Father in Spirit and truth' (Jn 4:23,24). With them we participate in the supreme *Opus divinum,* the glory that the eternal Son, who is truth, gives to the Father in the Holy Spirit of love. We join with them in the hymn which the triune God sings within himself. We are transported into that self-immolation whereby 'the Lamb standing between the throne and the four living creatures and the elders, a Lamb that had been slain' (Rv 5:6) offers himself forever to the Father, crying 'Abba, Father', and the Father gives himself to the Son in the joy of the Holy Spirit.

This is the 'glory of the Father and of the Son and of the Holy Spirit, as it was in the beginning' before all creation and as it 'is now and ever shall be, world without end'. This is the most profound mystery of the Godhead, the inexpressible and unfathomable 'Work of God' we think about when in the Divine Office we repeatedly say the *Gloria Patri*, the 'Glory be to the Father', rising from our seats 'out of honor and reverence to the Holy Trinity,' as Benedict twice explicitly directs (RB 9, 11).

We sense that surely here is the final mystery of humility. Now it becomes evident to us that the ultimate reason why our whole being must be transformed into humility, worship, self-surrender, is that God himself is wholly self-giving: the Father's giving of himself to the Son and the Son's giving of himself to the Father in the Holy Spirit who is essentially the self-giving Person, love. 'God is love, and he who abides in love abides in God, and God in him' (1 Jn 4:16).

And we are to 'become sharers of the divine nature' (2 Pt 1:4). The Father wants to give himself to us with that same self-giving with which he gives himself to the Son. 'May your love for me,' the Son prayed, 'live in them, and I in them' (Jn 17:26). Hence we too must have the attitude of Christ (Phil 2:5). We must offer to the Father what the Son offers him: the surrender of our whole being, heart and soul, in humility and love and adoration.

So it is that the Lord prays for us:

> *I consecrate myself for their sakes now, that they may be consecrated in truth . . . . I have given them the glory you gave me that they may be one, as we*

*are one—I living in them, you living in me—that*
*their unity may be complete. So shall the world*
*know that you sent me, and that you loved them*
*as you loved me. Father, all those you gave me*
*I would have in my company where I am, to see*
*this glory of mine which is your gift to me'*
*(Jn 17:19–24).*

# Liturgy is
# Community Prayer

ROM ALL we have been considering it becomes clear
why the *Opus Dei*—praise of God, worship of God—is
essentially community prayer. God's plan is 'to bring
all things in the heavens and on earth into one under Christ's
headship . . . . We were predestined to praise his glory'
(Eph 1:10, 12). All are to 'come to him, a living stone',
namely, Christ.

*You too are living stones, built as an edifice of*
*spirit, into a holy priesthood, offering spiritual*
*sacrifices acceptable to God through Jesus Christ*
*. . . . You are a chosen race, a royal priesthood, a*
*holy nation, a people he claims for his own to pro-*
*claim the glorious works of the One who called*
*you from darkness into his marvelous light (1 Pt*
*2,4 ff).*

Again and again St Benedict stresses this communal
character of the liturgy. All the members of the monastic

community, of the *corpus monasterii,* the 'monastic body' which is a facsimile of the Mystical Body of Christ, are strictly obliged to take part in the *Opus Dei* and to be there punctually. The most severe punishment meted out is exclusion from this pre-eminent community activity, choir prayer (RB 24, 25, 44).

Even when an individual performs the *Opus Dei* by himself, when he is saying the sacred words of liturgical prayer alone, he prays communally, in spiritual union with all who are likewise saying them. So for brethren who have to go so far to work that they cannot get to the oratory at the time of choir prayer, Benedict makes this ruling (RB 50):

> Let the brothers who are at work at a great distance, or on a journey, and cannot come to the oratory at the proper time (the abbot judging such to be the case) perform the Work of God there where they are laboring, in godly fear, and on bended knees. In like manner, let not those who are sent on a journey allow the appointed Hours to pass by; but, as far as they can, observe them by themselves, and not neglect to fulfil their obligation of divine service.

On their part, the brothers who are reciting the Office in choir at home are to remember those who cannot be present (RB 67):

> At the last prayer of the Work of God let a commemoration be always made of the absent.

At liturgical prayer, therefore, all those taking part must have a strong sense of solidarity and union in Christ. What Benedict says about the *Our Father* is a striking reference to this. Ordinarily the Lord's Prayer ending each liturgical Hour is said silently out of reverence and 'only the last part of the prayer is to be said aloud, so that all may answer, "But deliver us from evil" ' (RB 13). But twice a day, in the morning at Lauds and in the evening at Vespers, the entire Lord's Prayer is to be

ML besvar

*said aloud by the superior, so that all may hear it, on account of the thorns of scandal which are wont to arise; so that the brethren, by the covenant which they make in that prayer when they say, 'Forgive us as we forgive,' may cleanse themselves of such faults.*

From this prayer-community into which we are formed in the sacred liturgy by the communal worship of God, by God's word and sacrament, must grow the spirit of mutual charity which is sincerely benevolent, which plucks every thorn of uncharitableness from our heart and is willing and ready to forgive and forget. When our heart opens itself to God in worship, it must likewise open itself to the brothers with whom we are praying. When we receive divine grace in God's word and sacrament, we must also pass this grace on. It must be as in the triune God where the constant flow of self-giving unites all three divine Persons into one.

*I pray . . . that all may be one as you, Father, are in me, and I in you; I pray that they may be one in us (Jn 17:21).*

# The Outward Form of the Liturgy

THERE IS SOMETHING truly sublime and sacred about the liturgical choir prayer which brings us so close to God and unites us so intimately with one another. We can understand why St Benedict repeatedly calls for the greatest reverence and attention at the divine service and why he regulates the liturgy for his monks down to the smallest detail with great care and completeness.

In no less than eleven chapters he arranges the various times of prayer. As is clearly evident, he had made a thorough study of it. Various influences from already existing liturgical structures are recognizable. Some he originated. In others he followed the practice of the roman church (RB 13). He prescribed precise ceremonies, when to sit, when to stand. He determined the sequence in which, after the abbot, the psalms and antiphons are to be intoned. He made the rule that no one may 'presume to sing or to read except those who can so perform the office that the hearers may be edified. And let it be done with humility, gravity, and awe, and by those whom the abbot has appointed' (RB 47).

He was especially concerned that the signal for choir prayer be always given properly: 'Let the announcing of the hour for the Work of God, both by day and by night, be the abbot's care: either by signifying it himself, or by entrusting the duty to such a careful brother, that all things may be done at the appointed times' (RB 47). If anyone comes late to choir or 'makes a mistake in the recitation of psalm, responsory, antiphon, or lesson', he must 'humble himself by making satisfaction there before all', so that he may 'correct by humility what he did wrong through negligence' (RB 43, 45).

Just as the inner disposition of humility manifests itself outwardly in silence, speech, and bodily carriage, so too does the spirit of worship show itself in exterior reverence and in the deliberate manner in which the divine service is performed. Here too the *Opus Dei* on earth is a reproduction of the heavenly liturgy shown us by St John's Book of Revelation in scenes of wondrous harmony and radiant beauty. Just as the spirit of humility can be inferred from outward signs of humility, so also can fervor, the spirit of reverence, of

adoration, be inferred from the way the *Opus Dei* is performed. That is why St. Benedict set as a decisive criterion of
a monastic vocation that the novice be 'fervent in the Work
of God' (RB 58).

To be sure, as the outward signs of humility have no
meaning except from the spirit of humility, so also does the
form of liturgical prayer and the outward performance of the
*Opus Dei* derive authenticity and value only from within.
Therefore St Benedict, for all the importance he assigned to
the structure of the liturgy, made it clear that its form is not
the essential thing. At the conclusion of his organization of
the choir prayer, to which he gave such deep thought, he
wrote (RB 18):

> *If this arrangement of the psalms be displeasing to*
> *anyone, he should, if he think fit, order it*
> *otherwise.*

He insisted only that the entire psalter should by all means
be prayed each week (RB 18):

> *For those monks would show themselves very*
> *slothful in the divine service who said in the*
> *course of a week less than the entire psalter, with*
> *the usual canticles; since we read that our holy*
> *fathers resolutely performed in a single day what*
> *I pray we tepid monks may achieve in a whole*
> *week.*†

---

† St Benedict's directive to pray all one hundred fifty psalms every
week, which became universally obligatory for the Divine Office in the
roman rite, has now been changed by Vatican II's Constitution on the
Sacred Liturgy: 'The psalms are no longer to be distributed throughout
one week, but through some longer period of time' (Art. 91). This is
not only for the practical purpose 'that it may really be possible to observe the course of the Hours proposed in Article 89'. Since Benedict's
time fundamental modifications in religious and spiritual life have
undoubtedly occurred. Precious as the psalms are as prayer texts, for
our times they are no longer as much a prime source of the spiritual life
as they were earlier. Over the past 1400 years the Spirit of God has

Where the spirit of devotion, self-giving and adoration prevails, such an exhortation to zeal will not be necessary; and where this spirit fills the exterior form, the result is a beautiful inner harmony between 'mind and voice', between body and soul. There 'heavenly are joined with earthly things, divine with human' (from the *Exsultet* of the Easter vigil). There the liturgy truly becomes a 'Work of God', the most sublime work that mankind redeemed in Christ offers the Father, the most splendid affirmation of christian being. In its performance our hearts are opened so that God can accomplish his work in them, the work of sanctification and salvation in Jesus Christ, the eternal High Priest, who in the liturgical and sacramental actions brings us to the Father.

# The Spirit of Faith

I N CHAPTER 19, "Of the Discipline of saying the Divine Office', St Benedict twice stressed faith. 'We believe that the divine presence is everywhere . . . . Especially should we believe this, without any doubt, when we are assisting at the Work of God.'

Is it mere coincidence that Jn 6:29 says, 'This is the work

---

opened up many other wellsprings of prayer life. So also in the manner and method of praying there has been change and progress. What the Constitution in Art. 89c gives as a norm for the revision of the Hour known as Matins, that 'it is to be made up of fewer psalms and longer readings', is in full agreement with the wish that in the various Hours of the Office fewer psalms be imposed on us as an obligatory amount, but that we should pray these psalms more slowly, with greater recollection, more meditatively, and that 'the Office, both in choir and in common, be sung when this is possible', as Art. 99 suggests. St Benedict would certainly approve such a development, since it is wholly in accord with his spirit.

of God (*opus Dei*): have faith in the One whom he sent'? In faith the important thing is that basic attitude which the *Opus Dei,* the worship of God, expresses. What matters is that one accept as 'reality' what God says even when it surpasses his understanding, that he lets human wisdom and the human ego give way to make room for divine wisdom and divine reality. The very response to the 'Work of God' of the person who assents to God revealing is the 'Work of God' who in the word of faith gives man the personal Word of God, in such a way that 'Christ dwells in our hearts through faith' (Eph 3:17).

'Blest is she who believed that the Lord's words to her would be fulfilled', said Elizabeth to Mary (Lk 1:45). In an act of faith occurs that which occurred in Mary at the Annunciation. Mary surrendered herself completely to the divine message. She spoke an unconditional 'Yes' to what was asked of her. She submitted with all her being to the divine reality revealed to her. With perfect docility she accepted the heaven-sent invitation, laid herself open to the divine love which made her 'full of grace', offered herself as handmaid to the service of the Lord, who wanted to be 'with her'.

Her words, 'I am the servant of the Lord; let it be done to me as you say', express her whole faith, her boundless humility and willingness to serve, her profound adoration. And so 'it is done to her according to the word of the Lord'. What was said to her by the angel becomes reality in her. 'The Word became flesh and made his dwelling in her and revealed his glory, the glory of the only-begotten of the Father, full of grace and truth' (cf. Jn 1:14).

Faith, like adoration, is in the last analysis humility— submission to God—and *Opus Dei,* the Work of God, in its twofold meaning: God effecting his work of grace in man; and man opening himself and giving himself to God working in him. It is in this sense that St Benedict wants to teach us to 'believe that the divine presence is everywhere, and that the eyes of the Lord behold the good and the evil in every place'. It is in this faith that the monk at every moment listens for God's call, is conscious of being everywhere in the sight of God, at all times embraces with the full submission of his entire being the divine reality revealed to him in faith. This is the spirit of faith, the supernatural wisdom proper to the 'spiritual man', enabling him 'to recognize the gifts God has given us' and 'to appraise everything', in contrast to the 'natural man' to whom only the world of the senses is real and who 'does not accept what is taught by the Spirit of God' (1 Cor 2:12-15).

In this spirit of faith the monk 'believes that the abbot holds the place of Christ in the monastery' (RB 2) and obeys him 'out of reverence and love for Christ' (RB 63). In this spirit of faith he 'serves the sick in very deed as Christ himself, for he has said: "I was sick, and you visited me" ' (RB 36). It is this faith that inspires the Rule's directive:

> Let all guests that come be received like Christ himself, for he will say: 'I was a stranger and you took me in' . . . . In the salutation let all humility be shown. At the arrival or departure of all guests, let Christ, who is truly received in their persons, be adored in them, by bowing the head or even pros- trating on the ground (RB 53).

This spirit of faith sees the whole monastery as 'the house of God' (RB 31, 53, 64) and 'all the vessels and goods of the monastery as though they were the consecrated vessels of the altar' (RB 31).

There is no place and no circumstance in which we could not in faith be aware of God's presence. 'In the work of God, in the oratory, in the monastery, in the garden, on the road, in the field or wherever we may be, whether sitting, walking or standing . . . we believe that the divine presence is everywhere.' Everywhere we are conscious of being in that grace-filled union with God to which faith opens the way for us, which is made real and secure in humility, in the humble 'service of obedience to God's commands' (cf. RB Prologue). This faith receives its supernatural sanction and continuous growth from the sacred liturgy where we 'especially believe, without any doubt, in the presence of God', above all in the *mysterium fidei,* the eucharistic 'mystery of faith'.

Thus Benedict blends the *Opus Dei,* the liturgy, into christian life and ties it in with the whole purpose of Christians: 'to serve the Lord' in humble fear and submissive faith, to 'give him glory on earth by finishing the work he gave us to do' (cf. Jn 17:4).

# PERSONAL PRAYER

*We have seen how Benedict incorporated the
liturgy into the religious duties required of monks
and Christians. Because the* Opus Dei *is the most
profound expression of submission to God and at
the same time the fundamental means of union
with God, St Benedict assigned first place in the
monastic day to it. The set times of the liturgical
services are the supporting scaffolding, the enclos-
ing framework, for the activity of the entire day.*

*But St Benedict would protest if liturgical
prayer were said to be the only legitimate form of
communication with God, as has sometimes been
done. Alongside the communal praise of God,
alongside the public worship of God to which the
monk must daily devote himself at specified times
and in a specified manner, he expressly placed personal prayer, 'oratio' or 'oratio pura', the term
used by Cassian and the monks of old.†*

---

† It is of the greatest importance in the care of souls that *Opus Dei*
and *oratio*—liturgical prayer and personal prayer whether private or
public—be organically combined, somewhat as the Rule has it, and that
the faithful be properly instructed in both forms of prayer. Personal
prayer gives constantly renewed personal warmth and fervor to
liturgical prayer and prevents liturgy from becoming an empty form, a
merely external performance. And the liturgy is the ever-flowing

wellspring of supernatural strength and fruitfulness for personal prayer. It keeps personal spiritual life directed to what is essential. If the Liturgical Movement has so far not achieved what it set out to do and should have done, one of the reasons is that too little attention has been paid to this connection.

# The Nature of

# Personal Prayer

IN A NUMBER of passages in his Rule Benedict wrote of personal prayer (at the beginning of the Prologue, and in chapters 4, 20, 27, 28, 49, 52). Immediately after arranging choir prayer he treated of personal prayer specifically in Chapter 20, 'Of Reverence at [personal] Prayer':

> *If, when we wish to make any request to men in power, we presume not to do so except with humility and reverence; how much more ought we with all lowliness and purity of devotion to offer our supplications to the Lord God of all things? And let us remember that not for our much speaking, but for our purity of heart and tears of compunction shall we be heard. Our prayer, therefore, ought to be short and pure, except it be perchance prolonged by the inspiration of divine grace.*

In Chapter 52, 'Of the Oratory of the Monastery', St. Benedict directs:

> *When the Work of God is ended, let all go out with the utmost silence, paying due reverence to God, so that a brother, who perchance wishes to pray by himself, may not be hindered by another's*

*misconduct. If any one desire to pray in private,
let him go in quietly and pray, not with a loud
voice, but with tears and fervor of heart.*

These texts show clearly that personal prayer, 'supplications' for grace, must issue from the same spirit as divine worship in choir prayer: from the spirit of humility, from the acknowledgement of God's absolute power and glory and one's own helplessness and need of grace. But whereas in liturgical prayer this interior disposition expresses itself in the set form and measured flow of well-ordered and well-prepared communal prayer within the framework of the eucharistic and sacramental *Opus Dei* performed by the Church, in personal prayer it is given the possibility of greater freedom in time and duration as well as in wording.

In personal prayer the soul can open itself fully to the divine thoughts which enlightened it at liturgical prayer but on which it could not then linger, and can let itself be interiorly affected and moved by them to 'tears of compunction'. Now it can yield itself completely to the 'inspiration of divine grace'. Now it is not words that matter; 'Let us remember that not for our much speaking shall we be heard.'†

Personal prayer has at its heart the disposition of humility, *omnis humilitas,* all lowliness, the all-inclusive humility, the unqualified spirit of self-sacrifice that St Bene-

---

† These words obviously refer to what Our Lord said (Mt 6:7) about 'the pagans, who think they will win a hearing by the sheer multiplication of words'. He was by no means belittling community prayer, which must necessarily have a number of words, but people who perform their personal prayer in public, who 'stand and pray in synagogues or on street corners in order to be noticed' (Mt 6:5). Our Lord himself cherished both forms of prayer, as St Benedict noted. He took part in the communal liturgy in the temple, and his disciples continued to do this even after his ascension. Then again, especially at night, he withdrew for quiet prayer, 'with all lowliness and purity of devotion to offer supplications to the Father, the Lord God of all things.'

dict sought to instill. It is *puritatis devotio,* pure, unfeigned submissiveness to God; *intentio cordis,* fervor of heart, orientation of the inner man wholly to God, in docility and desire, 'truly seeking God' (RB 58) with all the strength of heart and soul, 'hearkening' to God in order to 'willingly receive and faithfully fulfil' his call (RB Prologue).

Now and again we should examine our theories and concepts of prayer in the light of what Holy Scripture and the masters of prayer, like St Benedict, tell us about it. Most people think only of the fact that *we* are seeking God and saying the words of prayer. But if prayer, as we surely believe, is a personal relationship to God, then there must also be place in it for God's speaking to us. In fact, the best form of prayer must necessarily be listening to God, being silent in his presence so that our soul may be wholly open to him, alert for his call, attentive in humility for the revelation of his will.

We have already discerned what is most significant about liturgical prayer, that we do not use our own human words but the words that God has previously given us, the inspired words of Holy Scripture whereby God speaks to us, whereby he brings grace and divine life to us. We repeat these words after God, as it were, listening for their hidden meaning, in 'reply' to what God said first. This is also the reason why in ancient liturgical tradition, to which Benedict conformed (RB 9-11), liturgical readings were always followed by a *responsorium,* a hymn of 'response', words of Holy Scripture, mostly from the psalms, in which the reading just heard could re-echo, sinking more deeply into the listening soul.

We have already considered the profound assertion of St Paul about the Holy Spirit praying within us:

> *The Spirit too helps us in our weakness, for we do not know how to pray as we ought; but the Spirit himself makes intercession for us with groanings that cannot be expressed in speech . . . . The Spirit intercedes for the saints as God himself wills (Rom 8:26,27).*

This is true not only of liturgical prayer but of any praying the Christian does. It is precisely in personal prayer, which is not as tied to words as liturgical prayer in common is, that greater freedom can be given to this listening for the prayer of the Spirit within us. Here the soul may surrender itself completely to 'the inspiration of divine grace', here it may let itself be wholly 'led by the Spirit of God . . . by the spirit of adoption through which we cry out, "Abba!" (that is, "Father")' (Rom 8:14, 15).

# Praying the Degrees of Humility

S T BENEDICT was not content with general references to personal prayer. Especially in the chapter on humility, the heart of his Rule, he gives us practical suggestions about it. What strikes one immediately is that to almost every degree of humility are added words of prayer taken from Holy Scripture, mostly psalm texts. Benedict did not merely want to give greater emphasis to his teachings by quoting from Scripture. These prayer formulas express the appropriate spiritual disposition to be produced in us.

In fact, we most likely have here the *oratio*, the personal prayer, of St Benedict himself put down in writing. In these prayer formulas, resembling what we call ejaculations, he has voiced his own striving and yearning for perfect humility and self-surrender to God. By saying these words over and over in prayer he familiarized himself with the thoughts we have already considered, and we too should use the same words to 'pray ourselves' into the same dispositions.

We can actually place twelve degrees of prayer alongside the twelve degrees of humility, and discern an intimate connection between the two. The whole quest for God as depicted by the degrees of humility is, of course, not possible at all without constant prayer. The thoughts we considered were converted into prayer time after time as if spontaneously, and each degree forced us to realize that without the power of God's grace we are nothing and can do nothing. That is why the first 'admonition' St Benedict gave us in the Prologue to take along on the way to God was that 'whatever good work we begin to do, we should beg of him with most earnest prayer to perfect'.

In the first degree of humility St Benedict placed on our lips words of prayer expressing fear of God, religious awe in the presence of his greatness and majesty, especially his omnipresence and omniscience. They are words like those of the Psalmist: 'God searches the heart and the soul . . . The Lord knows the thoughts of men . . . . You have understood my thoughts afar off . . . . The thought of man shall confess to you . . . . All my desire is before you.'

In the seclusion of his hermit's cave or in the solitude of his cell, while meditating on God's glory, his omnipresence and omniscience, overwhelmed by holy fear because conscious of the divine gaze boring into the depth of his soul, St Benedict surely must have used these psalm texts to voice the inward overpowering of his soul. He said words such as these over and over. He listened for their hidden meaning. By means of them the mystery of the all-knowing God's nearness sank deep into his soul. He became inwardly very quiet. He trembled with holy fear in the presence of God's majesty and holiness. He felt the nothingness, the sinfulness of human nature, and he adored God. 'With all lowliness and purity of devotion' he implored him for grace and mercy.

We use many words in prayer, far too many. We pray

'in multiloquio', with 'much speaking'. That is why we so
often 'say our prayers' carelessly and superficially. We do not
weigh our words, or measure their depth. We should go to the
saints' school of prayer. St Francis of Assisi could spend an
entire night repeating nothing more than, 'Deus meus et omnia, My God and my All'.

This is the sense of St Benedict's insistence that it is not
the number of words that matters but the depth from which
the prayer arises and into which it leads. 'Let us remember
that not for our much speaking shall we be heard.' We have
already noted how St Benedict wanted the Our Father
prayed, how seriously and how personally we should take the
petition, 'Forgive us—as we forgive' (RB 13). In the first
degree of humility he reminded us of the petition in which
'we beg of God in prayer that his will may be done in us'.
How many Our Fathers we say! But we say few in which we
take these and all the other petitions very seriously!

This is the purpose of the short prayer formulas Benedict
places on our lips in the first and the other degrees of
humility. We should say these words over and over, very
slowly and meditatively. We should assimilate them profoundly, listen for their hidden meaning, 'hear what God
proclaims' in us (Ps 84) by these words.

We should likewise discern the call of God in psalm texts
like these: 'Turn away from your own will . . . . Go not after
your lustful desires.' Such divinely inspired words tell us
what sin is in the sight of the all-holy God, what a terrible
thing is voluntary alienation from God, the separation from
God which is the penalty for surrendering to evil self-will or
sensual desire. So we should 'be ever mindful of all that God
has commanded, taking thought that those who despise God
will be consumed in hell for their sins, and that life everlasting is prepared for those who fear him.' By such reflections
the soul frees itself from evil, as the first degree of humility
wants: 'Keeping ourselves at all times from sin and vice,
whether of the thoughts, the tongue, the hands, the feet, or

our own will, let us thus hasten to cut off the desires of the flesh.' The prayers we say over and over as St Benedict directs us to do keep reminding us that 'we are always beheld from heaven by God, and that our actions are everywhere seen by the eye of the Divine Majesty, and are every hour reported to him by his angels'.

Frequent acts of contrition well up from our heart, acts of 'tearful compunction', because of all our unfaithfulness in the service of God, recalling the admonition of Chapter 4: 'Daily to confess one's past sins with tears and sighs to God'. An ardent yearning for perfect purity of heart is aroused in us, and without ceasing we pray most earnestly: 'Then shall I be unspotted before him, if I shall have kept myself from my iniquity'.

The practice of general and particular examination of conscience, which holds an important place in the ascetical life, is also organically incorporated into our spiritual striving. If while praying we become aware of the fact that 'the Lord knows the thoughts of men', we are continually compelled to take a probing look at the way we think, will, and act; we have to 'keep guard at all times over the actions of our life' (RB 4) and 'always be on the watch, lest, as the prophet says in the psalm, God should see us at any time declining to evil and become unprofitable'.

We see how inseparably the degrees of humility and prayer are joined together, just as in personal prayer the interior disposition of humility, which must be our aim, develops in us. In this fashion we should prayerfully ascend all the degrees of humility.

# Praying as Christ Prayed

A T THE SECOND DEGREE of humility we reflected upon the grandeur of the divine will. We seek to conform ourselves to it by acts of submission, of 'purity of devotion'. We united ourselves with the incarnate Son of God and made our own his words placed by Benedict on our lips: 'I came not to do my own will, but the will of him who sent me' (Jn 5:30), or other words used by Christ the Lord, like the psalm text which, as St Paul affirms, he said as the morning prayer of his life: 'I have come to do your will, O God' (Heb 10:7, Ps 40:8).

Here we can see who taught Benedict his way of praying— the divine Master himself. Holy Scripture attests that Christ prayed in such a way, using the divinely inspired words of the sacred text and 'fulfilling' them.

We may of course take other words of Scripture as well to beg for and give expression to the 'purity of devotion' which corresponds to the second degree of humility; we might use those of the Psalmist in Psalm 25: 'Your ways, O Lord, make known to me; teach me your paths', or in Psalm 143: 'Teach me to do your will, for you are my God. May your good spirit guide me on level ground'. All of Psalm 119 is a single act of submission to the holy will of God, a hymn of praise to the majesty of the divine law. A disciple of Benedict will be fond of repeating especially the verse which Benedict assigns for profession as the declaration of unreserved commitment to God: 'Uphold me, O Lord, according to your word, and I shall live: and let me not be confounded in my expectation' (Ps 119:116, RB 58). With St Paul we can ask, 'Lord, what is it I must do?' (Acts 22:10), or with the mother of Our Lord we can utter those incomparable words of submission with which she surrendered her whole being to God: 'I am the servant of the Lord. Let it be done to me as you say' (Lk 1:38).

We can also formulate the prayers ourselves. 'Lord, open me wide for you. Free me wholly for yourself, Lord; make me what you would have me be.' *The Imitation of Christ* (Book 3, Chapter 15) offers us words of this kind; its manner of prayer is in full accord with the kind of personal prayer the benedictine Rule teaches. Or there is the prayer of St Nicholas of Flue: 'Lord, take everything from me that hinders my going to you. Lord, give everything to me that helps me come to you. Lord, take me from myself and give me wholly to yourself.' Especially at times of crucial decisions, at times when we must fight our way through to complete submission to the divine will, we should pray in the spirit of the second degree of humility. We shall then find the right words spontaneously, not many, but sincere words that express what our Lord said, and Benedict summarized in this degree of humility: 'I came not to do my own will, but the will of him who sent me.'

In the third and fourth degrees of humility, we become by prayer and meditation ever more absorbed in picturing him who 'was made obedient even unto death, death on a cross'. We stir up our faith that in superiors, in confrères, in all persons, we meet Christ himself, that whatever is done 'for one of my least brothers' is done for the Lord (Mt 25:40). Prompted by such faith and prayer we 'adore Christ' in our fellow human beings (RB 53) and serve them 'in very deed as Christ himself' (RB 36) through humility put into practice. Repeatedly we renew our submission, our willingness to be wholly a victim, 'esteemed as sheep for the slaughter'.

In times of suffering and sorrow we shall more than once

drop to our knees before the crucifix or the tabernacle and repeat the words Benedict here places on our lips: 'You have proved us, O God; you have tried us as silver is tried by fire' (Ps 66:10). Benedict himself may have prayed this way in the tribulations of his life—after the failure at Vicovaro, during the painful persecution by the priest Florentius at Subiaco, when the destruction of his monastery was revealed to him in a bitter vision of the future—until ever reconciled anew to the divine will and filled with triumphant confidence in God he could say, 'But in all these things we overcome through him who has loved us' (Rm 8:37). He did not need many words. The few, profoundly understood and felt, were enough to express his struggle and sacrifice, just as our Lord on the Mount of Olives revealed the hidden depths of his soul in the few words he repeated over and over: 'My Father, if it is possible, let this cup pass me by. Still, let it be as you not I, would have it' (Mt 26:39).

In the fifth degree of humility we pray with the Psalmist, 'I will confess against myself my iniquities to the Lord: and you have forgiven the wickedness of my heart' (Ps 32:5), when we go to confession, when we make a manifestation of conscience to God's representative, at times when 'evil thoughts come into the heart' (RB 4), on days when we have to fight our way through to final surrender of our own ego as our holy Father here demands. Then when we have 'made known our way unto the Lord', filled with gratitude we can say after the manifestation of conscience, after sacramental confession: 'Confess to the Lord, for he is good, and his mercy endures forever' (Ps 136:1).

In the sixth and seventh degrees of humility we get still deeper insight into the Psalmist's words, 'I have been brought to nothing, and I knew it not: I am become as a beast before you, yet I am always with you' (Ps 73:22), when God takes up our schooling and gives us a taste of 'the meanest and worst of everything', when the consciousness of our unworthiness and nothingness lies heavy upon us, when we feel crushed by the burden of a great responsibility, when God permits every prop to the human ego to collapse. More and more clearly the mystery of the crucified, tortured and abandoned Saviour is disclosed to us, the mystery of his *kenosis,* his 'self-emptying', the mystery St Paul meant when he said that we have to be 'united with Christ through likeness to his death' (Rom 6:5). So close should the resemblance be that we can say with him, 'I am a worm and no man, the shame of men and the outcast of the people. I have been cast down, and confounded' (Ps 22:6, 88:15).

From such prayer and meditation saints have derived the strength to endure any degradation for the sake of Christ. They were aflame with holy 'zeal for humiliations' (RB 58). They knew that likeness to the death of Christ leads to 'a like resurrection', and they prayed gratefully, 'It is good for me that you have humbled me, that I may learn your commandments' (Ps 119:71).

We see how this prayer is nourished by the living word of Holy Scripture, how it is rooted in the reality and the nearness of God, which is liturgy's gift. As we know from the Dialogues of St Gregory (II.4), the monks of St Benedict had a short period of silent prayer following each liturgical hour. The thoughts and feelings inspired by the liturgy, the working of divine grace in the *Opus Dei,* should re-echo and burrow deep into the soul, like seed burying itself in the soil. Those who pray should, as is written about the mother of our Lord, 'treasure all these things and reflect on them' in their hearts (Lk 2:19). Yet, this personal prayer in common at the end of the Office should not last long:

> But let prayer made in common always be short:
> and at the signal given by the superior, let all rise
> together (RB 20).

Not everyone can devote himself to this mental prayer uninterruptedly for any great length of time. But every monk had to spend some time in prayer of this kind if he did not want to make himself guilty of punishable negligence.

Next to the liturgy, a prime source of mental prayer was the *lectio,* spiritual reading, to which Benedict assigned a large place in his daily order (RB 48)—especially the reading of 'the divinely-inspired books of the Old and New Testaments', then the books of 'the holy Catholic Fathers', and writings about the monastic life. Already in the chapter on silence (RB 6) we pointed out that St Benedict did not want this to be a hasty spiritual nibbling but a thorough perusal of what was read, a quest for new knowledge of 'how we may by a straight course reach our Creator' (RB 73). This reading itself turned into praying, 'seeking God' and finding God 'in purity of heart, in all lowliness and purity of devotion'.

# Stillness in Prayer

W E REALLY NEED to go to the school of prayer of someone like St Benedict to learn and practice the mental prayer that consists not of 'much speaking' but of 'purity of devotion', of spiritual absorption in the divine reality, of concentrating our heart on God. Everything in our life has become so full of unrest. The hustle and bustle and excessive drive of modern life has in many ways invaded our spiritual life too. We pile word on word, spiritual exercise on spiritual exercise, work of piety on work of piety, and perhaps even keep a record of them, like making entries in an account book. The *number* of spiritual exercises is often valued more highly than their content. Point by point the spiritual life is somehow predetermined, and little allowance is made for freedom of the spirit. Our praying and meditating follows a fixed pattern according to a well-rehearsed technique and therefore so easily becomes a mechanical routine. That is why, despite earnest effort and sincere desire, there is often so little genuine growth in the spiritual life, so little development of the full christian life. That is why it is often pious Christians who are immature in their whole attitude, narrow in mind and will, cramped, far from being 'that perfect man who is Christ come to full stature' (Eph 4:13).

All genuine spiritual growth requires freedom for God's creative power 'by the inspiration of divine grace', of which Benedict speaks in his chapter on prayer (RB 20), 'led by the Spirit of God', as St Paul says (Rom 8:14). If we want to 'have life and have it to the full' (Jn 10:10), we must open and surrender ourselves to the Spirit, and God 'does not ration his gift of the Spirit' (Jn 3:34); we must let ourselves be seized by 'the Lord who is the Spirit' in order to be 'transformed from glory to glory' (2 Cor 3:18). That is exactly why St Benedict wanted to make us very alert to the call of God, very docile, very humble, very responsive, 'in purity of devotion' setting our heart on God. Then 'God will vouchsafe to manifest by the Holy Spirit in his laborer' what Benedict at the close of the chapter on humility showed to be the goal of the spiritual life.

Stillness, silence was for St Benedict, as we have already seen, an essential component of training for the perfect life under his direction, and especially for true prayer. 'It becomes the disciple to be silent and to listen', he has already told us (RB 6), and we should, of course, all be disciples of God: 'It is written in the prophets: "They shall all be taught by God". Everyone who has heard the Father and learned from him comes to me' (Jn 6:45). When will this instruction by God more likely be given us than when we abide with him in prayer, than when we are silent, recollected, detached from everything external, waiting 'in purity of heart and with tears of compunction' for his word and imploring his grace?

This interior tranquillity is a fruit especially of the last degrees of humility. We summed up the eighth degree in the prayer of Holy Scripture, 'Lord God, with a sincere heart I have willingly given all these things' (1 Chr 29:17). *In simplicitate cordis,* literally, in simplicity of heart. Our spiritual life becomes ever more simple, but at the same time ever more profound. More and more, what is unessential falls away. More and more the 'one thing required' dominates everything. A spiritual peace and quiet comes over us. Our prayer becomes ever more *oratio pura* in the literal sense, a pure, simple, uncomplicated self-surrender, 'not in much speaking but in purity of heart', in that peacefulness of spiritual security, in that freedom from all earthly want and desire, to which this degree of humility leads us.

The ninth to eleventh degrees of humility are expressly intended to give us the spirit of *taciturnitas,* of silence, of inner composure in God. Here we may recall Chapter 6, 'Of the Practice of Silence', in which the wording is partially identical with expressions found in these degrees of humility, we may use the psalm text which introduces that chapter as the wording of our disposition and our prayer at this point: 'I said, I will take heed to my ways, that I sin not with my tongue. I have placed a watch over my mouth; I became dumb and was silent, and held my peace even from good things' (Ps 39:2,3).

# Prayer of Love

THE FIFTY-SEVENTH INSTRUMENT of good works in Chapter 4, 'To apply oneself frequently to prayer', ultimately becomes the 'praying always' of the Gospel (Lk 18:1). We are always aware, in faith, 'that the divine presence is everywhere'. 'In the work of God, in the oratory, in the monastery, in the garden, on the road, in the field or wherever we may be, whether sitting, walking or standing', we are aware of God, of judgment, of our responsibility. We stand in awe before him who will be our judge, and we say with the humble tax collector, 'Lord, I a sinner am not worthy to raise my eyes to heaven, bowed down and humbled on every side' (from the twelfth degree of humility). But 'having ascended all these degrees of humility, the monk will presently arrive at that love of God which, being perfect, casts out fear'. His prayer too will then become a prayer of love, a pure and holy self-oblation in 'unspeakable sweetness of love' (RB Prologue).

St Benedict does not enlarge upon this prayer of love; in the Rule his immediate purpose was to point out only 'a beginning of holiness' (RB 73). From indications given in his Rule and in his biography we can, however, infer how this prayer develops. It frees itself more and more from specific spoken words, especially human words, and is set aflame over and over again and more profoundly by the 'Word of God'. It becomes a constantly growing absorption in God and his mysteries 'in tears of compunction, in tears and fervor of heart'. It becomes prayer ardent with longing for God, with desire 'to advance ever more and more in godliness' (RB 62), with the 'spiritual longing' of which Chaper 49 speaks.

How often must the yearning St Benedict have repeated the psalm text he quoted in the Prologue: 'Lord, who shall dwell in your tabernacle, or who shall rest upon your holy hill?' (Ps 15:1) How often must he, heeding his own admonition in Chapter 4 (Instr. 46), have 'desired, with a special longing, everlasting life', perfect union with God!

Progressively this prayer becomes a prayer in the 'joy of the Holy Spirit' (RB 49), prayer 'by the inspiration of divine grace' (RB 20), an abiding in God, a surrender of self to the Holy Spirit who 'makes intercession for us with groanings that cannot be expressed in speech' (Rom 8:26). Indeed, it more and more takes on the characteristics which ascetical and mystical theology ascribes to 'affective prayer' and 'the prayer of simplicity', and then 'by the inspiration of divine grace' becomes the kind of prayer sometimes called 'acquired contemplation'.

Anyone who lets himself be led by the Spirit of God this way through the various stages of prayer may then be taken still higher by divine grace, 'to the height of perfection . . . to the lofty summits of doctrine and virtue' (RB 73), to so-called 'infused contemplation' and mystical union with God. To strive for that is of course no longer within our power. We can only ask humbly that in our prayer life too Our Lord 'may perfect what we have begun' (RB Prologue).†

The substance and goal of prayer thus filled with longing and love in the spirit of St Benedict is Jesus Christ, to whom prayer is directed ever anew. The monk may 'hold nothing dearer to him than Christ' (RB 5). He may 'prefer nothing to the love of Christ' (RB 4, Instr. 21), 'prefer nothing whatever to Christ' (RB 72). His image should always stand before the monk's eyes: the image of Christ the true King (RB Prologue), the image of the Good Shepherd (RB 27), the image of the Crucified, the image of the eternal Judge (RB 7). He is to see Christ in the abbot, in the brothers, in the guests, in the sick (RB 2, 36, 53). He is to imitate him in self-denial, in obedience, in patience (RB 4, Instr. 10, RB 5, 7). He should 'dash down on the [Rock] Christ' evil thoughts that come into his heart (RB Prologue, RB 4, Instr. 50, cf. Ps 137:9). 'By patience sharing in the sufferings of Christ', he should also 'deserve to be a partaker of his kingdom' (RB Prologue).

Benedict teaches a truly 'Christ-centered spirituality'. He himself lived and prayed wholly 'in Christ Jesus'. He died praying with Christ, united with him in the eucharistic meal. Here is the source of a St Bernard's ardent love for Christ, of a St Gertrude the Great's intimate union with Christ. Christ, however, is the way to the Father. The spirit of St Benedict constantly goes from Christ up to the mystery of the divine sonship, to the Father, 'who has

---

† Cf. Cuthbert Butler, *Benedictine Monachism,* (London, 1919; rpt. 1961) Ch. 6, 'St Benedict's Teaching on Prayer', and Ch. 7, 'Benedictine Mysticism'.

vouchsafed to count us in the number of his children' (RB Prologue) and to whom 'in the spirit of the adoption of children we cry Abba, Father' (RB 2, Rom 8:15), and to the mystery of the most holy Trinity. Holy fervor and ecstatic joy then filled his soul 'out of honor and reverence to the Holy Trinity' (RB 9). Everything earthly faded away, as it did in that sacred hour when the wonderful vision of the Godhead caused his soul to exult in blessed anticipation of eternal glory.

Thus did Benedict pray. Thus he teaches us to pray. With this method and teaching of prayer Benedict stands wholly within christian and monastic tradition. Cassian, whom he so highly esteemed, was a primary source for him, as parallel wording in part of his instructions on prayer shows. We can pursue the tradition right up to our own day in eastern monasticism, where the use of short but frequent prayer formulas, especially the so-called 'Jesus prayer',† constitutes an essential element of prayer life.

Nevertheless, while conforming with tradition, St Benedict preserved his spiritual self-reliance and independence precisely in his teaching on prayer. Here and there in the monastic tradition one finds a mechanization of prayer, trying for the greatest number of words possible, restriction to set forms and methods, even the development of a certain technique of bodily posture. Benedict has nothing of all this. The heart of his teaching on prayer is that all prayer flows from the basic disposition of humility governing all of life, from *puritas devotionis,* unreserved self-surrender to God in desire and docility, in faith and adoration.

The soul seeks to be completely open to 'the inspiration of divine grace', to the working of the Holy Spirit. 'Where the Spirit of the Lord is, there is freedom' (2 Cor 3:17). But

---

† 'Lord Jesus, Son of God, have mercy on me, a sinner.' Cf. Louis Bouyer, *Introduction to Spirituality* (Collegeville, MN, 1961) pp. 96-98, 'The Prayer of Jesus'.

prayer is not for that reason disorganized, not handed over to whimsy and caprice. Humility and love, to which humility leads, give measure and order to benedictine prayer.

# Benedictine

# Meditation

TO THIS MANNER of praying belongs the form of prayer called 'meditation', which is of such great importance in the development of the spiritual life. Systematic meditation as understood by the asceticism of later ages was unknown to Benedict and the monks of antiquity. If they fashioned their life, as Benedict's Rule shows it, out of the fundamental disposition of humility and endeavored prayerfully to ascend the degrees of humility; if in the *Opus Dei* their soul was absorbed in worshipping God seven times a day and they also 'at night arose to praise him' (RB 16), their whole life inevitably became meditation in the literal and true meaning of the word. The eyes of their souls were always fixed on God.

Systematic meditation became a necessary and definite means of spiritual progress only when constant awareness of God in the broad sense had more or less disappeared, when the *Opus Dei,* the liturgy, was no longer so deeply understood and practised that spiritual vigor continually flowed from it, when that inner bond between *Opus Dei* and *oratio,* between liturgical and personal prayer, upon which

Benedict laid so much stress, had been weakened.

The Father of Western Monasticism, who never clung obstinately to the traditional but was open to new spiritual value, who required the abbot of a monastery to have a store of knowledge from which he might 'bring forth new things and old' (RB 64), would nowadays no doubt assign a time for 'meditation' in the daily routine, as all monastic constitutions do. But in any case he would insist that this meditation not be some sort of independent spiritual exercise alongside other unrelated religious practices, but organically incorporated into the totality of the spiritual life. Furthermore, he could point out that he had already prescribed extra time for silent interior prayer at the close of each liturgical hour, a time of reflection and personal communication with God to reinforce and deepen the union with God gained in the liturgy, and at the same time the person praying could get ready for the transition from the direct service of God in worship to the active service of daily labor. Actually this was 'meditation' seven times a day.

Here too lies the answer to the question about the subject matter and method of benedictine meditation. The uniform theme of meditation of this kind is everything included in the concept of humility in its fullest extent as we meet it in the Holy Rule: God and all the mysteries of his being and our relationship to him, our spiritual striving in its entirety, the *Opus Dei* with its wealth of thought and treasury of grace—everything blended together into unity over and over again and directed to the sole purpose 'that God may be all in all' (1 Cor 15:28), 'that God may be glorified in all things' (RB 57).

The 'method' of meditation, however, is the form of personal prayer which we have derived from what the Holy Rule says: praying rather than merely reflecting; affective and volitional prayer, that is, application of our heart and of our will, rather than merely of our understanding, to God and divine truth. This does not mean that the intellect should be eliminated or should recede into the background. We have to fill our soul with ever new thoughts and incentives so that our prayer does not become impoverished. Especially if our prayer is to be a prayer of love, divine truth must be understood ever more profoundly so that our hearts may be set on fire by it.

That is exactly why Benedict provided for interior prayer at the end of the liturgy with its wealth of thought and its resources of grace. That is why he assigned such a large place in the daily order to spiritual reading. What matters in prayer is that intellect and will and feelings, our whole heart and soul and mind, be involved, that 'with all lowliness and purity of devotion' our entire person be given to God as his own and laid open to 'the inspiration of divine grace'.

# Other Forms and Practices of Piety

WHAT IS TRUE OF meditation is true also of other forms and practices of piety which have developed in the course of time. The concept of benedictine *oratio* is broad enough to allow any 'inspiration of divine grace' to evolve. But it is also precise enough to let us recognize whether something really is emanating from the free action of the Lord's Spirit. What is decisive is whether any form and practice of piety flows from the basic disposition of humility and merges with the main stream and overall purpose of the spiritual life: self-surrender to God through

Jesus Christ. All prayer that fits into this grand design and serves it is good and salutary.

We have spoken of the Christ-centered character of Benedict's spirituality, of the prayer of 'love for Christ, to which nothing may be preferred'. In particulars this love of Christ can take very diverse forms. It may draw one person more to the suffering Saviour, to the mystery of the cross, as it did St Bernard; another, to the Eucharist in which our Lord gives himself with his divinity and his humanity to us. Others, like St Gertrude, may let their life be dominated by the sublime theme of St John's Gospel: 'Christ in me, I in him.' It is always Christ at the center of everything: 'Jesus Christ, the same yesterday, today, and forever' (Heb 13:8).

When the Wise Men of the East were looking for the newborn king, 'they found the child with Mary his mother (Mt 2:11). Christ cannot be separated from Mary. Her name does not occur in the Holy Rule. But love of her is included in 'the love of Christ, to which nothing may be preferred'. Sons of St Benedict originated and were the first to use the hymns to the mother of God now sung daily by the entire Church in her praise, the marian antiphons at the conclusion of the Office. How ardently Mary was loved by St Bernard, who like no one else gave effect to Benedict's dictum, 'Prefer nothing whatever to Christ'! How intensely St Gertrude revered and loved Mary as 'the most worthy temple of the Holy Spirit', as 'the white lily of the radiant and ever serene Trinity', as 'the glowing rose, full of heavenly charm, from whom heaven's king was to be born'.

The image of Mary has constantly entered these reflections of ours too. In her humility and self-surrender we see humility's perfect exemplification. No other human being has ever consented to 'the Word of God' or spoken the *fiat* of total docility as she did. Consequently, neither has perfect love, attained through humility, developed in any other human soul as it did in hers. In no one else have St Paul's words, in which we find the most concise formulation of the substance and significance of humility, been realized as they were in her: 'The life I live now is not my own; Christ is living in me' (Gal 2:20).

In the same way veneration of the angels and saints also has its place in the broad expanse of benedictine *oratio* and *Opus Dei*. If already here on earth we should see and honor Christ in confrères, in the poor and the sick, all the more ought we do so in those in whom the image of Christ is now radiant in full unclouded brilliance. In his Rule Benedict speaks of 'the festivals of saints' (RB 14). His biography relates that on Monte Cassino he built oratories in honor of St John the Baptist and St Martin, the great patrons and prototypes of monasticism. Especially he reminded his monks again and again of God's angels, as monitors exhorting them to live in the presence of God, and as heavenly worshippers 'in whose sight we sing praises unto God' (RB 7,19). The angels and saints too belong to the 'armed ranks of the brothers' (RB 1) in which we 'fight for the Lord Christ, our true king' (RB Prologue). They help us fight the good fight to victory and take the way to God they did.

The family character of the benedictine Order, deriving from 'local stability', causes a bond with deceased members of the community to grow especially strong—not least with 'our holy father St Benedict' and with all the 'holy fathers' of our Order. We love them because we love Christ; they all 'held nothing dearer' than him (RB 5). The great number of saints and blesseds of the benedictine Order shows what a marvelous wealth of christian piety can develop when life is based on Benedict's Rule. How diverse are all these saints in their spiritual life: Gregory the Great, Boniface, Bede, Anselm or Bernard or Louis Blosius, Gertrude the Great, Mechtilde, all the way down to the monks and abbots of our times. Some day it would be a magnificent project, deserving the labor of many, to give an account of benedictine prayer and show its finest exemplifications, beginning with St Benedict himself, throughout the centuries of benedictine history.

Its title could well be the words of St Paul: 'One star differs from another in brightness' (1 Cor 15:41).

Yet the same light is reflected in all the stars. As diverse as these devotees of prayer were as regards particulars in the progress of their religious life, so akin were they all in that fundamental spiritual disposition from which benedictine prayer flows: humility, unconditional self-surrender to the Father through his Son Jesus Christ. They are akin in this too, that for them it was a vital necessity, taken for granted, 'to apply oneself frequently to prayer' (RB 4, Instr. 57), indeed 'to pray always'.

In this they were following faithfully their master's example and instructions on prayer. However much Benedict wanted freedom safeguarded in personal prayer especially, he just as definitely let it be understood that his disciples must be men of prayer. At any time of day the monks have access to the oratory without needing to ask permission (actually the only instance in the Rule): 'If anyone desire to pray in private, let him go in quietly and pray' (RB 52). During Lent the monks are to say 'extra prayers' and with redoubled zeal 'give themselves to prayer with tears, to holy reading, to compunction of heart' (RB 49). How much he expected every grace and blessing to come from prayer he expressed forcefully in Chapter 28, 'Of those who, being often corrected, do not amend':

> *If the abbot see that his labors are of no avail, let him add what is still more powerful—his own prayers and those of the brothers for him, that God, who is all-powerful, may work the cure of the sick brother.*

These faith-filled words, which apply to both kinds of prayer Benedict taught—the divine praise of the *Opus Dei* and the petitions of *oratio*—reveal the secret of all prayer: that the creative power and goodness of him who 'can do all things' bends down to the one praying in order to work miracles of grace and mercy in him. They also reveal the secret of the divine blessing resting upon Benedict's life and work. Because he was a true man of prayer he became the 'blessed one' (the meaning of 'Benedict'), the wonder-worker, the spiritual father and teacher of countless souls, a 'pillar in the temple of God', in the structure of the christian world.

To the extent that his sons and daughters give themselves to prayer in his spirit, the blessing of their father and master is imparted to them and others. Certainly Benedict's disciples today have nothing greater and more important in their power to give to mankind than in the spirit of their holy founder to pray rightly and teach others the art of genuine prayer. And all genuine prayer comes from one single source—humility.

# REMAINDER OF THE

# DAILY ORDER

CHAPTERS 21 TO 57:
'THAT IN ALL THINGS GOD MAY BE GLORIFIED'

A S 'IN THE WORK of God and in the oratory', so too everywhere else, 'in the monastery, in the garden, on the road, in the field or wherever he may be, whether sitting, walking or standing', the monk should 'not only in his heart, but also in his outer bearing, always show his humility to all who see him' (RB 7). What St Benedict sought to achieve through asceticism in his 'school of the Lord's service' was to focus all of man's thought and will and action on God. It is not enough to serve God by a few hours of prayer. The entire person with all his activities and occupations belongs to God so that 'God may be all in all' (1 Cor 15:28). 'All things must be brought into one under Christ's headship . . . . So must we praise his glory' (cf. Eph 1:10,12).

Therefore, after having laid down the fundamentals for the spiritual life of his monks in the first twenty chapters of his Rule, St Benedict turned to the remainder of the daily order from Chapter 21 on. He treated in detail the leadership and government of the monastery, the property of the monastery, the occupation of the monks outside the times of prayer, food and clothing, sleep; he established a penal code for the maintenance of monastic discipline. There is hardly any important area of life which the Holy Rule does not touch upon in one way or another. We hear about receiving guests, about caring for the needy and poor. The Rule provides for the case of monks sent on a journey, and we know from the biography of St Benedict that he engaged in apostolic and charitable activities and likewise sent his monks out for spiritual work and to found new monasteries. All these instructions and regulations of St Benedict are encompassed by the words of Chapter 57 with which he concludes this section of his Rule: 'Ut in omnibus glorificetur Deus: *That in all things God may be glorified*'.

In this way of life organized by St Benedict, which we shall briefly review in what follows, what is essential is that our natural activities and occupations be performed in the all-inclusive spirit of humility and humble self-surrender to God, that 'we believe that the divine presence' is not only at choir prayer but 'everywhere, and that the eyes of the Lord behold the good and the evil in every place' (RB 19). Thus the praise of God which is chanted in the Opus Dei reverberates throughout daily life, and it is not only 'the voice' of the one praying that 'accords with his mind', but all the rest of his life as well, so that 'in all things God may be glorified'.

# Respect for Others

I N OUR MEDITATION on the nature of faith we saw how
St Benedict wanted relations with one's neighbor to be
wholly determined by the spirit of humility. To guests, 'let
all humility be shown' as soon as 'in the salutation,' because
'Christ is received in their persons' (RB 53). On this basis,
how supernaturally profound and at the same time how
humanly refined all relations to one's neighbor become!

From this spirit of humility rooted in faith flows the
'reverence' with which, as St Benedict says with St Paul,
'brothers should in honor prefer one another' (RB 63, 72;
cf. Rom 12:10). It is sister to that fear of God which per-
meates all of life and embraces those who are the 'image and
likeness of God'. Every service to one's brother becomes
service 'for the honor of God' (RB 36).

St Benedict wanted all the shared life of his monastic
community to be filled with this supernatural reverence.
In Chapter 63, he wrote:

*In calling each other by name, let none
address another by his simple name; but let
the elders call the younger brethren 'Brothers',
and the younger call their elders 'Fathers', by
which is implied the reverence due a father.
But let the abbot, since he is considered to
represent the person of Christ, be called Lord
and Abbot, not that he has taken it upon
himself, but out of reverence and love for
Christ. Let him be mindful of this, and show
himself to be worthy of such an honor.
Wherever the brothers meet one another, let
the younger ask a blessing from the elder.
And when the elder passes by, let the younger*

*rise, and give place to him to sit down; nor let
the younger presume to sit with him, unless
the elder bid him, that it may come to pass
as it is written: 'In honor preferring one
another.'* Rom 12:10

To maintain this reverence for one another it is crucial that
the supernatural character of mutual relations never be lost
and that Christ be seen in one's neighbor. This is why
St Benedict strongly insisted that natural age may never
determine the order of seniority in the monastery but that
this order must correspond with the time each received his
special vocation to follow the Lord (RB 63). This is the reason too why he resolutely forestalled any attempt to make
something purely natural, such as kinship, spontaneous
attraction or aversion, the determining factor of mutual
relations.

*Care must be taken that on no occasion one monk
presume to defend another in the monastery, or
to take his part, even although they be connected
by some near tie of kinship. Let not the monks
dare to do this in any way whatsoever; because
therefrom may arise the most grievous occasion of
scandals. If any one transgress this rule, let him be
very severely punished (RB 69).*

*Let every occasion of presumption be banished
from the monastery. We ordain, therefore, that no
one be allowed to excommunicate or strike any of
his brethren, unless authority to do so shall have
been given him by the abbot. Let such as offend
herein be rebuked in the presence of all, that the
rest may be struck with fear (RB 70).*

It is on the basis of reverence and courteous humility such
as this that community life must flourish. It is beautifully
portrayed in Chapter 72 of the Holy Rule, 'Of the good zeal
which monks ought to have':

*Let monks . . . 'in honor prefer one another'.* Rom 12:10
*Let them very patiently endure one another's
infirmities, whether of body or of mind. Let
them vie with one another in obedience. Let
no one follow what he thinks good for himself, but rather what seems good for another.
Let them cherish fraternal charity with chaste
love, fear God, love their abbot with sincere
and humble affection, and prefer nothing
whatever to Christ. And may he bring us all
alike to life everlasting.*

# Bodily Needs

A SERIES OF CHAPTERS deals with bodily needs. As
regards food and drink and other physical requirements
St Benedict, with loving solicitude but also 'with some
misgiving', took pains to establish norms to meet the demands
of nature and at the same time 'consider the infirmity of the
weak' (RB 39, 40). What kindly consideration echoes from
the directive:

*For the daily meal . . . let there be at all seasons
of the year two dishes of cooked food, because
of the weakness of different people; so that he
who perchance cannot eat of the one, may make
his meal of the other.*

Nature is to get what it needs. But everything should be
directed to the ultimate purpose of life. 'Whether you eat or
drink—whatever you do—you should do all for the glory of
God' (1 Cor 10:31). With what religious solemnity Benedict
therefore invests the monastic meal! 'Reading must not be

wanting while the brothers eat at table' (RB 38). 'Not on bread alone is man to live' (Mt 4:4). Servers in the kitchen (RB 35) and the reader at table (RB 38) receive a ritual blessing before they take up their duties. During meals a grave, reverent silence must reign.

*The greatest silence must be kept at table, so that no whispering may be heard there, nor any voice except that of him who reads.*

A meal conducted in this way is in all truth a religious service. At such a meal it is understood, and explicitly insisted upon by St Benedict, that 'all surfeiting is to be avoided'. When physical needs are satisfied, body and soul are refreshed.

In this way natural life is elevated to the supernatural, a practical application of the principle 'That in all things God may be glorified'. This transfers humility, self-surrender to God, to the natural in human existence. Humility does not require renunciation of all natural joy and satisfaction; it demands only unquestioning subordination to the 'spirit'. It was said of St Bernard that he was so mortified in food and drink that without noticing it he consumed oil instead of water. But St Gertrude is said to have rejoiced when better food was placed on the table on feastdays, as children are happy when their parents have a party for them. Once when she was given a bunch of grapes she ate the tasty fruit, heartily enjoying the gift God had sent to her, and that night, it is said, Christ appeared to her with the grapes in his hand to show her his approval.

St Benedict's way of life has room for both saints' behavior. In the progress of the spiritual life he assigned no stage of its own to mortification of the body. He took it for granted that the monk will 'chastise the body', that he will 'love fasting' (RB 4, Instr. 11 and 13) and, especially during Lent, will offer voluntary sacrifices (RB 49). Bodily mortification however has no value in itself but derives it from the spirit which transforms the body from within, from the sublime awareness of

God which shapes & forms all of life both within and without.

As he did for food and drink, so St Benedict provided for all the other needs of life:

> *Let the abbot supply them with everything necessary: that is, a cowl, tunic, shoes, stockings, girdle, knife, pen, needle, handkerchief, and tablets; so that all plea of wanting anything may be taken away. Yet let the abbot always be mindful of these words of the Acts of the Apostles: 'Distribution was made to everyone, according as he had need' . . . . Let* Acts 4:35 *clothing be given to the brothers suitable to the nature and the climate of the place where they live; for in cold countries more is required, in warm countries less. This must therefore be considered by the abbot . . . . Let the abbot be careful about the size of the garments, that they be not too short for those who wear them, but of the proper length. When they receive new clothes let them always give up the old ones at once, to be put by in the wardrobe for the poor . . . . And let not the monks complain of the color or the coarseness of these things, but let them be such as can be got in the country where they live, or can be bought most cheaply . . . . (RB 55).*

Every now and then in the history of religious orders controversy has arisen over things like the color or style of the garb, as if the essence of perfection depended on it. *'Non causentur monachi'*, said St Benedict, 'Let monks not complain!' He always looked to what is essential. That is why his outlook remained ever broad and free, and his heart full of kindness and loving concern for everything. What he told the abbot was his own guiding norm: 'Let the abbot so arrange and dispose all things that souls may be saved, and

that the brothers may do what they have to do without just
cause for murmuring' (RB 41).

# The Monastery's

# Property

T HE MONASTERY, according to the Rule, is to have
material means at its disposal to provide adequate
support for the monastic community, and these possessions are to be competently managed.

> *The monastery ought if possible to be so consti-*
> *tuted that all things necessary, such as water, a*
> *mill, and a garden, and the various crafts may be*
> *contained within it (RB 66).*

Especially should the monastery have arable land and the
necessary manpower to farm it. St Benedict assumed that it
would also have a library (RB 48). But then again all these
things are not essential. If the monastery is poor and the
monks can only with difficulty procure their livelihood

> *let them not be saddened by this; because then are*
> *they truly monks, when they live by the labor of*
> *their hands, as did our fathers and the apostles.*
> *Yet let all be done with moderation, on account of*
> *the faint-hearted (RB 48). . . . Where the necessity*
> *of the place allows not even the aforesaid measure*
> *[of wine], but much less, or none at all, let those*
> *who dwell there bless God and not murmur*
> *(RB 40).*

The monks must always rise above earthly needs and see everything in relation to their final destiny, God.

> *This above all we admonish, that there be no murmuring among them (RB 40).*

About the cellarer, who is entrusted with administering the monastery's property and providing for exterior necessities, St Benedict says emphatically: '*Humilitatem ante omnia habeat:* Let him above all have humility' (RB 31). Earthly things harbor the danger of drawing one away from the divine and the supernatural. That is why anyone who has to be constantly occupied with earthly things must 'above all' possess the basic virtue of humility, even more than natural competence for his office. He must be very solidly grounded in unconditional self-surrender to God. His thinking and willing must have an especially strong orientation to God so that he views all the earthly and worldly things with which he has to deal in the light of God. 'Let him look upon all the vessels and goods of the monastery as though they were the consecrated vessels of the altar. Let him not think that he may neglect anything' (RB 31).

Things of earth need not stand in the way of love of God. Only when man sinfully closes himself to the grace of God do things become 'idols' and place themselves between God and man. But when man is, through genuine humility, freed from all resistance to God, creation is drawn without discord into the life of God, for he is 'the Lord of all'.

We may and should enjoy nature's beauty. St Benedict himself took pleasure in it. Otherwise he would not have chosen locations of extraordinary scenic grandeur for his foundations at Subiaco and Monte Cassino. His sons have followed the example of their father. How refreshing is Eigil's account of the founding of the monastery of Fulda, telling how St Sturmius at the bidding of St Boniface searched for weeks until he found 'the place already long since prepared by the Lord', and, 'delighted by the beauty of it, returned with joy'. Constant awareness of 'God, the Lord of all', continual 'praise of the Creator', sharpen one's vision also for the beauty of creation which mirrors God's glory. This is the spirit in which our fathers built splendid churches and monasteries, cultivated the arts and sciences, sought to bring everything true and good and beautiful into the 'service of the Lord'. In like manner their successors guard and foster the heritage of the past so that 'God may be glorified in all things'.

# Ora et Labora:

# Pray and Work

WITHOUT THIS SUPERNATURAL ORIENTATION all these things lose their significance and value, and in the eyes of God no longer have any right to exist. Characteristic of the spirit of St Benedict is Chapter 57, 'Of the Craftsmen of the Monastery', with which he concludes the organization of the various elements of the daily order.

> Should there be craftsmen in the monastery, let them work at their crafts in all humility, if the abbot give permission. But if any of them be puffed up by reason of his knowledge of his craft, in that he seems to confer some benefit on the monastery, let such a one be taken from it, and not exercise it again, unless, perchance, when he has humbled himself, the abbot bid him work at it anew.

Here it becomes unmistakably clear that St Benedict saw

humility as the monks' essential disposition. The merely human view judges the artist, the craftsman according to his skill and the quality of his work. Benedict did not first ask whether a brother were competent in his craft or brought material benefit to the monastery by his work, but whether he were humble in the exercise of his artistic talent, whether what he did served to glorify God or his own ego. If anyone did not have the spirit of humility, his entire work was worthless in the eyes of the holy patriarch. 'Let such a one be taken from his craft', even though he may be the best artist, the most capable craftsman, and however much material gain he may bring to the monastery.

What is said 'of the craftsmen' applies to every occupation. Where humility, orientation to God, is lacking, all activity is worthless in God's eyes. But where there is genuine humility, where God's glory is sought in labor, and all activity is motivated by the intention of serving God in true dedication, the results of labor are lasting even though visible production is minimal and recognition by the world non-existent.

A favorite expression of the benedictine attitude towards work is the ancient phrase, *Ora et labora:* Pray and work. The motto does not occur in the Holy Rule in these exact words. But it is in thorough agreement with the spirit of the Rule, not only because Benedict provided for a wise alternation of prayer and work in the life of his monks (cf. RB 48, 'Of the Daily Manual Labor'), but even more because he linked prayer and work closely. For St Benedict work too was a religious service, an *Opus Dei,* labor for God, and came under the heading: '*U.I.O.G.D.: Ut in omnibus glorificetur Deus:* That in all things God may be glorified'. For St Benedict work was never an end in itself. It must be fitted into the sublime over-all purpose of life: to attain to God by means of the 'Lord's service', by means of obedience.

The monk's daily labor is therefore determined and regulated by the schedule of choir prayer, and it is from this that earthly work too gets its consecration and its blessing.

Furthermore, the hours of manual labor alternate with periods of spiritual reading so that 'the spiritual craft' (RB 4) may not suffer because of artistic skill in things of earth (RB 48). Never may any earthly occupation so dominate that it obscures the spiritual goal, or through overexertion leads to spiritual harm.

> To brothers who are weak or delicate, let there be given such work or occupation as may prevent them either from being idle, or from being so oppressed by excessive labor as to be driven away. Their weakness must be taken into account by the abbot (RB 48).

That such a supernatural concept of labor is no detriment to zeal for work or to efficiency in work, but on the contrary makes great achievements all the more possible is sufficiently proved by the history of the benedictine Order.

In the second part of Chapter 57 Benedict speaks about the sale of the products of monastic labor.

> If any of the work of the artificers is to be sold, let those by whom the business is done see that they defraud not the monastery. Let them ever be mindful of Ananias and Saphira, lest perchance, they, and all who deal fraudulently with the goods of the monastery, should suffer in their souls the death which these incurred in the body. But with regard to the prices of such things, let not the vice of avarice creep in, but let them always be sold a little cheaper than by men in the world, that in all things God may be glorified (1 Pt 4:11).

Is it not significant that St Benedict makes this famous pronouncement, which can serve to sum up all his regulations for the monastic life, in connection with material things? Apparently, he feared most for the monastic spirit, for humility, when it is involved in what is earthly and material. Already in Chapter 2 he had earnestly warned the abbot:

> Above all let him not, overlooking or undervaluing

> *the salvation of the souls entrusted to him, be too*
> *solicitous for fleeting, earthly and perishable things.*

And in order to forestall any pretext, he continued:

> *And that he may not complain for want of*
> *worldly substance, let him remember what is*
> *written: 'Seek first the kingdom of God and*
> *his justice, and all these things shall be added*
> *unto you.' And again: 'Nothing is lacking to*     Mt 6:33
> *to those who fear him.'*     Ps 34:10

Our 'seeking the kingdom of God and his justice', our quest for God by way of humility, must be and must always remain 'first'. Only in this way do we fulfil the will of God and our christian and monastic vocation. Everything else belongs to what is 'added to' us if we seek in the right way what is first.

In his Rule St Benedict wrote nothing about the vast exterior activity which his Order would develop in the course of fourteen hundred years, yet it is wholly and entirely based on the Holy Rule. For the reason and to the extent that Benedict's sons 'sought the kingdom of God and his justice' were 'all these things added unto them': success in pastoral and missionary labors, economic prosperity, flourishing arts and sciences. If in the course of history 'all these things' were also taken away from them time and again, the reason was that the 'first' had taken second place. What is true of the monastic life is true in general of the credibility and effectiveness of Christianity in the world.

# St Benedict.

# Man of God

ITH WONDERFUL COHERENCE and consistency, in the spirit of humility, of total docility to the will of God, St Benedict gave form and substance to the life of his followers, down to the least details of the daily order. With ever greater force and intensity he sought to give unity to all thought and will and action, and direct them to the one purpose, 'that in all things God may be glorified'. One's entire person, body and soul, with everything that one is and has and does, must enter into God, so that God may be 'all in all'.

In his biography Gregory the Great calls St Benedict *vir Dei*, man of God. Perhaps no designation more succinctly and aptly sums up the essential character of St Benedict and what he had in mind for his 'school of the Lord's service'. Benedict was that, a man of God, a man for whom God was everything. 'To please God alone' (*soli Deo placere*) was the ardent desire of the 'pious and religious youth Benedict' who in the school of God matured into the 'perfect man', wholly committed to God and therefore also wholly filled with God. Out of the fullness of God he wrote his Rule, constituted the life of his monastic community as a perpetual 'divine service', and became for untold thousands a guide to God. Out of the fullness of God he worked his miracles. Even though the authenticity of individual incidents in St Gregory's biography of St Benedict may be questioned, one thing is certain: the delineation of

St Benedict's character is genuine and profound. He was completely at home in the world of God. He lived in God *velut naturaliter,* as it were naturally. He saw everything through the eyes of God, all of life with its many inter-relations, the world, people, things. For him, everything came under the heading *U.I.O.G.D.:* that in all things God may be glorified.

The most striking manifestation of this is the vision he had at the end of his life. In the divine light he saw the whole world in a single ray of the Eternal One's glory. 'The whole world was brought before his eyes, concentrated, as it were, in a single ray of the sun'. St Gregory explained this majestic vision profoundly:

> *When the soul sees God it sees how insignificant all creatures are. However little one may behold of the heavenly light, all that is created will appear small and trifling, for by the light of contemplation the range of his vision is enlarged to such an extent that his mind rises far above the world . . . . What wonder, then, that he saw the whole world before his eyes when his soul was raised far above the world by this light? . . . Rapt in the contemplation of God, he was privileged to see without any diffi-culty everything that is beneath God (*Dialogues II.35).

It is to such heights, above and beyond all creation, into God, that humility shows the way.

> *See that you follow the pattern shown you on the mountain! (Ex 25:40).*

# THE RULE OF SAINT BENEDICT

*Translated by*
*Dom Oswald Hunter Blair* OSB
*Abbot of Fort Augustus*

## PROLOGUE

Hearken, O my son, to the precepts of your master, and incline the ear of your heart; willingly receive and faithfully fulfil the admonition of your loving father, that you may return by the labor of obedience to him from whom you had departed through the sloth of disobedience. To you, therefore, my words are now addressed, whoever you are who, renouncing your own will, take up the strong and bright weapons of obedience in order to fight for the Lord Christ, our true king. In the first place, whatever good work you begin to do, beg of him with most earnest prayer to perfect; that he who has now vouchsafed to count us in the number of his children may not at any time be grieved by our evil deeds. For we must always so serve him with the good things he has given us, that not only may he never, as an angry father, disinherit his children, but may never, as a dreadful Lord, incensed by our sins, deliver us to everlasting punishment, as most wicked servants who would not follow him to glory.

Let us then at length arise, since the Scripture stirs us up, saying: 'It is time now for us to rise from sleep'. And our eyes being open to the deifying light, let us hear with

*Rom 13:11*

219

wondering ears what the divine voice admonishes us, daily crying out: 'Today if you

*Ps 95:8*          shall hear his voice, harden not your hearts'.
And again, 'He that has ears to hear, let him

*Rv 2:7*           hear what the Spirit says to the churches'.
And what says he? 'Come, my children,
hearken to me, I will teach you the fear of the
Lord. Run while you have the light of life,

*Ps 34:12, Jn 12:35* lest the darkness of death seize hold of you'.
And the Lord, seeking his own workman in
the multitude of the people to whom he thus
cries out, says again: 'Who is the man that will

*Ps 34:13*         have life, and desires to see good days?' And if
you, hearing him, answer, 'I am he', God says
to you: 'If you will have true and everlasting
life, keep your tongue from evil and your lips
that they speak no guile. Turn from evil, and

*Ps 34:14,15*      do good: seek peace and pursue it. And when
you have done these things, my eyes will be
upon you, and my ears will be open to your
prayers; and before you call upon me, I will
say unto you, "Behold, I am here".' What can
be sweeter to us, dearest brothers, than this
voice of the Lord inviting us? Behold in his
loving-kindness the Lord shows us the way
of life.

Having our loins, therefore, girded with
faith and the performance of good works, let
us walk in his paths by the guidance of the
Gospel, that we may deserve to see him who
has called us to his kingdom. And if we wish
to dwell in the tabernacle of his kingdom, we
shall by no means reach it unless we run to it
by our good deeds. But let us ask the Lord
with the prophet, saying to him: 'Lord, who
shall dwell in your tabernacle, or who shall

rest upon your holy hill?' After this question, *Ps 15:1*
brothers, let us hear the Lord answering and
showing to us the way to his tabernacle, and
saying: 'He that walks without stain and
works justice: he that speaks truth in his
heart, that has not done guile with his tongue:
he that has done no evil to his neighbor, and
has not taken up a reproach against his
neighbor': he that has brought the malignant *Ps 15:2,3*
evil one to naught, casting him out of his
heart with all his suggestions, and has taken
his bad thoughts, while they were yet young,
and dashed them down upon the (Rock)
Christ. These are they who, fearing the Lord, *Ps 137:9*
are not puffed up with their own good works,
but knowing that the good which is in them
comes not from themselves but from the
Lord, magnify the Lord who works in them,
saying with the prophet: 'Not unto us, O
Lord, not unto us, but unto your name give
the glory'. So the Apostle Paul imputed *Ps 115:1*
nothing of his preaching to himself, but said:
'By the grace of God I am what I am'. And *1 Cor 15:10*
again he says: 'He that glories, let him glory
in the Lord'. *2 Cor 10:17*

Hence also the Lord says in the Gospel:
'He that hears these words of mine, and does
them, is like a wise man who built his house
upon a rock: the floods came, the winds
blew, and beat upon that house, and it fell
not, because it was founded upon a rock'. *Mt 7:24,25*
And the Lord in fulfilment of these his words
is waiting daily for us to respond by our
deeds to his holy admonitions. Therefore are
the days of our life lengthened for the amendment of our evil ways, as says the apostle:

*Rom 2:4*
'Know you not that the patience of God is leading you to repentance?' For the merciful Lord says: 'I will not the death of a sinner, *Ez 33:11* but that he should be converted and live'.

Since then, brothers, we have asked of the Lord who is to inhabit his temple, we have heard his commands to those who are to dwell there: and if we fulfill those duties, we shall be heirs of the kingdom of heaven. Our hearts, therefore, and our bodies must be made ready to fight under the holy obedience of his commands; and let us ask God to supply by the help of his grace what by nature is not possible to us. And if we would arrive at eternal life, escaping the pains of hell, then— while there is yet time, while we are still in the flesh, and are able to fulfill all these things by the light which is given us—we must hasten to do now what will profit us for all eternity.

We have, therefore, to establish a school of the Lord's service, in the setting forth of which we hope to order nothing that is harsh or rigorous. But if anything be somewhat strictly laid down, according to the dictates of sound reason, for the amendment of vices or the preservation of charity, do not therefore fly in dismay from the way of salvation, whose beginning cannot but be strait and difficult. But as we go forward in our life and in faith, we shall with hearts enlarged and the unspeakable sweetness of love run in the way of God's commandments; so that never departing from his guidance, but persevering in his teaching in the monastery until death, we may by patience share in the sufferings of Christ, that we may deserve to be partakers of his kingdom. Amen.

# CHAPTER 1
## *Of the several kinds of monks and their way of life*

It is well known that there are four kinds of monks. The first are the cenobites: that is, those in monasteries, who live under a rule or an abbot. The second are the anchorites or hermits: that is, those who, not in the first fervor of religious life, but after long probation in the monastery, have learned by the help and experience of many to fight against the devil; and going forth well armed from the ranks of their brethren to the single-handed combat of the desert, are able, without the support of others, to fight by the strength of their own arm, God helping them, against the vices of the flesh and their evil thoughts. A third and most baneful kind of monks are the sarabaites, who have been tried by no rule nor by the experience of a master, as gold in the furnace; but being soft as lead, and still serving the world in their works, are known by their tonsure to lie to God. These in twos or threes, or even singly, without a shepherd, shut up, not in the Lord's sheep-folds, but in their own, make a law to themselves in the pleasure of their own desires; whatever they think fit or choose to do, that

they call holy; and what they like not, that
they consider unlawful.

The fourth kind of monks are those called
gyrovagues, who spend all their lives-long
wandering about divers provinces, staying in
different cells for three or four days at
a time, ever roaming, with no stability,
given up to their own pleasures and to
the snares of gluttony, and worse in all
things than the sarabaites. Of the most
wretched life of these it is better to say
nothing than to speak. Leaving them alone
therefore, let us set to work, by the help of
God, to lay down a rule for the cenobites,
that is, the strongest kind of monks.


## CHAPTER 2
*What kind of man the abbot ought to be*

An abbot who is worthy to rule over the
monastery ought always to remember what
he is called, and correspond to his name of
superior by his deeds. For he is believed to
hold the place of Christ in the monastery,
since he is called by his name, as the apostle
says: 'You have received the spirit of the
adoption of children, in which we cry Abba,
Father'. And, therefore, the abbot ought not
(God forbid) to teach, or ordain, or command
anything contrary to the law of the Lord; but
let his bidding and his doctrine be infused into the minds of his disciples like the leaven of
divine justice.

*Rom 8:15*

Let the abbot be ever mindful that at the
dreadful judgment of God an account will

have to be given both of his own teaching and
of the obedience of his disciples. And let him
know that to the fault of the shepherd shall
be imputed any lack of profit which the father
of the household may find in his sheep. Only
then shall he be acquitted, if he shall have
bestowed all pastoral diligence on his unquiet
and disobedient flock, and employed all his
care to amend their corrupt manner of life:
then shall he be absolved in the judgment of
the Lord, and may say to the Lord with the
prophet: 'I have not hidden your justice in
my heart, I have declared your truth and your
salvation, but they contemned and despised
me'. And then at length the punishment of    *Ps 40:11, Is 1:2*
death shall be inflicted on the disobedient
sheep.

Therefore, when anyone receives the name
of abbot, he ought to govern his disciples by a
two-fold teaching: that is, he should show
forth all goodness and holiness by his deeds
rather than his words: declaring to the intelli-
gent among his disciples the commandments
of the Lord by words: but to the hard-
hearted and the simple-minded setting forth
the divine precepts by the example of his
deeds. And let him show by his own actions
that those things ought not to be done which
he has taught his disciples to be against the
law of God; lest, while preaching to others, he
should himself become a castaway, and God
should say to him in his sin: 'Why do you
declare my justice, and take my covenant in
your mouth? You have hated discipline, and
have cast my words behind you'. And again:    *Ps 50:16,17*
'You who saw the mote in your brother's eye,

*Mt 7:3* did you not see the beam in your own?'

Let him make no distinction of persons in the monastery. Let not one be loved more than another, unless he be found to excel in good works or in obedience. Let not one of noble birth be put before him that was formerly a slave, unless some other reasonable cause exist for it. But if upon just consideration it should so seem good to the abbot, let him arrange as he please concerning the place of any one whomsoever; but, otherwise, let them keep their own places; because, whether bond or free, we are all one in Christ, and bear an equal rank in the service of one Lord, *Rom 2:11* 'for with God there is no respecting of persons'. Only for one reason are we preferred in his sight, if we be found to surpass others in good works and in humility. Let the abbot, then, show equal love to all, and let the same discipline be imposed upon all according to their deserts.

For the abbot in his doctrine ought always to observe the bidding of the apostle, wherein *2 Tm 4:2* he says: 'Reprove, entreat, rebuke'; mingling, as occasions may require, gentleness with severity; showing now the rigor of a master, now the loving affection of a father, so as sternly to rebuke the undisciplined and restless, and to exhort the obedient, mild, and patient to advance in virtue. And such as are negligent and haughty we charge him to reprove and correct. Let him not shut his eyes to the faults of offenders; but as soon as they appear, let him strive with all his might to root them out, remembering the fate of Eli, *1 Sam 2:27-36* the priest of Shiloh. Those of good disposition

and understanding let him, for the first or
second time, correct only with words; but
such as are froward and hard of heart, and
proud, or disobedient, let him chastise with
bodily stripes at the very first offence, knowing that it is written: 'The fool is not
corrected with words'. And again, 'Strike       *Pr 29:19*
your son with the rod, and you shall deliver
his soul from death'.                            *Pr 23:14*

The abbot ought always to remember what
he is and what he is called, and to know that
to whom more is committed, more is required;
and he must consider how difficult and arduous a task he has undertaken, of ruling souls
and adapting himself to many dispositions.
Let him so accommodate and suit himself to
the character and intelligence of each, winning
some by kindness, others by reproof, others
by persuasion, that not only may he suffer no
loss in the flock committed to him, but may
even rejoice in their virtuous increase.

And above all let him not, overlooking or
undervaluing the salvation of the souls entrusted to him, be too solicitous for fleeting,
earthly, and perishable things; but let him ever
bear in mind that he has undertaken the
government of souls, of which he shall have
to give an account. And that he may not complain for want of worldly substance, let him
remember what is written: 'Seek first the
kingdom of God and his justice, and all these
things shall be added unto you'. And again:    *Mt 6:33*
'Nothing is wanting to them that fear him'.     *Ps 34:10*

And let him know that he who has undertaken the government of souls, must prepare
himself to render an account of them. And

whatever may be the number of the brethren
under his care, let him be certainly assured
that on the day of judgment he will have to
give an account to the Lord of all these souls,
as well as of his own. And thus, being ever
fearful of the coming inquiry which the
Shepherd will make into the state of the flock
committed to him, while he is careful on
other men's account, he will be solicitous also
on his own. And so, while correcting others
by his admonitions, he will be himself cured
of his own defects.


CHAPTER 3
*Of calling the brothers to council*

As often as any important matters have to be
transacted in the monastery, let the abbot
call together the whole community, and himself declare what is the question to be settled.
And, having heard the counsel of the brothers,
let him consider within himself, and then do
what he shall judge most expedient. We have
said that all should be called to council,
because it is often to the younger that the
Lord reveals what is best. But let the brothers
give their advice with all subjection and
humility, and not presume stubbornly to
defend their own opinion; but rather let the
matter rest with the abbot's discretion, that
all may submit to whatever he shall judge to
be best. Yet, even as it becomes disciples to
obey their master, so does it behove him
to order all things prudently and with justice.
    Let all, therefore, follow the Rule in all

things as their guide, and let no man rashly depart from it. Let no one in the monastery follow the will of his own heart: nor let any one presume insolently to contend with his abbot, either within or without the monastery. But if he should so presume, let him be subjected to the discipline appointed by the Rule. The abbot himself, however, must do everything with the fear of God and in observance of the Rule: knowing that he will have without doubt to render to God, the most just Judge, an account of all his judgments. If it happen that less important matters have to be transacted for the good of the monastery, let him take counsel with the seniors only, as it is written: 'Do all things with counsel, and you shall not afterwards repent it'.

*Sir 32:24*

## CHAPTER 4
*What are the instruments of good works*

In the first place, to love the Lord God with all one's heart, all one's soul, and all one's strength:

2. Then one's neighbor as oneself.
3. Then not to kill.
4. Not to commit adultery.
5. Not to steal.
6. Not to covet.
7. Not to bear false witness.
8. To honor all men.
9. Not to do to another what one would not have done to oneself.
10. To deny oneself, in order to follow

Christ.

11.  To chastise the body.

12.  Not to seek after delicate living.

13.  To love fasting.

14.  To relieve the poor.

15.  To clothe the naked.

16.  To visit the sick.

17.  To bury the dead.

18.  To help in affliction.

19.  To console the sorrowing.

20.  To keep aloof from worldly actions.

21.  To prefer nothing to the love of Christ.

22.  Not to give way to anger.

23.  Not to harbor a desire of revenge.

24.  Not to foster guile in one's heart.

25.  Not to make a feigned peace.

26.  Not to forsake charity.

27.  Not to swear, lest perchance one forswear oneself.

28.  To utter truth from heart and mouth.

29.  Not to render evil for evil.

30.  To do no wrong to anyone, yea, to bear patiently wrong done to oneself.

31.  To love one's enemies.

32.  Not to render cursing for cursing, but rather blessing.

33.  To bear persecution for justice's sake.

34.  Not to be proud;

35.  Not given to wine;

36.  Not a glutton;

37.  Not drowsy;

38.  Not slothful;

39.  Not a murmurer;

40.  Not a detractor.

41.  To put one's hope in God.

42.  To attribute any good one sees in oneself to God, and not to oneself.

43. But to recognize and always impute to oneself the evil that one does.

44. To fear the day of judgment.

45. To be in dread of hell.

46. To desire with a special longing everlasting life.

47. To keep death daily before one's eyes.

48. To keep guard at all times over the actions of one's life.

49. To know for certain that God sees one everywhere.

50. To dash down on the (Rock) Christ one's evil thoughts, the instant that they come into the heart:

51. And to lay them open to one's spiritual father.

52. To keep one's mouth from evil and wicked words.

53. Not to love much speaking.

54. Not to speak vain words or such as move to laughter.

55. Not to love much or excessive laughter.

56. To listen willingly to holy reading.

57. To apply oneself frequently to prayer.

58. Daily to confess one's past sins with tears and sighs to God, and to amend them for the time to come.

59. Not to fulfil the desires of the flesh: to hate one's own will.

60. To obey in all things the commands of the abbot, even though he himself (which God forbid) should act otherwise: being mindful of that precept of the Lord: 'What they say, do; but what they do, do not'.   *Mt 23:3*

61. Not to wish to be called holy before one is so: but first to be holy, that one

may be truly so called.

62. Daily to fulfil by one's deeds the commandments of God.

63. To love chastity.

64. To hate no man.

65. Not to give way to jealousy and envy.

66. Not to love strife.

67. To fly from vainglory.

68. To reverence the seniors.

69. To love the juniors.

70. To pray for one's enemies in the love of Christ.

71. To make peace with an adversary before the setting of the sun.

72. And never to despair of God's mercy.

Behold, these are the tools of the spiritual craft, which, if they be constantly employed day and night, and duly given back on the day of judgment, will gain for us from the Lord that reward which he himself has promised— 'which eye has not seen, nor ear heard; nor has it entered into the heart of man to conceive what God has prepared for them that love him'. And the workshop where we are to labor at all these things is the cloister of the monastery, and stability in the community.

*1 Cor 2:9*

## CHAPTER 5
### *Of obedience*

The first degree of humility is obedience without delay. This becomes those who hold nothing dearer to them than Christ, and who on account of the holy servitude which they have taken upon them, either for fear of hell

or for the glory of life everlasting, as soon as
anything is ordered by the superior, suffer no
more delay in doing it than if it had been
commanded by God himself. It is of these
that the Lord says: 'At the hearing of the ear
he has obeyed me'. And again, to teachers he    *Ps 18:45*
says: 'He that hears you hears me'.              *Lk 10:16*

Such as these, therefore, leaving immediately their own occupations and forsaking
their own will, with their hands disengaged,
and leaving unfinished what they were about,
with the speedy step of obedience follow by
their deeds the voice of him who commands;
and so as it were at the same instant the
bidding of the master and the perfect fulfilment of the disciple are joined together in the
swiftness of the fear of God by those who
are moved with the desire of attaining eternal
life. These, therefore, choose the narrow
way, of which the Lord says: 'Narrow is the
way which leads to life'; so that living not by    *Mt 7:14*
their own will, nor obeying their own desires
and pleasures, but walking according to the
judgment and command of another, and
dwelling in community, they desire to have
an abbot over them. Such as these without
doubt fulfil that saying of the Lord: 'I came
not to do mine own will, but the will of him
who sent me'.                                     *Jn 6:38*

But this very obedience will then only be
acceptable to God and sweet to men, if what
is commanded be done not fearfully, tardily,
nor coldly, nor with murmuring, nor with an
answer showing unwillingness; for the obedience which is given to superiors is given to
God, since he himself has said: 'He that hears

Lk 10:16
you, hears me'. And it ought to be given by disciples with a good will, because 'God loves a cheerful giver'. For if the disciple obey with ill-will, and murmur not only with his lips but even in his heart, although he fulfil the command, yet it will not be accepted by God, who regards the heart of the murmurer. And for such an action he shall gain no reward; nay, rather, he shall incur the punishment due murmurers, unless he amend and make satisfaction.

2 Cor 9:7

## CHAPTER 6
### Of the practice of silence

Let us do as says the prophet: 'I said, I will take heed to my ways, that I sin not with my tongue, I have placed a watch over my mouth; I became dumb and was silent, and held my peace even from good things'. Here the prophet shows that if we ought at times to refrain even from good words for the sake of silence, how much more ought we to abstain from evil words, on account of the punishment due to sin. Therefore, on account of the importance of silence, let leave to speak be seldom granted even to perfect disciples, although their conversation be good and holy and tending to edification; because it is written: 'In much speaking you shall not avoid sin'; and elsewhere: 'Death and life are in the power of the tongue'. For it becomes the master to speak and to teach, but it beseems the disciple to be silent and to listen. And therefore, if anything has to be asked of the superior, let it be done with all humility and

Ps 39:2,3

Pr 10:19

subjection of reverence. But as for buffoonery or idle words, such as move to laughter, we utterly condemn them in every place, nor do we allow the disciple to open his mouth in such discourse.

## CHAPTER 7
### *Of humility*

The Holy Scripture cries out to us, brothers, saying: 'Every one that exalts himself shall be humbled, and he who humbles himself shall be exalted'. In saying this, it teaches us *Lk 14:11* that all exaltation is a kind of pride, against which the prophet shows himself to be on his guard when he says: 'Lord, my heart is not exalted nor mine eyes lifted up; nor have I walked in great things, nor in wonders above me.' For why? 'If I did not think humbly, but *Ps 13:1* exalted my soul: like a child that is weaned from his mother, so will you requite my soul'. Whence, brothers, if we wish to arrive *Ps 131:2* at the highest point of humility, and speedily to reach that heavenly exaltation to which we can only ascend by the humility of this present life, we must by our ever-ascending actions erect such a ladder as that which Jacob beheld in his dream, by which the angels appeared to him descending and ascending. This descent and ascent signifies nothing *Gn 28:12* else than that we descend by self-exaltation and ascend by humility. And the ladder thus erected is our life in the world, which, if the heart be humbled, is lifted up by the Lord to heaven. The sides of the same ladder we understand to be our body and soul, in which our divine vocation has placed various degrees of humility or discipline, which we must ascend.

The first degree of humility, then, is that a man, always keeping the fear of God before his eyes, avoid all forgetfulness; and that he be ever mindful of all that God has commanded, bethinking himself that those who despise God will be consumed in hell for their sins, and that life everlasting is prepared for them that fear him. And keeping himself at all times from sin and vice, whether of the thoughts, the tongue, the hands, the feet, or his own will, let him thus hasten to cut off the desires of the flesh.

Let him consider that he is always beheld from heaven by God, and that his actions are everywhere seen by the eye of the Divine Majesty, and are every hour reported to him by his angels. This the prophet tells us, when he shows how God is ever present in our thoughts, saying: 'God searches the heart and the reins'. And again: 'The Lord knows the thoughts of men'. And he also says: 'You have understood my thoughts afar off'; and 'The thought of man shall confess to you'. In order, therefore, that he may be on his guard against evil thoughts, let the humble brother say ever in his heart: 'Then shall I be unspotted before him, if I shall have kept myself from my iniquity'.

We are, indeed, forbidden to do our own will by Scripture, which says to us: 'Turn away from your own will'. And so too we beg God in prayer that his will may be done

*Ps 7:10*

*Ps 94:11*

*Ps 139:3*

*Ps 76:11*

*Ps 18:24*

*Sir 18:30*

in us. Rightly therefore are we taught not to
do our own will, if we take heed to the warning of Scripture: 'There are ways which to
men seem right, but the ends thereof lead to
the depths of hell'; or, again, when we trem-    *Pr 16:25*
ble at what is said of the careless: 'They are
corrupt and have become abominable in their
pleasures'. And in regard to the desires of the    *Ps 53:2*
flesh, we must believe that God is always
present to us, as the prophet says to the
Lord: 'O Lord, all my desire is before you'.    *Ps 38:10*

Let us be on our guard, then, against evil
desires, since death has its seat close to the
entrance of delight; wherefore the Scripture
commands us, saying: 'Go not after your
evil desires'. Since, therefore, 'The eyes of the    *Sir 18:30*
Lord behold the good and the evil', and 'The    *Pr 15:3*
Lord is ever looking down from heaven upon
the children of men, to see who has understanding or is seeking God'; and since the    *Ps 14:2,3*
works of our hands are reported to him day
and night by the angels appointed to watch
over us; we must be always on the watch,
brothers, lest, as the prophet says in the psalm,
God should see us at any time declining to
evil and become unprofitable; and lest, though
he spares us now, because he is merciful and
expects our conversion, he should say to us
hereafter: 'These things you did and I held
my peace'.    *Ps 50:21*

The second degree of humility is, that a
man love not his own will, nor delight in fulfilling his own desires; but carry out in his
deeds that saying of the Lord: 'I came not to
do mine own will, but the will of him who
sent me'. And again Scripture says: 'Self-will    *Jn 6:38*

has punishment, but necessity wins the crown'.

The third degree of humility is, that a man for the love of God submit himself to his superior in all obedience; imitating the Lord, of whom the apostle says: 'He was made
*Phil 2:8*     obedient even unto death'.

The fourth degree of humility is, that if in this very obedience hard and contrary things, nay even injuries, are done to him, he should embrace them patiently with a quiet conscience, and not grow weary or give in, as the Scripture says: 'He that shall persevere to the
*Mt 24:13*     end shall be saved'. And again: 'Let your
*Ps 27:14*     heart be comforted, and wait for the Lord'. And showing how the faithful man ought to bear all things, however contrary, for the Lord, it says in the person of the afflicted: 'For you we suffer death all the day long; we
*Ps 44:22*     are esteemed as sheep for the slaughter'. And secure in their hope of the divine reward, they go on with joy, saying: 'But in all these things we overcome, through him who has
*Rom 8:37*     loved us'. And so in another place Scripture says: 'You have proved us, O God; you have tried us as silver is tried by fire; you have led us into the snare, and have laid tribulations on
*Ps 66:10,11*  our backs'. And in order to show that we ought to be under a superior, it goes on to
*Ps 66:12*     say: 'You have placed men over our heads'. Moreover, fulfilling the precept of the Lord by patience in adversities and injuries, they who are struck on one cheek offer the other: to him who takes away their coat they leave also their cloak; and being forced to walk one
*Mt 5:39-41*   mile, they go two. With Paul the apostle, they

bear with false brethren, and bless those that curse them.

The fifth degree of humility is, not to hide from one's abbot any of the evil thoughts that beset one's heart, or the sins committed in secret, but humbly to confess them. Concerning which the Scripture exhorts us, saying: 'Make known your way unto the Lord, and hope in him'. And again: 'Confess to the Lord, for he is good, and his mercy endures forever'. So also the prophet says: 'I have made known to you mine offence, and mine iniquities I have not hidden. I will confess against myself my iniquities to the Lord: and you have forgiven the wickedness of my heart'.

The sixth degree of humility is for a monk to be contented with the meanest and worst of everything, and in all that is enjoined him to esteem himself a bad and worthless laborer, saying with the prophet: 'I have been brought to nothing, and I knew it not: I am become as a beast before you, yet I am always with you'.

The seventh degree of humility is that he should not only call himself with his tongue lower and viler than all, but also believe himself in his inmost heart to be so, humbling himself, and saying with the prophet: 'I am a worm and no man, the shame of men and the outcast of the people: I have been exalted, and cast down, and confounded'. And again: 'It is good for me that you have humbled me, that I may learn your commandments'.

The eighth degree of humility is for a monk to do nothing except what is authorized by

*2 Cor 11:26*

*Ps 37:5*

*Ps 106:1*

*Ps 32:5*

*Ps 73:22,23*

*Pss 22:7, 88:16*

*Ps 119:71*

the common rule of the monastery, or the example of the seniors.

The ninth degree of humility is, that a monk refrain his tongue from speaking, keeping silence until a question be asked him, as the Scripture shows: 'In much talking you shall not avoid sin', and, 'The talkative man shall not be directed upon the earth'.

Pr 10:19
Ps 140:12

The tenth degree of humility is, that he be not easily moved and prompt to laughter; because it is written: 'The fool lifts up his voice in laughter'.

Sir 21:23

The eleventh degree of humility is that when a monk speaks, he do so gently and without laughter, humbly, gravely, with few and reasonable words, and that he be not noisy in his speech, as it is written: 'A wise man is known by the fewness of his words'.

The twelfth degree of humility is that the monk, not only in his heart, but also in his very bearing, always show his humility to all who see him: that is, in the Work of God, in the oratory, in the monastery, in the garden, on the road, in the field or wherever he may be, whether sitting, walking or standing, with head always bent down, and eyes fixed on the earth, that he ever think of the guilt of his sins, and imagine himself already present before the terrible judgment-seat of God: always saying in his heart what the publican in the Gospel said with his eyes fixed on the earth: 'Lord, I a sinner am not worthy to raise mine eyes to heaven'. And again, with the prophet: 'I am bowed down and humbled on every side'.

Lk 18:13
Ps 119:107

Having, therefore, ascended all these degrees

of humility, the monk will presently arrive at
that love of God which, being perfect, casts
out fear: whereby he shall begin to keep,
without labor, and as it were naturally and
by custom, all those precepts which he had
hitherto observed through fear: no longer
through dread of hell, but for the love of
Christ, and of a good habit and a delight in
virtue: which God will vouchsafe to manifest
by the Holy Spirit in his laborer, now cleansed
from vice and sin.

## CHAPTER 8
### *Of the Divine Office at night*

In winter time, that is, from the first of
November until Easter, the brothers shall rise
at what may be reasonably calculated to be
the eighth hour of the night; so that having
rested till some time past midnight, they may
rise having had their full sleep. And let the
time that remains after the Night Office be
spent in study by those brothers who have
still some part of the psalter and lessons to
learn. But from Easter to the first of November let the hour for the Night Office be so
arranged that, after a very short interval,
during which the brothers may go out for the
necessities of nature, Lauds, which are to be
said at day-break, may follow without delay.

CHAPTER 9
*How many psalms are to be said
at the Night Hours*

Ps 70:2

Ps 51:17

*To avoid what
may seem too
great a departure
from the text of
the Holy Rule,
the Vulgate num-
bering of the
psalms has been
retained in
Chapters 9–18,
with the Hebrew
numbering given in
parentheses.
Throughout the
rest of the transla-
tion, the Hebrew
numbering is used
exclusively.*

In winter time, after beginning with the verse,
'O God, come to my assistance; O Lord, make
haste to help me', with the *Gloria,* let the
words, 'O Lord, you will open my lips, and
my mouth shall declare your praise', be next
repeated thrice; then the third psalm, with a
*Gloria,* after which the ninety-fourth (95)*
psalm is to be said or sung, with an antiphon.
Next let a hymn follow, and then six psalms
with antiphons. These being said, and also a
versicle, let the abbot give the blessing: and,
all being seated, let three lessons be read by
the brethren in turns, from the book on the
lectern. Between the lessons let three responsories be sung, two of them without a
*Gloria,* but after the third let the reader say
the *Gloria:* and as soon as he begins it, let all
rise from their seats out of honor and
reverence to the Holy Trinity. Let the divinely
inspired books, both of the Old and New
Testaments, be read at the Night Office, and
also the commentaries upon them written by
the most renowned, orthodox and catholic
Fathers. After these three lessons with their
responsories, let six more psalms follow, to
be sung with an *Alleluia.* Then let a lesson
from the apostle be said by heart, with a
verse and the petition of the litany, that is,
*Kyrie eleison.* And so let the Night Office
come to an end.

CHAPTER 10
*How the Night Office is to be said*
*in summer time*

From Easter to the first of November let the
same number of psalms be recited as prescribed above; only that no lessons are to be
read from the book, on account of the short-
ness of the night: but instead of those three
lessons let one from the Old Testament be
said by heart, followed by a short responsory,
and the rest as before laid down; so that never
less than twelve psalms, not counting the
third and ninety-fourth (95th), be said at the
Night Office.

CHAPTER 11
*How the Night Office is to be said on Sundays*

On Sunday let the brothers rise earlier for the
Night Office, which is to be arranged as
follows. When six psalms and a versicle have
been sung (as already prescribed), all being
seated in order in their stalls, let four lessons
with their responsories be read from the book,
as before: and to the last responsory only let
the reader add a *Gloria,* all reverently rising as
soon as he begins it. After the lessons let six
more psalms follow in order, with their
antiphons and versicle as before; and then let
four more lessons, with their responsories, be
read in the same way as the former. Next let
three canticles from the prophets be said, as
the abbot shall appoint, which canticles are
to be sung with an *Alleluia.* After the versicle,

and the blessing given by the abbot, let four more lessons from the New Testament be read as before; and at the end of the fourth responsory, let the abbot begin the hymn, *Te Deum laudamus.* After the hymn, let the abbot read the lesson from the Gospel, while all stand in awe and reverence. The Gospel being ended, let all answer *Amen.* Then let the abbot go on with the hymn, *Te decet laus;* and after the blessing has been given, let them begin Lauds. This order for the Night Office is always to be observed on Sunday, alike in summer and in winter, unless perchance (which God forbid) they rise too late, in which case the lessons or responsories must be somewhat shortened. Let all care, however, be taken that this not happen; but if it should, let him, through whose neglect it has come to pass, make satisfaction for it in the oratory.

CHAPTER 12
*How the solemn Office of Lauds
is to be said*

At Lauds on Sunday let the sixty-sixth (67th) psalm first be said straight on, without an antiphon. After this let the fiftieth (51st) psalm be said, with an *Alleluia,* and then the hundred and seventeenth (118th) and the sixty-second (63d). Then the *Benedicite* and psalms of praise, a lesson from the Apocalypse, said by heart, a responsory, a hymn, a versicle, a canticle out of the Gospel, and the litany, and so end.

CHAPTER 13
*How Lauds are to be said on week-days*

On week-days let Lauds be celebrated in the
manner following: Let the sixty-sixth (67th)
psalm be said without an antiphon, as on Sundays, and somewhat slowly, in order that all
may be in time for the fiftieth (51st), which
is to be said with an antiphon. After this let
two other psalms be said according to custom;
that is, on Monday, the fifth and thirty-fifth
(36th): on Tuesday, the forty-second (43d) and
fifty-sixth (57th): on Wednesday, the sixty-
third (64th) and sixty-fourth (65th): on Thursday, the eighty-seventh (88th) and eighty-ninth
(90th): on Friday, the seventy-fifth (76th) and
ninety-first (92d): and on Saturday, the hundred and forty-second (143d) and the canticle
from Deuteronomy, which must be divided
into two *Glorias.* But on the other days let
canticles from the prophets be said, each on
its proper day, according to the practice of
the Roman Church. Then let the psalms of
praise follow, and after them a lesson from
the apostle, to be said by heart, a responsory,
a hymn, a versicle, a canticle out of the
Gospel, the litany, and so conclude.

The Office of Lauds and Vespers, however,
must never conclude without the Lord's
Prayer being said aloud by the superior, so
that all may hear it, on account of the thorns
of scandal which are wont to arise; so that the
brothers, by the covenant which they make
in that prayer when they say 'Forgive us as we
forgive', may cleanse themselves of such
faults. But at the other Offices let the last

part only of the prayer be said aloud, so that all may answer, 'But deliver us from evil'.

CHAPTER 14

*How the Night Office is to be said
on saints' days*

On the festivals of saints, and all other solemnities, let the Office be ordered as we have prescribed for Sundays: except that the psalms, antiphons, and lessons suitable to the day are to be said. Their number, however, shall remain as we have appointed above.

CHAPTER 15

*At what times of the year*
Alleluia *is to be said*

From the holy feast of Easter until Pentecost, without interruption, let *Alleluia* be said with the psalms and with the responsories. From Pentecost until the beginning of Lent it is to be said at the Night Office with the six latter psalms only. But on every Sunday out of Lent let the Canticles, Lauds, Prime, Tierce, Sext and None be said with *Alleluia:* Vespers, however, with an antiphon. The responses are never to be said with *Alleluia,* except from Easter to Pentecost.

## CHAPTER 16
*How the Work of God is to be done
in the daytime*

As the prophet says: 'Seven times in the day
have I given praise to you'. And we shall
observe this sacred number of seven if, at
the times of Lauds, Prime, Tierce, Sext,
None, Vespers and Compline, we fulfil the
duties of our service. For it was of these hours
of the day that he said: 'Seven times in the
day have I given praise to you'; just as the
same prophet says of the night watches: 'At
midnight I arose to give you praise'. At these
times, therefore, let us sing the praises of our
Creator for the judgments of his justice: that
is, at Lauds, Prime, Tierce, Sext, None,
Vespers and Compline; and at night let us
arise to praise him.

*Ps 119:164*

*Ps 119:62*

## CHAPTER 17
*How many psalms are to be sung
at these Hours*

We have now disposed the order of the
psalmody for the Night Office and for Lauds;
let us proceed to arrange for the remaining
Hours. At Prime, let three psalms be said
separately and not under one *Gloria.* The
hymn at this Hour is to follow the verse,
*Deus in adjutorium,* before the psalms be
begun. Then at the end of the three psalms,
let one lesson be said, with a versicle, the
*Kyrie eleison,* and the collect. Tierce, Sext
and None are to be recited in the same way,

that is, the verse, the hymn proper to each
Hour, three psalms, the lesson and versicle,
*Kyrie eleison,* with the collect. If the community be large, let the psalms be sung with
antiphons: but if small, let them be sung
straight forward. Let the Vesper Office consist of four psalms with antiphons: after the
psalms a lesson is to be recited; then a responsory, a hymn and versicle, the canticle from
the Gospel, the litany and Lord's Prayer, and
finally the collect. Let Compline consist of
the recitation of three psalms to be said
straight on without antiphons; then the hymn
for that Hour, one lesson, the versicle, *Kyrie
eleison,* the blessing and the collect.

CHAPTER 18

*In what order the psalms are to be said*

First of all let this verse be said: 'O God,
come to my assistance; O Lord, make haste
to help me', and the *Gloria,* followed by the
hymn proper to each Hour. At Prime on Sunday four parts of the hundred and eighteenth
(119th) psalm are to be said. At the other
Hours, that is, Tierce, Sext and None, let three
parts of the same psalm be said. At Prime on
Monday let three psalms be said, namely, the
first, second and sixth; and so in the same
way every day until Sunday let three psalms
be said at Prime in order, up to the nineteenth (20th); the ninth and seventeenth
(18th), however, being divided into two
*Glorias.* It will thus come about that at the
Night Office on Sunday we shall always begin

with the twentieth (21st) psalm.

At Tierce, Sext and None on Monday are to be said the nine remaining parts of the hundred and eighteenth (119th) psalm, three parts at each Hour. This psalm having thus been said through in two days, that is, Sunday and Monday, let the nine psalms from the hundred and nineteenth (120th) to the hundred and twenty-seventh (128th) be said on Tuesday at Tierce, Sext and None—three at each Hour. And these psalms are to be repeated at the same Hours every day until Sunday; the arrangement, moreover, of hymns, lessons and versicles remaining the same throughout, so as always to begin on Sunday from the hundred and eighteenth (119th) psalm.

Vespers are to be sung every day with four psalms. And let these begin from the hundred and ninth (110th), and go on to the hundred and forty-seventh, omitting those of their number that are set apart for other Hours—that is, from the hundred and seventeenth (118th) to the hundred and twenty-seventh (128th), the hundred and thirty-third (134th), and the hundred and forty-second (143rd). All the rest are to be said at Vespers. And as there are three psalms wanting, let those of the aforesaid number which are somewhat long be divided, namely the hundred and thirty-eighth (139th), the hundred and forty-third (144th), and the hundred and forty-fourth (145th). But let the hundred and sixteenth (117th), as it is short, be joined to the hundred and fifteenth (116th). The order of the psalms at Vespers being thus disposed, let the rest, that is, the lessons, responses, hymns, verses, and canticle, be said as already laid down. At Compline the same psalms are to be repeated every day: namely the fourth, ninetieth (91st), and hundred and thirty-third (134th).

The order of psalmody for the Day Hours being now arranged, let all the remaining psalms be equally distributed among the seven Night Offices, dividing the longer psalms among them, and assigning twelve to each night. Above all, we recommend that if this arrangement of the psalms be displeasing to anyone, he should, if he think fit, order it otherwise; taking care in any case that the whole psalter of a hundred and fifty psalms be recited every week, and always begun afresh at the Night Office on Sunday. For those monks would show themselves very slothful in the divine service who said in the course of a week less than the entire psalter, with the usual canticles; since we read that our holy fathers resolutely performed in a single day what I pray we tepid monks may achieve in a whole week.

### CHAPTER 19
*Of the discipline of saying the Divine Office*

We believe that the divine presence is everywhere, and that the eyes of the Lord behold the good and the evil in every place. Especially should we believe this, without any doubt, when we are assisting at the work of God. Let us, then, ever remember what the prophet

says: 'Serve the Lord in fear'; and again, 'Sing   *Ps 2:11*
wisely' and, 'In the sight of the angels I will   *Ps 47:8*
sing praises unto you'. Therefore let us con-   *Ps 138:1*
sider how we ought to behave ourselves in the
presence of God and of his angels, and so
assist at the Divine Office, that our mind and
our voice may accord together.

## CHAPTER 20
### *Of reverence at prayer*

If, when we wish to make any request to men
in power, we presume not to do so except
with humility and reverence, how much more
ought we with all lowliness and purity of
devotion to offer our supplications to the
Lord God of all things? And let us remember
that not for our much speaking, but for our
purity of heart and tears of compunction shall
we be heard. Our prayer, therefore, ought to
be short and pure, except it be perchance prolonged by the inspiration of divine grace. But
let prayer made in common always be short:
and at the signal given by the superior, let all
rise together.

## CHAPTER 21
### *Of the deans of the monastery*

Should the community be large, let there be
chosen from it certain brothers of good
repute and holy life, and appointed deans.
Let them carefully direct their deaneries in
all things according to the commandments

of God and the will of their abbot. And let
such men be chosen deans as the abbot may
safely trust to share his burdens: let them not
be chosen according to order, but for the
merit of their lives and for their wisdom and
learning. And should any one of them, being
puffed up with pride, be found worthy of
blame, and after being thrice corrected, refuse
to amend, let him be deposed, and one who is
worthy put in his place. And we order the
same to be done with regard to the prior.

## CHAPTER 22
### *How the monks are to sleep*

Let them sleep each one in a separate bed,
receiving bedding suitable to their manner of
life, as the abbot shall appoint. If possible, let
all sleep in one place: but if the number does
not permit this, let them repose by tens or
twenties with the seniors who have charge of
them. Let a candle burn constantly in the
room until morning. Let them sleep clothed,
and girded with belts or cords but not with
knives at their sides, lest perchance they
wound themselves in their sleep—and thus be
always ready, so that when the signal is given
they may rise without delay, and hasten each
to forestall the other in going to the Work of
God, yet with all gravity and modesty. Let not
the younger brethren have their beds by
themselves, but among those of the seniors.
And when they rise for the Work of God, let
them gently encourage one another, because
of the excuses of the drowsy.

## CHAPTER 23
### *Of excommunication for offences*

If any brother shall be found contumacious,
or disobedient, or proud, or a murmurer, or
in any way transgressing the Holy Rule, and
contemning the orders of his seniors, let him,
according to our Lord's commandment, be
once or twice privately admonished by his
elders. If he does not amend, let him be
rebuked in public before all. But if even then
he does not correct himself, let him be subjected to excommunication, provided that he
understand the nature of the punishment.
Should he, however, prove incorrigible, let
him undergo corporal chastisement.

## CHAPTER 24
### *What the measure of excommunication should be*

The measure of excommunication or chastisement should be meted out according to the
gravity of the offence, the estimation of which
shall be left to the judgment of the abbot. If
any brother be found guilty of lighter faults,
let him be excluded from the common table.
And this shall be the rule for one so deprived:
he shall intone neither psalm nor antiphon in
the oratory, nor shall he read a lesson, until
he have made satisfaction. Let him take his
meals alone, after those of the brothers, so
that if, for example, the brothers eat at the
sixth hour, let him eat at the ninth: if they
eat at the ninth, let him eat in the evening,

until by proper satisfaction he obtain pardon.

## CHAPTER 25
### *Of graver faults*

Let the brother who is found guilty of a more grievous offence be excluded both from the table and from the oratory, and let none of the brothers consort with him or speak to him. Let him be alone at the work enjoined him, and continue in penance and sorrow, remembering that dreadful sentence of the apostle, 'That such a one is delivered over to Satan for the destruction of the flesh, that his spirit may be saved in the day of the Lord'. Let him take his portion of food alone, in the measure and at the time that the abbot shall think best for him. Let none of those who pass by bless him nor the food that is given him.

*1 Cor 5:5*

## CHAPTER 26
### *Of those who, without leave of the abbot, consort with the excommunicate*

If any brother presume without the abbot's leave to hold any intercourse whatever with an excommunicated brother, or to speak with him, or to send him a message, let him incur the same punishment of excommunication.

## CHAPTER 27
*How careful the abbot should be
of the excommunicate*

Let the abbot show all care and solicitude
towards the offending brothers, for 'they
that are whole need not a physician, but they
that are sick'. To which end he ought, as a     *Mt 9:12*
wise physician, to use every means in his
power, sending some brothers of mature years
and wisdom, who may, as it were secretly,
console the wavering brother, and induce him
to make humble satisfaction. Let them comfort him, that he be not overwhelmed by
excess of sorrow; but as the apostle says, 'Let
charity be strengthened towards him', and     *2 Cor 2:8*
let all pray for him. For the abbot is bound
to use the greatest care, and to strive with all
possible prudence and zeal, not to lose any
one of the sheep committed to him. He must
know that he has undertaken the charge of
weak souls, and not a tyranny over the
strong; and let him fear the threat of the
prophet, through whom God says: 'What you
saw to be fat that you took to yourselves, and
what was diseased you cast away'. Let him imi-     *Ez 34:3*
tate the loving example of the Good Shepherd,
who, leaving the ninety and nine sheep on
the mountains, went to seek one which had
gone astray, on whose weakness he had such
compassion that he vouchsafed to lay it on his
own sacred shoulders and so bring it back to
the flock.

## CHAPTER 28
*Of those who, being often corrected,
do not amend*

If any brother who has been frequently corrected for some fault, or even excommunicated, does not amend, let a more severe
chastisement be applied: that is, let the
punishment of stripes be administered to
him. But if even then he does not correct
himself, or perchance (which God forbid),
puffed up with pride, even wishes to defend
his deeds, then let the abbot act like a wise
physician. If he has applied fomentations and
the unction of his admonitions, the medicine
of the Holy Scriptures, and the last remedy of
excommunication or corporal chastisement,
and if he see that his labors are of no avail, let
him add what is still more powerful, his own
prayers and those of all the brothers for him,
that God, who is all-powerful, may work the
cure of the sick brother. But if he be not
healed even by this means, then at length let
the abbot use the sword of separation, as the
apostle says: 'Put away the evil one from
you'. And again: 'If the faithless one depart,
let him depart', lest one diseased sheep should
taint the whole flock.

1 Cor 5:13
1 Cor 7:15

## CHAPTER 29
*Whether the brothers who leave
the monastery are to be received again*

If any brother who through his own fault
departs or is cast out of the monastery be

willing to return, let him first undertake to
amend entirely the fault for which he went
away; and then let him be received back into
the lowest place, that thus his humility may
be tried. Should he again depart, let him be
taken back until the third time, knowing that
after this all return will be denied him.

## CHAPTER 30
### How the younger boys are to be corrected

Every age and understanding should have its
proper measure of discipline. As often, therefore, as boys or others under age, or unable
to understand the greatness of the penalty of
excommunication, commit faults, let them be
punished by severe fasting or sharp stripes, in
order that they may be cured.

## CHAPTER 31
### What kind of man the cellarer of the
### monastery is to be

Let there be chosen out of the community, as
cellarer of the monastery, a man wise and of
mature character, temperate, not a great
eater, not haughty, nor headstrong, nor arrogant, not slothful, nor wasteful, but a God-
fearing man, who may be like a father to the
whole community. Let him have the care of
everything, but do nothing without leave of
the abbot. Let him take heed to what is
commanded him, and not sadden his brothers.
If a brother ask him for anything

unreasonably, let him not treat him with contempt and so grieve him, but reasonably and with all humility refuse what he asks for amiss. Let him be watchful over his own soul, remembering always that saying of the apostle, that 'he that has ministered well, purchases to himself a good degree'. Let him have special care of the sick, of the children, of guests and of the poor, knowing without doubt that he will have to render an account of them all on the day of judgment. Let him look upon all the vessels and goods of the monastery as though they were the consecrated vessels of the altar. Let him not think that he may neglect anything: let him not be given to covetousness, nor wasteful, nor a squanderer of the goods of the monastery; but do all things in proper measure, and according to the bidding of his abbot.

*1 Tm 3:13*

Let him above all things have humility; and to him on whom he has nothing else to bestow, let him give at least a kind answer, as it is written: 'A good word is above the best gift'. Let him have under his care all that the abbot may enjoin him, and presume not to meddle with what is forbidden him. Let him distribute to the brothers their appointed allowance of food, without arrogance or delay, that they be not scandalized; mindful of what the Word of God declares him to deserve who 'shall scandalize one of these little ones', namely, 'that a millstone be hanged about his neck and that he be drowned in the depths of the sea'. If the community be large, let him be given helpers, by whose aid he may with peace of mind

*Sir 18:17*

*Mt 18:6*

discharge the office committed to him. Let
such things as are necessary be given and
asked for at befitting times, that no one may
be troubled nor grieved in the house of God.


CHAPTER 32
*Of the iron tools and property*
*of the monastery*

Let the abbot appoint brothers, on whose
manner of life and character he can rely, to
the charge of the iron tools, clothes, and
other property of the monastery; and let him
consign to their care, as he shall think fit, the
things to be kept and collected after use. Of
these let the abbot keep a list, so that as the
brothers in turn succeed to different employ-
ments, he may know what he gives and
receives back. If anyone treat the property of
the monastery in a slovenly or negligent manner, let him be corrected; and if he does not
amend, let him be subjected to the discipline
of the Rule.


CHAPTER 33
*Whether monks ought to have*
*anything of their own*

The vice of private ownership is above all to
be cut off from the monastery by the roots.
Let none presume to give or receive anything
without leave of the abbot, nor to keep anything as their own, either book or writing-
tablet or pen, or anything whatsoever; since

they are permitted to have neither body nor will in their own power. But all that is necessary they may hope to receive from the father of the monastery; nor are they allowed to keep anything which the abbot has not given, or at least permitted them to have. Let all things be common to all, as it is written: 'Neither did anyone say that anything which he possessed was his own'. But if anyone should be found to indulge in this most baneful vice, and after one or two admonitions does not amend, let him be subjected to correction.

*Acts 4:32*

### CHAPTER 34
*Whether all ought alike to receive
what is needful*

As it is written: 'Distribution was made to every man, according as he had need'. Herein we do not say that there should be respecting of persons—God forbid—but consideration for infirmities. Let him, therefore, that has need of less give thanks to God and not be grieved; and let him who requires more be humbled for his infirmity and not made proud by the kindness shown to him; and so all members of the family shall be at peace. Above all, let not the evil of murmuring show itself by the slightest word or sign on any account whatever. If anyone be found guilty herein, let him be subjected to severe punishment.

*Acts 4:35*

CHAPTER 35
*Of the weekly servers in the kitchen*

Let the brothers wait on one another in turn,
so that none be excused from the work of the
kitchen, except he be prevented by sickness
or by some more necessary employment; for
thus is gained a greater reward and an increase
of charity. But let assistance be given to the
weak, that they may not do their work with
sadness; and let all have help according to the
number of the community and the situation
of the place. If the community be large, let
the cellarer be excused from work in the kitchen, and also those, as already mentioned,
who are occupied in more urgent business.
Let the rest serve each other in turn with
all charity. Let him who ends his week in the
kitchen make all things clean on Saturday
and wash the towels with which the brothers
dry their hands and feet. Let both him who
goes out and him who is coming in wash the
feet of all. Let him hand over to the cellarer
the vessels of his office, clean and whole; and
let the cellarer deliver the same to him who
enters, that he may know what he gives and
what he receives.

Let the weekly servers each take a cup of
drink and a piece of bread over and above the
appointed portion, one hour before the time
for refection, that so they may serve their
brothers when the hour comes without murmuring or great labor. On solemn days, however, let them forbear until after Mass. On
Sunday, as soon as Lauds are ended, let both
the incoming and the outgoing servers fall on

*Ps 86:17*

*Ps 70:2*

their knees before all in the oratory and ask
their prayers. Let him who is ending his week,
say this verse: 'Blessed are you, Lord God,
who have helped me and comforted me';
which being thrice repeated, he shall receive
the blessing. Let him that is beginning his
week follow, and say: 'O God, come to my
assistance: O Lord, make haste to help me'.
Let this likewise be thrice repeated by all;
and having received the blessing, let him enter
on his office.

CHAPTER 36
*Of the sick brothers*

*Mt 25:36,40*

Before all things and above all things care is
to be had of the sick, that they be served in
very deed as Christ himself, for he has said:
'I was sick, and you visited me', and, 'What
you have done unto one of these little ones,
you have done unto me'. And let the sick
themselves remember that they are served for
the honor of God, and not grieve by un-
necessary demands the brothers who serve
them. Yet must they be patiently borne
with, because from such as these is gained a
more abundant reward. Let it be, therefore,
the abbot's greatest care that they suffer no
neglect. And let a cell be set apart by itself
for the sick brothers, and one who is God-
fearing, diligent, and careful be appointed to
serve them. Let the use of baths be allowed
the sick as often as may be expedient; but to
those who are well, and especially to the
young, let it be granted more seldom. Let the

use of flesh meat also be permitted to the sick and to those who are very weak, for their recovery; but when they are restored to health, let all abstain from meat in the accustomed manner. The abbot must take all possible care that the sick be not neglected by the cellarer or servers; because whatever is done amiss by his disciples is laid to his charge.

## CHAPTER 37
### *Of old men and children*

Although human nature is of itself drawn to feel pity for these two times of life, namely, old age and infancy, yet the authority of the Rule should also provide for them. Let their weakness be always taken into account, and the strictness of the Rule respecting food be by no means kept in their regard; but let a kind consideration be shown for them, and let them eat before the regular hours.

## CHAPTER 38
### *Of the weekly reader*

Reading must not be wanting while the brothers eat at table; nor let any one who may chance to have taken up the book presume to read, but let him who is to read throughout the week begin upon the Sunday. After Mass and Communion, let him ask all to pray for him, that God may keep from him the spirit of pride. And let this verse be said

Ps 51:17

thrice in the oratory, he himself beginning it:
'O Lord, you shall open my lips, and my
mouth shall declare your praise'. And so,
having received the blessing, let him enter on
his reading. The greatest silence must be kept
at table, so that no whispering may be heard
there, nor any voice except that of him who
reads. And whatever is necessary for food or
drink let the brothers so minister to each
other that no one need ask for anything: but
should anything be wanted, let it be asked for
by a sign rather than by the voice. And let no
one presume to put any question there, either
about the reading or about anything else, lest
it should give occasion for talking, unless perchance the superior should wish to say a few
words for the edification of the brothers. Let
the brother who is reader for the week take
a little bread and wine before he begins to
read, on account of the Holy Communion,
and lest it be hard for him to fast so long.
Afterwards let him take his meal with the
weekly cooks and other servers. The brothers
are not to read or sing according to their
order, but those only who may edify the
hearers.

## CHAPTER 39
### *Of the measure of food*

We think it sufficient for the daily meal,
whether at the sixth or the ninth hour, that
there be at all seasons of the year two dishes
of cooked food, because of the weakness of
different people; so that he who perchance

cannot eat the one, may make his meal of the other. Let two dishes, then, suffice for all the brothers; and if there be any fruit or young vegetables, let a third be added. Let one pound weight of bread suffice for the day, whether there be but one meal or both dinner and supper. If they are to sup, let a third part of the pound be kept back by the cellarer, and given to them for supper. If, however, their work chance to have been hard, it shall be in the abbot's power, if he think fit, to make some addition, avoiding above everything, all surfeiting, that the monks be not overtaken by indigestion. For there is nothing so adverse to a Christian as gluttony, according to the words of Our Lord: 'See that your hearts be not overcharged with surfeiting'. *Lk 21:34* And let not the same quantity be allotted to children of tender years, but less than to their elders, moderation being observed in every case. Let everyone, except the very weak and the sick, abstain altogether from the flesh of four-footed animals.

## CHAPTER 40
### Of the measure of drink

Everyone has his proper gift from God, one after this manner, another after that. And, therefore, it is with some misgiving that we appoint the measure of other men's living. Yet, considering the infirmity of the weak, we think that one pint of wine a day is sufficient for each; but let those to whom God gives the endurance of abstinence know that they shall

have their proper reward. If, however, the
situation of the place, the work, or the heat
of summer require more, let it be in the power
of the superior to grant it, taking care in every
thing that surfeit or drunkenness creep not in.
And although we read that wine ought by no
means to be the drink of monks, yet since in
our times monks cannot be persuaded of this,
let us at least agree to drink not to satiety, but
sparingly; because 'wine makes even the wise

*Sir 19:2* to fall away'. But where the necessity of the
place allows not even the aforesaid measure,
but much less, or none at all, let those who
dwell there bless God and not murmur. This
above all we admonish, that there be no
murmuring among them.

## CHAPTER 41
### *At what hours the brothers*
### *are to take their meals*

From holy Easter until Pentecost let the
brothers dine at the sixth hour, and sup in the
evening. But from Pentecost throughout the
summer (unless they have to work in the
fields, or are harrassed by excessive heat) let
them fast on Wednesdays and Fridays until
the ninth hour, but on other days dine at
the sixth. Should they have field labor, or
should the heat of the summer be very great,
they must always take their dinner at the
sixth hour. Let the abbot provide for this, and
let him so arrange and dispose all things that
souls may be saved, and that the brothers may
do what they have to do without just cause

for murmuring. From the fourteenth of September until the beginning of Lent let them always dine at the ninth hour; and during Lent, until Easter, in the evening. And let the hour of the evening meal be so ordered that they have no need of a lamp while eating, but let all be over while it is yet daylight. At all times, whether of dinner or supper, let the hour be so arranged that everything be done by daylight.

## CHAPTER 42
### *That no one may speak after Compline*

Monks should love silence at all times, but especially during the hours of the night. Therefore, on all days, whether of fasting or otherwise, let them sit down all together as soon as they have risen from supper (if it be not a fast-day) and let one of them read the *Conferences* [of Cassian], or the lives of the Fathers, or something else which may edify the hearers. Not, however, the Heptateuch, or the Books of Kings, for it will not profit those of weak understanding to hear those parts of Scripture at that hour: they may, however, be read at other times. If it be a fast-day, then a short time after Vespers let them assemble for the reading of the *Conferences,* as we have said; four or five pages being read, or as much as time allows, so that during the reading all may gather together, even those who may have been occupied in some work enjoined them. Everyone then being assembled, let them say Compline; and when that is finished,

let none be allowed to speak to any one. And
if any one be found to evade this rule of
silence, let him be subjected to severe punishment; unless the presence of guests should
make it necessary, or the abbot should
chance to give any command. Yet, even then,
let it be done with the utmost gravity and
moderation.


## CHAPTER 43
### *Of those who come late*
### *to the Work of God, or to table*

At the hour of Divine Office, as soon as the
signal is heard, let everyone, leaving whatever
he had in hand, hasten to the oratory with all
speed, and yet with seriousness, so that no
occasion be given for levity.

Let nothing, then, be preferred to the
Work of God. And should any one come to
the Night Office after the *Gloria* of the
ninety-fourth (95th) psalm (which for this
reason we wish to be said very slowly and
protractedly), let him not stand in his order
in the choir, but last of all, or in the place set
apart by the abbot for the negligent, so that
he may be seen by him and by all, until, the
Work of God being ended, he has made satisfaction by public penance. The reason why
we have judged it fitting for them to stand in
the last place or apart is that, being seen by
all, they may amend for very shame. For, if
they were to remain outside the oratory,
someone perchance would return to his place
and go to sleep, or at all events would sit down

outside, and give himself to idle talk, and thus an occasion would be given to the evil one. Let him therefore enter, that he may not lose the whole and may amend for the future. At the day Hours, let him who comes to the Work of God after the Verse and the *Gloria* of the first psalm which follows it stand in the last place, as ordered above, and not presume to join with the choir in the Divine Office until he has made satisfaction, unless perchance the abbot shall permit him so to do, on condition, however, that he afterwards do penance.

If any one, through his own negligence and fault, come not to table before the Verse, so that all may say this and the prayer together and together sit down to table, let him be once or twice corrected. If after this he does not amend, let him not be admitted to share in the common table, but be separated from the companionship of all and eat alone, his portion of wine being taken from him, until he has made satisfaction and amends. Let him be punished in like manner who is not present also at the Verse which is said after meals. And let no one presume to take food or drink before or after the appointed hour: but should a brother be offered anything by the superior, and refuse to take it, if he afterwards desire either what he before refused, or anything else, he shall receive nothing whatever, until he has made proper satisfaction.

CHAPTER 44
*Of those who are excommunicated,
how they are to make satisfaction*

Let him who for graver offences is excommunicated from the oratory and table prostrate himself at the door of the oratory,
saying nothing, at the hour when the Work of
God is being performed, lying prone, with his
face upon the ground, at the feet of all who
go out from the oratory. Let him continue to
do this until the abbot judge that he has made
satisfaction; and then, coming at the abbot's
bidding, let him cast himself at his feet and at
the feet of all, that they may pray for him.
After this, if the abbot so order, let him be
received back into the choir, in such a place
as he shall appoint; yet so, that he presume
not to intone psalm or lesson or anything
else in the oratory, unless the abbot again
command him. And at all the Hours, when
the Work of God is ended, let him cast himself on the ground, in the place where he is
standing, and so make satisfaction, until such
time as the abbot bid him cease therefrom.
But let those who for lighter faults are excommunicated only from the table make
satisfaction in the oratory so long as the
abbot shall command, and continue so doing
until he bless them and say it is enough.

CHAPTER 45
*Of those who make mistakes
in the oratory*

If any one makes a mistake in the recitation
of psalm, responsory, antiphon, or lesson,
and does not humble himself by making
satisfaction there before all, let him be subjected to severer punishment, as one who
would not correct by humility what he did
wrong through negligence. But children for
such faults are to be whipped.

CHAPTER 46
*Of those who offend
in any other matters*

If any one, while at work in the kitchen or
the cellar, in serving the brothers, in the
bakehouse or the garden, or at any other
occupation or in any place whatever, com-
mits any fault, or breaks or loses anything, or
transgresses in any other way, and does not
come immediately before the abbot and community, and of himself confess and make
satisfaction for his fault, if it is made known
by another, he shall be subjected to more
severe correction. If, however, the guilt of his
offence be hidden in his own soul, let him
manifest it to the abbot only, or to his spiritual seniors, who know how to heal their own
wounds, and will not disclose or publish
those of others.

## CHAPTER 47
### *Of signifying the hour for the Work of God*

Let the announcing of the hour for the Work of God, both by day and night, be the abbot's care; either by signifying it himself, or by entrusting the duty to such a careful brother, that all things may be done at the appointed times. Let the psalms and antiphons be intoned by those whose duty it is, each in his order, after the abbot. Let no one presume to sing or to read except those who can so perform the office that the hearers may be edified. And let it be done with humility, gravity, and awe, and by those whom the abbot has appointed.

## CHAPTER 48
### *Of the daily manual labor*

Idleness is an enemy of the soul; and hence at certain seasons the brothers ought to occupy themselves in the labor of their hands, and at others in holy reading. We think, therefore, that the times for each may be disposed as follows: from Easter to the first of October, let them, in going from Prime in the morning, labor at whatever is required of them until about the fourth hour. From the fourth hour until near the sixth let them apply themselves to reading. And when they rise from table, after the sixth hour, let them rest on their beds in perfect silence; or if any one perchance desire to read, let him do so in such a way as not to disturb any one else. Let None be said in good time, at about the middle of the eighth hour: and then let them again work at whatever has to be done until Vespers. And if the needs of the place, or their poverty, oblige them to labor themselves at gathering in the crops, let them not be saddened thereat; because then are they truly monks, when they live by the labor of their hands, as did our fathers and the apostles. Yet let all be done with moderation, on account of the faint-hearted.

From the first of October to the beginning of Lent let them apply themselves to reading until the end of the second hour. Let Tierce be then said, and until the ninth hour let all labor at the work that is enjoined them. When the first signal for None is given, let everyone break off from his work, and be ready as soon as the second signal is sounded. After their meal, let them occupy themselves in their reading or in learning the psalms. During Lent, let them apply themselves to reading from morning until the end of the third hour, and then until the end of the tenth labor at whatever is enjoined them. And in these days of Lent let each one receive a book from the library, and read it all through in order. These books are to be given out at the beginning of Lent. Above all, let one or two seniors be appointed to go round the monastery at the hours when the brothers are engaged in reading, and see that there be no slothful brother giving himself to idleness or to foolish talk, and not applying himself to his reading, so that he is thus not only useless to himself, but a distraction to others. If such a one be

found (which God forbid) let him be corrected once and a second time; and if he does
not amend, let him be subjected to the
chastisement of the Rule, so that the rest may
be afraid. And let not one brother associate
with another at unseasonable hours.

On Sunday, let all occupy themselves in
reading, except those who have been appointed to the various offices. But if any one
should be so negligent and slothful, as to be
either unwilling or unable to study or to
read, let some task be given him to do, that he
be not idle. To brothers who are weak or delicate, let there be given such work or occupation as to prevent them from being idle, or
from being so oppressed by excessive labor
as to be driven away. Their weakness must be
taken into account by the abbot.

CHAPTER 49
*Of the observance of Lent*

Although the life of a monk ought at all times
to have about it a lenten character, yet since
few have strength enough for this, we exhort
all, at least during the days of Lent, to keep
themselves in all purity of life, and to wash
away during that holy season the negligences
of other times. This we shall worthily do, if
we refrain from all sin and give ourselves to
prayer with tears, to holy reading, compunction of heart, and abstinence. In these days,
then, let us add something to our wonted
service; as private prayers and abstinence
from food and drink, so that every one of his

own will may offer to God, with joy of the
Holy Spirit, something beyond the measure
appointed him, withholding from his body
something of his food, drink and sleep,
refraining from talking and mirth, and await-
ing holy Easter with the joy of spiritual
longing. Let each one, however, make known
to his abbot what he is offering, and let it
be done with his blessing and permission:
because what is done without leave of the
spiritual father shall be imputed to presumption and vainglory, and deserve no reward.
Everything, therefore, is to be done with the
approval of the abbot.

CHAPTER 50
*Of the brothers who are working
at a distance from the oratory,
or are on a journey*

Let the brothers who are at work at a great
distance, or on a journey, and cannot come to
the oratory at the proper time (the abbot
judging such to be the case) perform the
Work of God there where they are laboring,
in godly fear and on bended knees. In like
manner, let not those who are sent on a
journey allow the appointed Hours to pass by,
but, as far as they can, observe them by
themselves, and not neglect to fulfil their
obligation of divine service.

## CHAPTER 51
*Of the brothers who go not very far off*

Let the brother who is sent out on any business, and hopes to return that same day to the monastery, not presume to eat while away, even although pressed by anyone to do so, unless perchance he has been bidden by his abbot. If he does otherwise, let him be excommunicated.

## CHAPTER 52
*Of the oratory of the monastery*

Let the oratory be what it is called, a place of prayer; and let nothing else be done or kept there. When the Work of God is ended, let all go out with the utmost silence, paying due reverence to God, so that a brother, who perchance wishes to pray by himself, may not be hindered by another's misconduct. If anyone desires to pray in private, let him go in quietly and pray, not with a loud voice, but with tears and fervor of heart. And let it not be permitted, as we have said, to remain in the oratory when the Work of God is finished, except for a like purpose, lest hindrance be caused to others.

## CHAPTER 53
*Of receiving guests*

Let all guests that come be received like Christ himself, for he will say: 'I was a

stranger and you took me in'. And let fitting    *Mt 25:35*
honor be shown to all, especially to such as
are of the household of the faith, and to
strangers. When, therefore, a guest is an-
nounced, let him be met by the superior or
the brothers with all due charity. Let them
first pray together, and thus associate with
one another in peace; but the kiss of peace
must not be offered until after prayer, on
account of the delusions of the devil. In this
salutation let all humility be shown. At the
arrival or departure of all guests, let Christ—
who indeed is received in their persons—be
adored in them, by bowing the head or even
prostrating on the ground.

When the guests have been received, let
them be led to prayer, and then let the
superior, or any one he may appoint, sit with
them. The law of God is to be read before the
guest for his edification; and afterwards let all
kindness be shown him. The superior may
break his fast for the sake of the guest, unless
it happen to be a principal fast day, which
may not be broken. The brothers, however,
shall observe their accustomed fasting. Let
the abbot pour water on the hands of the
guests, and himself, as well as the whole
community, wash their feet; after which let
them say this verse: 'We have received your
mercy, O God, in the midst of your temple'.    *Ps 48:10*
Let special care be taken in the reception of
the poor and of strangers, because in them
Christ is more truly welcomed. For the very
fear men have of the rich procures them
honor.

Let the kitchen for the abbot and guests be

apart by itself, so that strangers, who are
never wanting in a monastery, may not disturb the brothers by coming at unlooked-for
hours. Let two brothers, who are well able
to fulfil the duty, be placed in this kitchen
for a year; and let help be afforded them as
they require it, so that they may serve without murmuring. When they have not much
to occupy them there, let them go forth to
other work, wherever they may be bidden.
And not only with regard to them, but in all
the offices of the monastery, let there be such
consideration shown that when there is need
of help it may be given them, and that when
they are without work, they do whatever
they are commanded. Let the care of the
guest-house, also, be entrusted to a brother
whose soul is possessed with the fear of God.
Let there be sufficient beds prepared there
and let the house of God be wisely governed
by prudent men. Let no one, except he be
bidden, on any account associate or converse
with the guests. But if he chance to meet or
to see them, after humbly saluting them, as
we have said, and asking their blessing, let him
pass on, saying that he is not permitted to
talk with a guest.

CHAPTER 54

*Whether a monk ought to receive*
*letters, or tokens*

By no means let a monk be allowed to
receive, either from his parents or anyone
else, or from his brothers, letters, tokens, or

any gifts whatever, or to give them to others, without permission of the abbot. And if any thing be sent to him, even by his parents, let him not presume to receive it until it has been made known to the abbot. But even if the abbot order it to be received, it shall be in his power to bid it be given to whom he pleases; and let not the brother to whom it may have been sent be grieved, lest occasion be given to the devil. Should anyone, however, presume to act otherwise, let him be subjected to the discipline of the Rule.

## CHAPTER 55
### Of the clothes and shoes
### of the brothers

Let clothing be given to the brothers suitable to the nature and the climate of the place where they live; for in cold countries more is required, in warm countries less. This must therefore be considered by the abbot. We think, however, that in temperate climates a cowl and a tunic should suffice for each monk, the cowl to be of thick stuff in winter, but in summer something worn or thin; likewise a scapular for work, and shoes and stockings to cover their feet. And let not the monks complain of the color or coarseness of these things, but let them be such as can be got in the country where they live or can be bought most cheaply.

Let the abbot be careful about the size of the garments, that they be not too short for those who wear them, but of the proper

length. When they receive new clothes let
them always give up the old ones at once, to
be put aside in the wardrobe for the poor. For
it is sufficient for a monk to have two tunics
and two cowls for wearing at night, and also
for washing: whatever is over and above this is
superfluous and ought to be cut off. In the
same way, let them give up their shoes, and
whatever else is worn out, when they receive
new ones. Let those who are sent on a journey receive drawers from the wardrobe, and
on their return restore them washed. Their
cowls and tunics also, which are to be a little
better than those they ordinarily wear, let
them receive from the wardrobe when setting
out on their journey, and give them back on
their return.

For their bedding let a straw mattress,
blanket, coverlet, and pillow suffice. These
beds must be frequently inspected by the
abbot, to see if any private property be dis-
covered therein. And if any one should be
found to have anything which he has not
received from the abbot, let him be subjected
to the most severe discipline. In order that
this vice of private ownership may be rooted
out entirely, let the abbot supply them with
all necessaries: that is, a cowl, tunic, shoes,
stockings, girdle, knife, pen, needle, handker-
chief, and tablets; so that all plea of wanting
anything may be taken away. Yet let the abbot always be mindful of those words of the
Acts of the Apostles: 'Distribution was made
to every one, according as he had need'. Let
him, therefore, consider the infirmities of
such    as    are    in    want,    and    not    the

*Ac 4:35*

the ill-will of the envious. Nevertheless, in all his judgments, let him think of the retribution of God.

## CHAPTER 56
### *Of the abbot's table*

Let the table of the abbot be always with the guests and strangers. But as often as there are few guests, it shall be in his power to invite any of the brothers. Let him take care, however, always to leave one or two seniors with the brothers for the sake of discipline.

## CHAPTER 57
### *Of the artificers of the monastery*

Should there be artificers in the monastery, let them work at their crafts in all humility, if the abbot gives permission. But if any of them be puffed up by reason of his knowledge of his craft, in that he seems to confer some benefit to the monastery, let such a one be taken from it and not exercise it again, unless, perchance, when he has humbled himself, the abbot bid him work at it anew. And if any of the work of the artificers is to be sold, let those by whom the business is done see that they defraud not the monastery. Let them ever be mindful of Ananias and Sapphira, lest perchance, they, and all who deal fraudulently with the goods of the monastery, should suffer in their souls the death which these incurred in the body. But with regard to the prices of such things, let not the vice of avarice creep in, but let them always be sold a little cheaper than by men in the world, that in all things God may be glorified.

## CHAPTER 58
*Of the discipline of receiving
brothers into religion*

To him that newly comes to change his life, let not an easy entrance be granted, but, as the apostle says, 'Try the spirits if they be of God'. If, therefore, he that comes perseveres in knocking, and after four or five days seems patiently to endure the wrongs done to him and the difficulty made about his coming in, and to persist in his petition, let entrance be granted him, and let him be in the guest-house for a few days. Afterwards let him go into the novitiate, where he is to meditate and study, to take his meals and to sleep. Let a senior, one who is skilled in gaining souls, be appointed over him to watch him with the utmost care, and to see whether he is truly seeking God, and is fervent in the Work of God, in obedience, and in humiliations. Let all the hard and rugged paths by which we walk towards God be set before him. And if he promises steadfastly to persevere, after the lapse of two months let this Rule be read through to him, with these words: 'Behold the law, under which you desire to fight. If you can observe it, enter in; if you cannot, freely depart.' If he still stands firm, let him

*1 Jn 4:1*

be taken back to the aforesaid cell of the
novices, and again tried with all patience.
And, after a space of six months, let the Rule
be again read to him, that he may know
to what he comes. Should he still persevere,
after four months let the same Rule be read
to him once more. And if, having well considered within himself, he promises to keep it
in all things, and to observe everything that is
commanded him, then let him be received into
the community, knowing that he is now
bound by the law of the Rule, so that from
that day forward he cannot depart from the
monastery or shake from off his neck the
yoke of the Rule, which after such prolonged
deliberation he was free either to refuse or to
accept.

Let him who is to be received make before
all, in the oratory, a promise of stability, conversion of life, and obedience, in the presence
of God and of his saints, so that, if he should
ever act otherwise, he may know that he will
be condemned by him whom he mocks. Let
him draw up this promise in writing, in the
name of the saints whose relics are in the altar, and of the abbot there present. And let
him write it with his own hand; or at least, if
he does not know how, let another write it at
his request, and let the novice put his mark to
it, and place it with his own hand upon the
altar. When he has done this, let the novice
himself immediately begin this verse: 'Uphold
me, O Lord, according to your word, and I
shall live: and let me not be confounded
in my expectation'. And this verse let the    *Ps 119:116*
whole community thrice repeat, adding

thereto *Gloria Patri.* Then let the newly-received brother cast himself at the feet of all, that they may pray for him, and from that day let him be counted as one of the community. Whatever property he has let him first bestow on the poor, or by a solemn deed of gift make over to the monastery, keeping nothing of it all for himself, as knowing that from that day forward he will have no power even over his own body. Forthwith, therefore, in the oratory, let him be stripped of his own garments, wherewith he is clad, and be clothed in those of the monastery. And let the garments that are taken from him be laid by and kept in the wardrobe, so that if ever, by the persuasion of the devil, he consent (which God forbid) to leave the monastery, he may be stripped of the monastic habit and cast forth. But the form of his profession, which the abbot took from the altar, shall not be given back to him, but be kept in the monastery.

## CHAPTER 59
### *Of the sons of nobles or of poor men that are offered*

If any nobleman shall perchance offer his son to God in the monastery, let the parents, should the boy be still in infancy, make for him the written promise as aforesaid; and together with the oblation let them wrap that promise and the hand of the child in the altar-cloth and so offer him up. With respect to his property, they must in the same document promise under oath that they will never either themselves, or through anyone else, or in any way whatever, give him anything, or the means of having anything. Or else, if they are unwilling to do this, and desire to offer something as an alms to the monastery for their own advantage, let them make a donation of whatever they please to the monastery, reserving to themselves, if they will, the income thereof during their life. Thus let all possibility of expectation be excluded whereby the child might be deceived and so perish (which God forbid), as we have learned by experience may happen. Let those who are poorer do in like manner. But those who have nothing whatever may simply make the promise in writing, and, with the oblation, offer their son before witnesses.

CHAPTER 60
*Of priests who may wish to dwell
in the monastery*

If anyone in priestly orders asks to be received into the monastery, let consent not be too quickly granted him; but if he persists in his request, let him know that he will have to observe all the discipline of the Rule, and that nothing will be relaxed in his favor, according as it is written: 'Friend, wherefore are you come?' Let him, nevertheless, be *Mt 26:50* allowed to stand next the abbot, to give the blessing, and to say Mass, if the abbot bid him do so. Otherwise, let him presume to do nothing, knowing that he is subject to the discipline of the Rule; but rather let him give an example of humility to all. And if there be a question of any appointment, or other business in the monastery, let him expect the position due to him according to the time of his entrance and not that which was yielded to him out of reverence for the priesthood. If any clerics should desire in the same way to be admitted into the monastery, let them be placed in a middle rank; but in their case also, only on condition that they promise observance of the Rule, and stability therein.

## CHAPTER 61
### *Of stranger monks, how they are to be received*

If any monk who is a stranger come from distant parts and desire to dwell in the monastery as a guest, and if he be content with the customs which he there finds, and does not trouble the monastery by any superfluous wants, but is satisfied with what he finds, let him be received for as long a time as he will. And if reasonably and with humility he reprove and point out what is amiss, let the abbot prudently mark his words, in case God perchance has sent him for this very end. If afterwards he desire to bind himself to remain there, let not his wish be denied him, especially since during the time he was a guest his manner of life could well be ascertained.

But if during that time he was found burdensome or prone to vice, not only must he not be admitted among the brothers, but he must even be courteously bidden to depart, lest others should be corrupted by his evil living. If, however, he is not such as to deserve to be sent away, let him not merely on his own asking be received and admitted into the community, but even be persuaded to remain, that the others may be taught by his example; because in every place we serve one God, and fight under one King. And if the abbot perceive him to be a man of this kind, he may put him in a somewhat higher place. It shall be in the abbot's power to assign not only to a simple monk, but also to any of the aforesaid priests or clerics, a higher place than that due to them by their entrance into the monastery, if he see that their lives are such as to deserve it. But let the abbot take care never to receive a monk from any known monastery without his own abbot's consent and letters of recommendation; as it is written: 'What you will not have done to yourself, do not to another'.                    *Tb 4:16*

## CHAPTER 62
### *Of the priests of the monastery*

If any abbot desire to have a priest or deacon ordained for his monastery, let him choose from among his monks one who is worthy to fulfil the priestly office. And let him that is ordained beware of arrogance and pride, and presume to do nothing that is not commanded him by the abbot, knowing that he is now all the more subject to regular disci-

pline. Let him not, by reason of his priesthood, become forgetful of the obedience and
discipline of the Rule, but advance ever more
and more in godliness. Let him always keep
the place due to him according to his entrance
into the monastery, except with regard to his
office at the altar, or unless the choice of the
community and the will of the abbot should
raise him to a higher place for the merit of his
life. Nevertheless, let him know that he must
observe the rules prescribed by the deans or
prior. Should he presume to do otherwise, he
shall be judged, not as a priest, but as a
rebel; and let recourse be had to the intervention of the bishop. If even then he will
not amend, and his guilt is clearly shown, let
him be cast forth from the monastery, provided his contumacy be such that he will not
submit to or obey the Rule.

## CHAPTER 63
### *Of the order of the community*

Let everyone keep that place in the monastery which the time of his entering religion,
the merit of his life, or the appointment of the
abbot shall determine. And let not the abbot
disquiet the flock committed to him, nor by
an undue use of his authority ordain anything
unjustly; but let him ever bear in mind that he
will have to give an account to God of all his
judgments and all his deeds. Therefore in that
order which they hold, or which he shall have
appointed, let the brothers receive the kiss of
peace, approach to Communion, intone the

psalms, and stand in choir. And in no place whatever let age decide the order, or be prejudicial to it; for Samuel and Daniel, when but children, judged the elders. Excepting, therefore, those whom (as we have said) the abbot has promoted with some special object, or for distinct reasons has degraded, let all the rest stand in the order of their coming to religion, so that, for example, he who entered the monastery at the second hour of the day must know that he is lower than he who came at the first hour, whatever may be his age or dignity. The children are to be kept under discipline at all times and by everyone.

Let the younger brothers, then, reverence their elders, and the elder love the younger. In calling each other by name, let none address another by his simple name, but let the elders call the younger brethren *Brothers,* and the younger call their elders *Nonnus,* by which is implied the reverence due to a father. But let the abbot, since he is considered to represent the person of Christ, be called Lord and Abbot, not that he has taken it upon himself, but out of reverence and love for Christ. Let him be mindful of this, and show himself to be worthy of such an honor. Wherever the brothers meet one another, let the younger ask a blessing from the elder. And when the elder passes by, let the younger rise, and give place to him to sit down; let not the younger presume to sit with him, unless the elder bid him, that it may come to pass as it is written: 'In honor preferring one another'. Let young *Rom 12:10* children and boys take their places in the oratory, or at table, with all due discipline.

In other places, also, wherever they may be, let them be under proper care and discipline, until they come to the age of understanding.


## CHAPTER 64
### *Of the appointment of the abbot*

In the appointing of an abbot, let this principle always be observed, that he be made abbot whom all the brothers with one consent in the fear of God, or even a small part of the community with more wholesome counsel, shall elect. Let him who is to be appointed be chosen for the merit of his life and the wisdom of his teaching, even though he should be the last in order in the community. But if all the brothers with one accord (which God forbid) should elect a man willing to acquiesce in their evil habits, and these in some way come to the knowledge of the bishop to whose diocese that place belongs, or of the abbots or neighboring Christians, let them not suffer the consent of these wicked men to prevail, but appoint a worthy steward over the house of God, knowing that for this they shall receive a good reward, if they do it with a pure intention and for the love of God, as, on the other hand, they will sin if they neglect it.

Let him that has been appointed abbot always bear in mind what a burden he has received, and to whom he will have to give an account of his stewardship; and let him know that it beseems him more to profit his brothers than to preside over them. He must,

therefore, be learned in the law of God, that
he may know whence to bring forth new
things and old; he must be chaste, sober, *Mt 13:52*
merciful, ever preferring mercy to justice,
that he himself may obtain mercy. Let him
hate sin, and love the brothers. And even in
his corrections, let him act with prudence,
and not go too far, lest while he seeks too
eagerly to scrape off the rust, the vessel be
broken. Let him keep his own frailty ever
before his eyes, and remember that the
bruised reed must not be broken. And by *Is 42:3*
this we do not mean that he should suffer
vices to grow up but that prudently and with
charity he should cut them off in the way he
shall see best for each, as we have already
said; and let him study rather to be loved
than feared. Let him not be violent or over
anxious, not exacting or obstinate, not jeal-
ous or prone to suspicion, or else he will
never be at rest. In all his commands, whether
concerning spiritual or temporal matters, let
him be prudent and considerate. In the works
which he imposes, let him be discreet and
moderate, bearing in mind the discretion of
holy Jacob, when he said: 'If I cause my flocks
to be overdriven, they will all perish in one
day'. Taking, then, the testimonies, borne by *Gn 33:13*
these and like words, to discretion, the
mother of virtues, let him so temper all
things, that the strong may have something to
strive after, and the weak nothing at which to
take alarm. And, especially, let him observe
this present Rule in all things, so that, having
faithfully fulfilled his stewardship, he may
hear from the Lord what the good servant

heard, who gave wheat to his fellow-servants
in due season: 'Amen, I say unto you, over all

*Mt 24:47*         his goods shall be place him'.


## CHAPTER 65
### *Of the prior of the monastery*

It happens very often that by the appointment of the prior grave scandals arise in
monasteries, since there are some who, puffed
up by the evil spirit of pride, and deeming
themselves to be second abbots, take upon
themselves to tyrannize over others, and so
foster scandals and cause dissensions in the
community: especially in those places where
the prior is appointed by the same priest or
the same abbots as appoint the abbot himself. How foolish this is may easily be seen;
for from the moment of his appointment an
incentive to pride is given to him, the
thought suggesting itself that he is freed from
the authority of his abbot, since he has been
appointed by the very same persons. Hence
are stirred up envy, quarrels, backbiting,
dissensions, jealousy, and disorders. And while
the abbot and prior are at variance with one
another, it must needs be that their own souls
are endangered by reason of their disagree-
ment; and those who are their subjects, while
favoring one side or the other, run to destruction. The evil of this peril falls on the heads of
those who by their action have been the cause
of such disorders.

    We foresee, therefore, that it is expedient
for the preservation of peace and charity, that

the ordering of the monastery depend upon the will of the abbot. If possible, let all the affairs of the monastery be attended to (as we have already arranged) by deans, as the abbot shall appoint; so that, the same office being shared by many, no one may become proud. But if the needs of the place require it, and the community ask for it reasonably and with humility, and the abbot judge it expedient, let him himself appoint a prior, whomsoever he shall choose with the counsel of brothers who fear God. Let the prior reverently do whatever is enjoined him by his abbot, and nothing against his will or command; for the more he is raised above the rest, so much the more carefully ought he to observe the precepts of the Rule. And if the prior be found culpable or deceived by the haughtiness of pride, or be proved a contemner of the holy Rule, let him be admonished by words until the fourth time, and then let the correction of regular discipline be applied to him. But if even then he does not amend, let him be deposed from the office of prior, and another, who is worthier, be substituted in his place. If afterwards he be not quiet and obedient in the community, let him be expelled from the monastery. Nevertheless, let the abbot bear in mind that he must give an account to God of all his judgments, lest perchance the flame of envy or jealousy be kindled in his soul.

## CHAPTER 66
### *Of the porter of the monastery*

At the gate of the monastery let there be placed a wise old man who knows how to give and receive an answer, and whose ripeness of years suffers him not to wander. He ought to have his cell near the gate, so that they who come may always find someone at hand to give them an answer. As soon as anyone shall knock, or a poor man call to him, let him answer, 'Thanks be to God', or bid God bless him, and then with all mildness and the fear of God let him give reply without delay, in the fervor of charity. If the porter needs help, let him have with him one of the younger brothers.

The monastery, however, ought if possible to be so constituted that all things necessary, such as water, a mill, and a garden, and the various crafts may be contained within it, so that there may be no need for the monks to wander abroad, for this is by no means expedient for their souls. And we wish this Rule to be frequently read in the community, that none of the brothers may excuse himself on the plea of ignorance.

## CHAPTER 67
### *Of brothers who are sent on a journey*

Let the brothers who are about to be sent on a journey commend themselves to the prayers of all the brothers and of the abbot, and at the last prayer of the Work of God let a commemoration be always made of the absent. Let the brothers who return from a journey, on the very day that they come back, lie prostrate on the floor of the oratory at all the canonical Hours, while the Work of God is being performed, and beg the prayers of all on account of their transgressions, in case they should perchance upon the way have seen or heard anything harmful, or fallen into idle talk. And let no one presume to relate to another what he may have seen or heard outside the monastery, for thence arise manifold evils. If anyone shall so presume, let him be subjected to the punishment prescribed by the Rule. And he shall undergo a like penalty who dares to leave the enclosure of the monastery, or to go anywhere, or do anything, however trifling, without permission of the abbot.

## CHAPTER 68
### *If a brother be commanded to do impossibilities*

If on any brother there be laid commands that are hard and impossible, let him receive with all mildness and obedience the orders of him who bids him. But if he sees the weight of the burden altogether to exceed his strength, let him seasonably and with patience lay before his superior the reasons of his incapacity to obey, without showing pride, resistance, or contradiction. If, however, after this the superior still persists in his command, let the younger know that it is

expedient for him, and let him obey for the
love of God, trusting in his assistance.

<br>

CHAPTER 69
*That no one presume to defend another
in the monastery*

Care must be taken that on no occasion one
monk presume to defend another in the
monastery, or to take his part, even though
they be connected by some near tie of kinship. Let not the monks dare to do this in
any way whatsoever, because therefrom may
arise the most grievous occasion of scandals.
If anyone transgress this rule, let him be very
severely punished.

<br>

CHAPTER 70
*That no one presume to strike another*

Let every occasion of presumption be banished from the monastery. We ordain, therefore, that no one be allowed to excommunicate or strike any of his brothers, unless
authority to do so shall have been given him
by the abbot. Let such as offend herein be
rebuked in the presence of all, that the rest
may be struck with fear. With regard to the
children, however, let them be kept by all
under diligent and watchful discipline until
their fifteenth year, yet this, too, with
measure and discretion. For if anyone presume, without leave of the abbot, to chastise
such as are above that age, or show undue

severity even to the children, he shall be subjected to the discipline of the Rule, because it is written: 'What you would not have done to yourself, do not to another'.    *Tb 4:16*


## CHAPTER 71
### *That the brothers be obedient one to the other*

Not only is the excellence of obedience to be shown by all to the abbot, but the brothers must also obey one another, knowing that by this path of obedience they shall come to God. The commands, then, of the abbot or the superiors appointed by him (to which we allow no private orders to be preferred) having the first place, let all the younger brothers obey their elders with all charity and vigilance. And should anyone be found refractory, let him be corrected. But if a brother be rebuked by the abbot, or any of his superiors, for the slightest cause, or if he perceive that the mind of any superior is even slightly angered or moved against him, however little, let him at once, without delay, cast himself on the ground at his feet, and there remain doing penance until that feeling be appeased, and he gives him the blessing. If anyone should disdain to do this, let him either be subjected to corporal chastisement, or, if he remain obdurate, let him be expelled from the monastery.

## CHAPTER 72
*Of the good zeal which monks
ought to have*

As there is an evil zeal of bitterness which separates from God and leads to hell, so there is a good zeal which keeps us from vice and leads to God and life everlasting. Let monks, therefore, exert this zeal with most fervent love; that is, 'in honor preferring one an-

*Rom 12:10*

other'. Let them most patiently endure one another's infirmities, whether of body or of mind. Let them vie with one another in obedience. Let no one follow what he thinks good for himself, but rather what seems good for another. Let them cherish fraternal charity with chaste love, fear God, love their abbot with sincere and humble affection, and prefer nothing whatever to Christ. And he may bring us all alike to life everlasting.

## CHAPTER 73
*That the whole observance of perfection
is not set down in this Rule*

We have written this Rule in order that, by observing it in monasteries, we may show ourselves to have some degree of goodness of life and a beginning of holiness. But for him who would hasten to the perfection of reli- gion, there are the teachings of the holy Fathers, the following whereof brings a man to the height of perfection. For what page or what word is there in the divinely-inspired books of the Old and New Testaments that is not a most unerring rule for human life? Or what book of the holy catholic Fathers does not loudly proclaim how we may by a straight course reach our Creator? Moreover, the *Conferences of the Fathers,* their *Institutes* and their *Lives,* and the Rule of our holy Father Basil, what are these but the instruments whereby well-living and obedient monks attain to virtue? But to us, who are slothful and negligent and of evil lives, they are cause for shame and confusion. Whoever, therefore, you are that hasten to your heavenly country, fulfil by the help of Christ this least of Rules which we have written for beginners, and then at length you shall arrive, under God's protection, at the lofty summits of doctrine and virtue of which we have spoken above.

# SELECTED BIBLIOGRAPHY

Walter M. Abbott, ed. *The Documents of Vatican II.* New York: Herder and Herder, Association Press, 1966. Decree on the Appropriate Renewal of the Religious Life, 466-482.

Thomas Aquinas. *Summa Theologica,* II-IIae, q. 161, a. 1-6, *De humilitate.*

Louis Bouyer. *Introduction to Spirituality,* tr. Mary Perkins Ryan. Collegeville, Minn.: Liturgical Press, 1961.

Cuthbert Butler. *Benedictine Monachism: Studies in Benedictine Life and Rule.* London: Longmans, Green & Co., 1919.

P. Delatte. *The Rule of St. Benedict, A Commentary,* tr. J. McCann. London: Burns Oates, 1921. Reprint: Latrobe, Penn., 1950.

Timothy Fry, ed. *RB 1980 The Rule of St. Benedict.* Collegeville, Minn.: Liturgical Press, 1981.

G. Gilleman. *New Catholic Encyclopedia, 'Humility'.* New York: McGraw-Hill, 1967.

Idlefons Herwegen. *St. Benedict: A Character Study,* tr. P. Nugent. St. Louis: Herder, 1924.

David Knowles. *The Benedictines.* Florida: The Abbey Press, 1962.

Jean Leclercq, François Vandenbroucke, and Louis Bouyer. *The History of Christian Spirituality,* vol. 2, *The Spirituality of the Middle Ages.* London: Burns Oates, 1968; rpt. New York: Seabury.

Jean Leclercq. *The Love of Learning and the Desire for God,* tr. C. Misrahi. New York: Fordham University Press, 1961.

T. Lindsay. *Saint Benedict: His Life and Work.* London: Burns Oates, 1949.

C. Marmion. *Christ the Ideal of the Monk.* St. Louis: Herder, 1922.

T. Maynard. *Saint Benedict and His Monks.* New York, P. J. Kenedy, 1954.

Justin McCann. *Saint Benedict.* New York: Sheed and Ward, 1937; rpt. rev. ed. New York: Doubleday Image Books, 1958.

Thomas Merton. *Basic Principles of Monastic Spirituality.* Gethsemani, 1957.

—— *The Climate of Monastic Prayer.* Cistercian Publications, 1969.

—— *Contemplation in a World of Action.* New York: Doubleday Image Books, 1973.

—— *Monastic Peace*. Gethsemani, 1958.

—— *The Silent Life*. New York: Farrar, Strauss, Cudahy, 1957.

G. Morin. *The Ideal of the Monastic Life Found in the Apostolic Age,* tr. C. Gunning. New York: Benziger, 1914.

Claud Peifer. *Monastic Spirituality*. New York: Sheed and Ward, 1966.

Daniel Rees, ed. *Consider Your Call*. London–Kalamazoo: SPCK– Cistercian Publications, 1978.

B. Sause. *The School of the Lord's Service*. St. Meinrad, Ind.: Grail, 1948.

I. Schuster. *Saint Benedict and His Times,* tr. G. Roettger. St Louis: Herder, 1951.

G. Thils. *Christian Holiness*. Tielt, Belgium: Lannoo Publ., 1961.

W. Tunink. *Vision of Peace*. New York: Farrar, Strauss, 1963.

I. Van Houtryve. *Benedictine Peace,* tr. Leonard J. Doyle. Westminster, Md.: Newman Press, 1950.

Hubert Van Zeller. *Approach to Monasticism*. New York: Sheed and Ward, 1960.

—— *The Holy Rule. Notes on St. Benedict's Legislation for Monks*. New York: Sheed and Ward, 1958.

Ambrose Wathen. *Silence: The Meaning of Silence in the Rule of St. Benedict*. Washington, D.C.: Cistercian Publications, 1973.

M. Wolter. *The Principles of Monasticism,* tr. B. Sause. St. Louis: Herder, 1962.

CISTERCIAN PUBLICATIONS INC.

# TITLES LISTING

## THE CISTERCIAN FATHERS SERIES

### THE WORKS OF
### BERNARD OF CLAIRVAUX

### THE WORKS OF WILLIAM OF
### SAINT THIERRY

### THE WORKS OF AELRED OF RIEVAULX

### THE WORKS OF GILBERT OF
### HOYLAND

### OTHER EARLY CISTERCIAN WRITERS

## THE CISTERCIAN STUDIES SERIES

### MONASTIC TEXTS

* *Temporarily out of print* † *Forthcoming*